São Paulo in the Twenty-First Century

This book analyzes in detail the main social, economic, and special transformation of the city of São Paulo. In the last 30 years, São Paulo has become a more heterogeneous and less unequal city. Contrary to some expectations, the recent economic transformations did not produce social polarization, and the localized processes of spaces production (the plural is increasingly important) are more and more key to define their respective growth patterns, social conditions, forms of housing production, service availability, and urban precariousness. In other dimensions, however, inequalities remain present and strong, and certain disadvantaged areas have changed little and are still marked by strong social inequalities. The metropolis remains heavily segregated in terms of race and class in a clear hierarchical structure.

The book shows that it is necessary to escape from dual and polarity interpretations. This does not lead to the complete disappearance of a crudely radial and concentric structure (not only due to geographic path dependence) but superposes other elements over it, leading to more complexes and continuous patterns. A general summary of these elements could perhaps be stated as pointing to greater social and spatial heterogeneity, accompanied by smaller, but reconfigured, inequalities.

Eduardo Cesar Leão Marques is a livre-docente professor at the Department of Political Science at the University of São Paulo and researcher at the Center for Metropolitan Studies.

Routledge Advances in Sociology

For a full list of titles in this series, please visit www.routledge.com

171 **Sharing Lives**
Adult Children and Parents
Marc Szydlik

172 **The Reflexive Initiative**
On the Grounds and Prospects of Analytic Theorizing
Edited by Stanley Raffel and Barry Sandywell

173 **Social Movements in Violently Divided Societies**
Constructing Conflict and Peacebuilding
John Nagle

174 **Challenging Identities**
European Horizons
Edited by Peter Madsen

175 **Cool Nations**
Media and the Social Imaginary of the Branded Country
Katja Valaskivi

176 **Thanatourism and Cinematic Representations of Risk**
Screening the End of Tourism
Rodanthi Tzanelli

177 **The Decent Society**
Planning for Social Quality
Pamela Abbott, Claire Wallace and Roger Sapsford

178 **The Politics and Practice of Religious Diversity**
National Contexts, Global Issues
Edited by Andrew Dawson

179 **São Paulo in the Twenty-First Century**
Spaces, Heterogeneities, Inequalities
Edited by Eduardo Cesar Leão Marques

São Paulo in the Twenty-First Century
Spaces, Heterogeneities, Inequalities

Edited by
Eduardo Cesar Leão Marques

LONDON AND NEW YORK

First published 2016 by Routledge

2 Park Square, Milton Park, Abingdon, Oxfordshire OX14 4RN
52 Vanderbilt Avenue, New York, NY 10017

Routledge is an imprint of the Taylor & Francis Group, an informa business

First issued in paperback 2020

Copyright © 2016 Taylor & Francis

The right of the editor to be identified as the author of the editorial material, and of the authors for their individual chapters, has been asserted in accordance with sections 77 and 78 of the Copyright, Designs and Patents Act 1988.

All rights reserved. No part of this book may be reprinted or reproduced or utilised in any form or by any electronic, mechanical, or other means, now known or hereafter invented, including photocopying and recording, or in any information storage or retrieval system, without permission in writing from the publishers.

Notice:
Product or corporate names may be trademarks or registered trademarks, and are used only for identification and explanation without intent to infringe.

Library of Congress Cataloging-in-Publication Data
CIP data has been applied for.

ISBN: 978-1-138-65560-7 (hbk)
ISBN: 978-0-367-59656-9 (pbk)

Typeset in Sabon
by Apex CoVantage, LLC

Contents

List of Figures	vii
List of Tables	ix
Acknowledgments	xi
Introduction: Heterogeneities and Inequalities in a Southern Metropolis EDUARDO CESAR LEÃO MARQUES	1
1 São Paulo Histories, Institutions and Legacies EDUARDO CESAR LEÃO MARQUES	31

PART I
Economic Processes and Social Structure

2 Socioeconomic Transformations and Social Structure EDUARDO CESAR LEÃO MARQUES, ROGÉRIO JERÔNIMO BARBOSA AND IAN PRATES	57
3 Labor Market, Income Inequalities and Poverty ROGÉRIO JERÔNIMO BARBOSA AND IAN PRATES	73

PART II
Demographic Dynamics and Segregation

4 Population Dynamics and Migration: 1991–2010 JOSÉ MARCOS PINTO DA CUNHA	101
5 Diverse Demographic Trajectories and Heterogeneity EDUARDO CESAR LEÃO MARQUES AND CAROLINA REQUENA	120

6 The Social Spaces of the Metropolis in the 2000s 138
EDUARDO CESAR LEÃO MARQUES

7 Inequalities and Residential Segregation by
Race and Class 160
DANILO FRANÇA

PART III
Processes of Space Production

8 The Dynamics of São Paulo's Favelas: Socioeconomic
Conditions and Territorial Patterns 177
CAMILA PEREIRA SARAIVA

9 Public Housing Production 196
EDUARDO CESAR LEÃO MARQUES AND LEANDRO DE PÁDUA RODRIGUES

10 Private-Sector Housing Developments: Who Produces
What, How and Where? 214
TELMA HOYLER

11 Mobility Inequalities in a Road Transport System 228
CAROLINA REQUENA

Contributors 241
Index 243

Figures

1	Location of the São Paulo metropolitan region (SPMR) in Brazil and South America.	xii
2	SPMR.	xiii
1.1	Expansion of the SPMR, 1881 to 2002.	41
2.1	Distribution of EGP classes, SPMR, 1991, 2000 and 2010.	63
3.1	Counterfactual decomposition: effects of education.	83
3.2	Counterfactual decomposition: (in)formality effects.	85
3.3	Counterfactual decomposition: class structure effects (EGP).	86
3.4	Employment generation and unemployment balance per household income. SPMR, 1991–2000 and 2000–2010.	88
4.1	Intrametropolitan migratory flows over 4,500 people, SPMR, 2005/2010.	112
5.1	Demographic growth, weighting areas, SPMR, 1991–2000.	124
5.2	Demographic growth by weighting area, SPMR, 2000–2010.	125
6.1	Distribution of groups, SPMR, 2010.	152
6.2	Types of residences in the Western region.	154
7.1	LISA Maps of the concentration of social groups, 2010.	169
8.1	Types of favelas, Guarapiranga and Billings reservoirs, Southern SPMR, 2010.	190
9.1	Location of housing projects by MCMV Program band, SPMR.	204
10.1	Number of residential units and amount released (1985–2013).	218
10.2	Location of private-sector developments, Cycle 1 (1985–1993).	224
10.3	Location of private-sector developments, Cycle 3 (2005–2013).	224
11.1	Vehicle ownership rate, income and car use: SPMR, 2007.	234
11.2	Location quotient of trips by individual modes (map A) and collective modes (map B), SPMR, 2007.	236

Tables

2.1	Relative income and ISEI in the EGP classes, SPMR, 2000 and 2010.	65
2.2	Educational level by class, SPMR, 2000 and 2010 (%).	66
4.1	Average annual population growth rates by areas: Brazilian Metropolitan Districts and the Federal District—1991 and 2010.	108
4.2	Intrametropolitan migrants by educational level and share of migrants and groups of municipalities.	113
5.1	Population and demographic growth, SPMR—1920 to 2010.	122
6.1	Dissimilarity Indexes between classes, SPMR, 2010.	144
6.2	Proportional distribution of classes and groups, SPMR, 2010 (%).	146
6.3	Differences between proportions in the areas: 2000/2010, SPMR (%).	150
7.1	Racial inequalities in income by educational level, SPMR, 2000 and 2010.	164
7.2	Dissimilarity Index between racial group and socio-occupational strata in the SPMR, 2000 and 2010.	167
8.1	Socioeconomic indicators in São Paulo and in favelas, 1991, 2000 and 2010.	183
8.2	Socioeconomic indicators in São Paulo, favelas, their neighboring areas, and urbanized favelas 1991, 2000, and 2010.	185
9.1	Distances for housing projects to centralities—MCMV, COHAB and CDHU (km).	206
9.2	Average social characteristics of the area surrounding projects (1000 meters), 2010.	208

Acknowledgments

First and foremost, we would like to thank the Center for Metropolitan Studies (CEM) for providing the research environment in which this book was produced. Without the academic discussions held at the Center and the contributions of many colleagues in seminars, meeting and informal conversations, this book would be impossible.

The book would not be possible also without the generous and substantial financial support received from the São Paulo Research Foundation (Fapesp) and National Council for Scientific and Technological Development (CNPq) for the development of the research project on which this book is based. Fapesp also financed a post-doc fellowship for the organizer at the Bartlett School of University College London, during which most of the two first chapters of this book were written.

Finally, we would also like to thank Marcos Campos for the final critical reading of the chapters, David Rogers for the translation and revision of the manuscripts and Gabriela Trindade for the help with the Index.

www.fflch.usp.br/centrodametropole/
urbanpoliticscem.wordpress.com

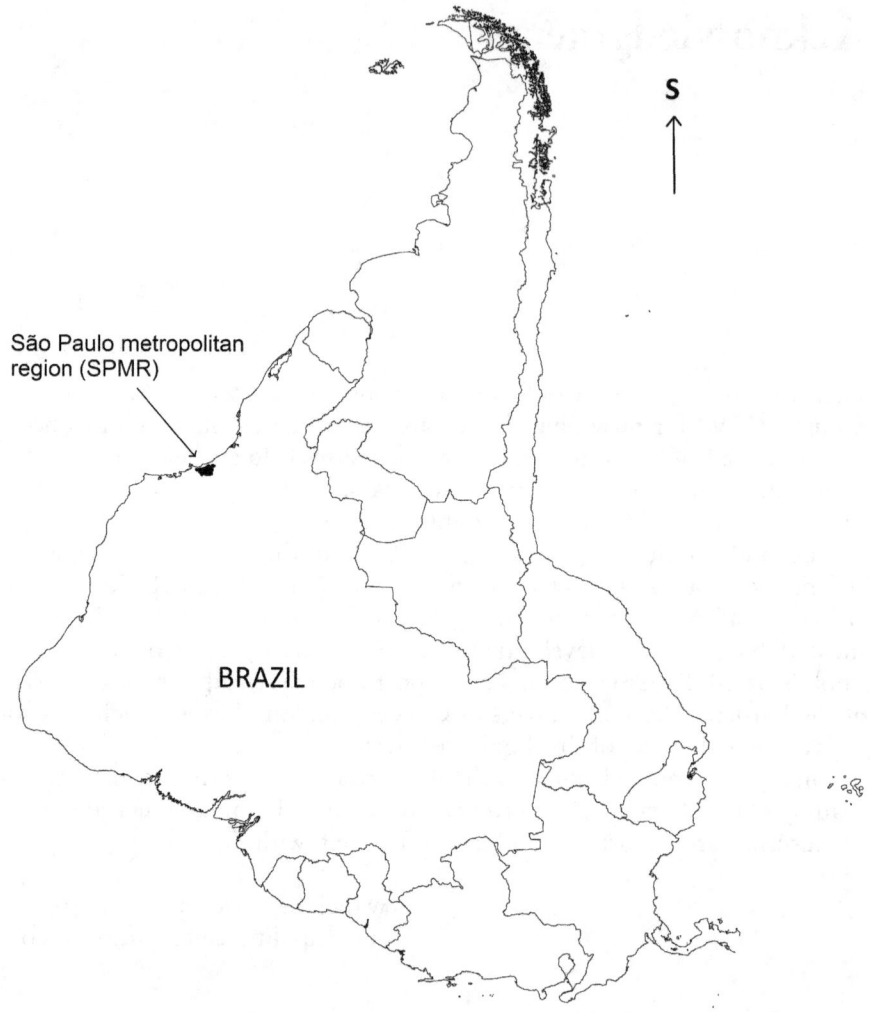

Figure 1 Location of the São Paulo metropolitan region (SPMR) in Brazil and South America.

Source: Center for Metropolitan Studies (CEM), inspired by Uruguayan artist Joaquin Torres Garcia, 1943.

Figure 2 SPMR.
Source: CEM.

Introduction
Heterogeneities and Inequalities in a Southern Metropolis

Eduardo Cesar Leão Marques

The city of São Paulo is now the largest and most important Latin American metropolis, home to the world's third-largest metropolitan population and possessing the 10th-largest urban gross domestic product (GDP) in 2010, according to United Nations estimates. The 39 municipalities making up the metropolitan region accounted for around 19 percent of Brazil's GDP and 10 percent of its population during the same year. This large and dynamic metropolis has grown at a fast pace, especially over the last 50 years, leaping from 4.8 million inhabitants in 1960 to 19.7 million in 2010. This has meant accommodating a demographic increase equivalent to 1.3 times the total population of Paris's metropolitan area or twice the population of contemporary Greater London in just half a century. During the same period, São Paulo has added a productive capacity comparable in scale to the entire economy of Chile or Hong Kong.

At the same time, though, around 15 percent of the city's population lives below the poverty line (PL), while nearly 2.8 million inhabitants live in precarious settlements or favelas. São Paulo's iconic income inequalities may be summarized by the fact that while the average income of the richest 10 percent of its residents was equivalent to just over US$4,000 per month in 2010, its poorest 40 percent only received about US$100 per month. Large and dynamic, rich and poor, but especially complex and unequal, São Paulo has for decades challenged analysts from various disciplines and theoretical affiliations. The goal of this book is to give a detailed account of São Paulo at the eve of the 21st century. Although these elements are associated with politics and policies in the city, as well as to urban sociability and culture, this book is devoted to portray broadly its recent economic, social and spatial transformations.

The book provides a monography of one particular city, although some might add that the city itself is host to many smaller cities (Canevacci 1993). Just the same, the book contributes to the recent "comparative gesture" (Robinson 2011), since local processes are analyzed in relation to other cases and theories. Monographic studies may set out from parochial concepts, as Kantor & Savitch argue (2005), and develop case-centered approaches that lead to fragmentation, as critiqued by Rodgers et al. (2011), or may be constructed in dialogue with other cases by continuously connecting their analysis with existing concepts and theories. In this case, the intellectual aim of the project is not to compare attributes, as in Gugler (2004) and Gilbert (1996), nor to construct general laws. Instead, it involves comparing processes and relations (Robinson 2011) and seeking to develop modest generalizations (Rihoux & Ragin 2009) that may identify multiple causalities (Pickvance 1986). This is the case of this book, aimed at contributing to bringing "the experience of cities of the 'South' . . . to rethink urban knowledge and urban theory" (McFarlane 2010, p. 726).

On the other hand, the complexity of the subject (which is common to large and heterogeneous metropolises) creates great difficulties for the application of one single theoretical framework to capture and explain all its processes. As will be discussed later in this introduction, instead of talking about urban theory, therefore, it may be more appropriate to discuss urban theories in plural what may specify differently the tasks of comparative urbanism.

Reflecting its importance, São Paulo has been intensely investigated ever since the 1970s, when urban studies began in Brazil and international comparisons frequently included Latin American cities. These studies formed part of the international discussions on development, dependency, marginality and urban peripheries that set the paradigm for studying cities in the region. Indeed, the international literature still focuses on Latin America through this paradigm, making very few connections with the local literature and taking almost no account of the social and spatial changes that have happened over the last 40 years.

Between the 1960s and the 1990s, São Paulo experienced a combination of rapid economic and demographic growth with regressive public policies and repressive political conditions. The social and spatial consequences of this scenario were studied by Camargo (1976), Oliveira (1982) and Kowarick (1979). As a result, the city developed a large urban fabric marked by considerable inequalities in terms of opportunity, wealth and living conditions. From the viewpoint of urban form, the period consolidated a center-periphery structure with wealthy social groups inhabiting central spaces where services and amenities were available, contrasting with vast precarious regions on the city outskirts, irregularly occupied by the recently migrated working poor (Bonduki & Rolnik 1982, Durham 1988, Santos 1982).

The 1980s and 1990s brought changes to these patterns in part due to national-level processes. In the last few decades, Brazil has experienced major political changes following the consolidation of democracy and the return to regular and competitive elections. Moreover, several public sectors have been reformed through the establishment of national policy systems regulated and primarily funded by the federal government, with state and municipal responsibilities for policy implementation. It should be observed that although neoliberalism has been a clear factor in economic policies (Portes & Roberts 2005), the impact of neoliberal ideas on Brazilian social policies has tended to be slight, possibly due to the strength of the democratization processes in the 1980s and 1990s. These changes had a profound impact on public policies and service provision, improving access to services, albeit with varying standards of quality and a high spatial (and social) heterogeneity in terms of service distribution.

The macroeconomic policies of the 1990s followed the Latin American turn from industrialization through import substitution to liberalization and economic opening, while the 2000s were characterized by the return of strong rates of economic growth. This initially led to rising metropolitan poverty and unemployment in the 1990s, combined with declining wages and labor formalization, followed by a reversal of these processes in the 2000s, when poverty levels, income inequality and unemployment declined, while labor formalization and average wages increased. As in other urban areas of Latin America, the social situation in Brazilian cities has improved since the turn of the new century. Migration flows, fertility rates and demographic growth have also fallen substantially since the 1980 (Guzmán 2006).

As a result, São Paulo over the last 30 years has become a productively, socially and spatially more heterogeneous city. It has also became less unequal in terms of income, the labor market and living conditions, even in its areas of precarious housing. Contrary to the expectations of studies informed by general descriptions of globalization, economic restructuring and neoliberalism, the recent economic transformations have not led to social polarization. Also contrary to the hypotheses sustaining spatial polarization, the localized processes involved in producing spaces in São Paulo (and, as we shall see, the plural in processes and spaces is increasingly important) have become more and more important in terms of defining their respective growth patterns, social conditions, forms of housing production, service availability and urban precariousness. In other aspects, however, such as service quality and the effectiveness of policies, inequalities remain persistent and strong. While the majority of urban areas now experience better living conditions, some disadvantaged areas have changed little and are still driven by strong social inequalities. The structure of the metropolis remains highly segregated along race and class boundaries, forming a clear hierarchical structure. The recent transformations have not led to the complete disappearance of a broadly radial and concentric structure with the richest social groups at the center, albeit overlapping with other elements, leading to the development of more continuous mosaic patterns. Contrary to the forecasts made by a substantial portion of the international literature, though, the city experienced processes usually taken to be decoupled, if not antagonistic: its historical center has become more popular and elite areas more exclusive, but at the same time peripheral regions have become more socially mixed with the growth of intermediate social groups. A general summary of these elements can perhaps be taken to indicate greater social and spatial heterogeneity, accompanied by smaller but reconfigured inequalities.

Local studies have attempted to account for these changes by focusing their attention on specific processes such as the production of gated communities (Caldeira 2000); the relationships among poverty, social inequality and segregation (Marques & Torres 2005); the various forms of precarious housing (Kowarick 2009); sociability patterns in poverty (Marques 2012); the role of informality in urban relations and processes (Telles 2010); and the multiple forms in which sociability is regulated on the periphery, in particular the increase in violence (Feltran 2011, Perlman 2004, Zaluar 2010), changing associative life and sociability and not only in Brazilian cities (Rodgers et al. 2011).

However, with the exception of gated communities, intensely analyzed by the literature in Brazil and beyond (Duren 2006, Salcedo et al. 2008), most of the international literature appears unaware of the recent analyses of Latin American cities, published almost solely in Portuguese. In fact, a generalizing view of these metropolitan areas still dominates at the international level, a legacy of the structuralist models of the 1960s and 1970s. These models have always faced considerable difficulty in accounting for differences and local processes, actors and dynamics in different cities, but now they also appear very weakly connected to the intense processes of change evident over recent decades.

Since this volume takes comparison as its point of departure, it is essential to explore the recent debates on comparative urbanism in this introduction as well as situate São Paulo and urban Latin America within the tradition of comparative studies more generally. This will afford us a clearer understanding of the specific contribution made by this book while at the same time as providing a comparative framework for expanding the lessons derived from specific processes in São Paulo to other cities and engaging with the diverse theories mobilized over the course of the individual chapters. The following section therefore examines the recent debate in comparative urbanism, discussing the traditional role played by Latin American metropolises in comparative theories and identifying some of the historical processes that have constructed Latin American cities. The final section of the introduction presents the structure of the book and outlines the main findings reported in each chapter.

Comparisons, Latin American Cities and São Paulo

Although it is not the objective of this introduction to critically access the diverse positions encountered in the recent comparative debate, some general elements need to be discussed to clarify the position adopted by this book before we proceed to Latin American cities and São Paulo. The recent debate on comparative urbanism (Edensor & Jayne 2012, Hart 2004, McCann & Ward 2010, McFarlane 2010, Nijman 2007, Robinson 2006 and 2011, Roy 2011 and 2014, Ward 2010) has revived interest in comparing cities, especially by emphasizing the importance of North-South and South-South comparisons for the study of "ordinary cities" (Robinson 2006). This can help us avoid imposing external models on empirical realities, engaging in parochialism or treating these cities (and their internal parts) as abnormalities or legacies of the past.

The reasons for this are twofold. First, as already underlined by Robinson (2011), almost all the theories presently available to investigate urban phenomena were produced with the social realities of cities from the so-called Global North in mind. Contrary to this idea, recent comparative debates have declared that "all cities are starting points for theorizing" (Robinson 2014, p. 7), including those "beyond the West" (Edensor & Jayne 2012). In this sense, the production of monographic studies on cities located in the Global South can inform the development of new theories or the revision of existing ones by enabling the consideration of the full range of phenomena under study, reducing "asymmetric ignorance" (Robinson 2006). This is a relatively uncontroversial claim, we presume.

Second and more importantly, however, the debate emphasizes that the very specificity of the historical processes responsible for constructing cities like São Paulo introduces the need to account for new realities, processes and combinations of factors, challenging existing explanations, especially when we consider the multiple conjunctural causalities (Ragin 1987) and plural causalities (Pickvance 1986) usually present in urban phenomena. Hence the postcolonial approach is correct when it states that several facets of southern cities fail to fit into existing theories, except as abnormalities, absences and failures, establishing an opposition between modernity and tradition or (still) incomplete modernity (Robinson 2006).

I would like to state, however, that this is more or less true depending on the subject or theme under analysis. For some research topics, the conditions in southern cities may be more similar to the ones present in the (northern) cities that inspired existing theories, while others may make no sense for those cities, their histories and urban experiences. Due to this, at least a part of the recent polemic on the generalizability of existing explanations may be exaggerated by two reasons. First because considering the complexity of the urban, it is highly improbable that one single "robust urban theory" (Roy 2009, p. 820), from the North or the South, may explain all urban and metropolitan phenomena. Second, considering the diversity of theories we need to account for processes and cities, authors in the recent polemic depart from different research subjects—namely sociability and urban experience (Roy 2011 and 2015) and urban economics (Scott & Storper 2015), and consequently, they may be all right but exaggerating their arguments.[1]

Let's consider, for example, one subject marked by cultural and local specificities: everyday sociability and urban culture. These are culturally embedded and deeply influenced by the ways through which people make sense of their lives as well as by the internal dynamics of the diverse social groups in which they participate and interact. For this field, therefore, theories produced from specific urban experiences may present serious limitations. This is not to say that existing theories have no place in the study of these facets of southern cities. Classical models such as those of Simmel and the Chicago School, for example, obviously tell us something about the everyday sociability of a favela in Rio de Janeiro or São Paulo. These cities (and their favelas) clearly share some common aspects with Berlin and Chicago: capitalist economies, modern states and active democratic institutions to mention just some of the broader similarities. On the other hand, however, southern cities followed different historical paths beyond these general macro characteristics and experienced the construction of different forms of modernity (Robinson 2006). Consequently, people living in these cities, especially in poorer regions like the Brazilian favelas, experience radically different family structures and dynamics, forms of insertion in labor market, housing conditions and relations with the state and institutions in general (the law and informality, among other aspects).

Theories produced solely on the basis of the realities and ontologies of cities of the North present serious limitations, therefore, when it comes to analyzing sociability in a Brazilian city[2] or in Mumbai (Roy 2011). For this reason, the contemporary shift of comparison towards the South calls for theories embedded in places outside mainstream urban studies, which opens up multiple possibilities for different themes, ontologies of modernity (Robinson 2006) and geographies of theory (Roy 2011).

In fact, even among the heterogeneous and artificial set of cities of the "South," many differences remain to be explained. Informality is itself an extremely complicated category insofar as it is defined as the ahistorical opposite of some formal (and sometimes abstract) pattern (Roy & Alsayyad 2004). Even this feature, therefore, classically assumed to be typical of southern cities (Gugler & Gilbert 1982), comes in many socially, territorially and institutionally distinct forms, introducing the need for studies conceptually decentered not only from the "formal" (and the North) but also from any generic "Southern" pattern.

Other authors contributing to this debate have stressed the importance of setting out from a relational perspective when making comparisons in line with the recent turn of much geographical studies toward flows, interactions and multiplicity (Massey 2005) as well as toward "interconnected trajectories of sociospatial change" (Hart 2004). For authors like Ward (2010), McCann and Ward (2010) and Hart (2004), traditional comparative perspectives (e.g., Kantor & Savitch 2005) proceed from a static, discrete and self-containing understanding of the cities under comparison. This leads to a formalistic understanding of geographic scales, following institutional boundaries rather than processes, as well as a restrictive understanding of causalities associated with a search for law-like theories. As an alternative, Ward (2010) and McCann and Ward (2010) emphasize the need to foreground the interconnections among cities through their historical constructions, accounting for processes occurring simultaneously at different scales.

Similarities and differences among cities, in this sense, have to be understood as multiple points of convergence and divergence within interlocked historical trajectories (Ward 2010). Each city thus includes diverse features at different scales, shaping contradictory historical outcomes that cannot be captured by single labels, as in Savitch (1988), or by broad generalizations, as in Goldfrank and Schrank (2009). This alternative approach has produced some important results, especially in the study of the interdependencies between subjects and places, such as policy mobilities and the circulation of knowledge (McCann & Ward 2010).

At the same time, though, it is not entirely evident to me that this will lead to a widespread epistemological turn in urban theory as Roy (2011) suggests. My disagreement resides in the fact that cities are complex (and contradictory) sets of socially constructed territories, processes and actors. Consequently, no general urban theory—or theoretical critique—can explain a city or group of cities or their internal processes, actors and consequences. Indeed, we can ask whether this was ever possible for any northern city. The field of urban studies is composed of many thematic theories explaining different phenomena or even various facets of the same phenomena, historically constructed within specific traditions and debates. Moreover, inhabitants of southern cities (including the poor and their spaces) are not the "other" of northern cities, and if they do live specific urban experiences, they also share experiences with northern inhabitants (and their spaces) as well as with elite social groups in their own cities. Consequently, the recent comparative turn away from the North as a center has a greater impact for some theories of the urban than for others. This may seem obvious, but an extreme emphasis on "slum ontologies" (Roy 2011) or on claiming that "the centre of theory making must move to the global South" (Roy 2009, p. 820) can also be read as another "general concept of the urban" (Scott & Storper 2015) intended to counterbalance.

This is especially the case for those existing theories that focus on subjects and causalities that are indeed universally present and not just globally present in the sense given by Roy (2015). As a consequence, studies focusing social groups or regions of southern cities with similar conditions to northern realities or characterized by formal labor markets, structured land markets under commodified private property, Western living standards and family structures, for example, dialogue better with existing, mainstream theories. This is always the case for the majority of economic processes since the economic logic is present even in the absence of formalized structures, institutions and relationships, even if with specific characteristics. This is why Scott and Storper's (2015) critique of comparative urbanism is based on urban economics and the "land nexus." Although economic relations are always embedded in their societies (Granovetter 1985), the prevalence of economic calculations in any market economy leads much of what happens in urban real estate markets to be structured by the logic of land values, land exchanges and land valorization. The substantial variations in how these work thus fall into Tilly's (1984) "variation finding" category—the existence of one general statement about phenomena that take many different historical forms.

This is true even for geographical locations typical of southern cities. To illustrate this, let's return to Brazilian favelas but looking this time at land transactions and not sociability. Land in Brazil—with the exception of indigenous land—is fully commodified, which is not necessarily the norm in the Global South. However, a substantial proportion of the poor live on land that is not legally owned and involves several types of land squats (favelas), informal settlements, informal renting and sales and even informal (invaded or rented) occupation of housing developments. These have all developed on the margins of the legal system but also in some kind of dialogue with the state.[3] The absence of legal property does not block economic transactions, and in fact these areas are sites of intense and dynamic informal markets. Land transactions in such areas differ from those in a London neighborhood, for example, and involve "different mechanisms of land-market operation" (Roy & Alsayyad 2004). However, they are also regulated by institutions that lend them stability and through which people can make sense of their lives and plan their own strategies. In these parts of the city, then, property is exchanged, and prices are formed through more or less the same kind of economic logic found in the formal neighborhoods of these cities (or indeed in London neighborhoods), associated with bids for locations and uses and expectations of land valorization. The use of housing projects units (which cannot be sold formally) is also rented and sold informally in a similar manner.

These markets may be devalued and entail lower prices than the rest of the city (Baltrusis 2009), but they function along similar lines, including speculation (Santos 1982). Prices tend to change dynamically in a similar way as do formal land markets—with changes in land use, with expectations of public works construction or other amenities, with renovations, as well as with institutional changes that secure tenure (closing the gaps between formal and informal markets).

In this sense, understanding informal land use in Brazilian favelas does not require the complete reconstruction of existing economic theories, merely their adaptation to local conditions. It could be added (correctly) that understanding the circulation of the wealth produced by one specific land transaction—which economic circuits it will feed and what effects it may have on social mobility, for example—are completely dependent on Polanyian dimensions of the economy that are located beyond the range of traditional economic models and call for new geographies of theory (Roy 2015). However, to comprehend how prices are formed and how they influence locations and uses, we simply have to adapt the knowledge accumulated by urban economics.

In sum, the recent debate on comparative urbanism has brought many important insights, although the controversies surrounding the refounding of urban theory may have been somewhat exaggerated. First, this may be because there is no single and unified urban theory, but different theoretical approaches within different traditions and, second, because existing theories may be appropriate for analyzing certain phenomena at a broader level, but may become too limited in geographical and historical terms when we turn to examine other topics. Instead, these call for a denser restructuring of existing knowledge that takes into account the processes revealed by studies of southern cities.

Latin American Cities in Comparative Studies

This position in mind, we can turn now to examine the presence of Latin American cities in international comparative studies. There are at least two reasons for discussing Latin America here and not just São Paulo. First, urbanization in the region's many countries and cities has resulted from historical processes that were intertwined, notwithstanding the many differences nested within them. Second, Latin America has already been the subject of important and broad-ranging comparative theories. Some of these—development theory and dependency theory—still inform many contemporary international studies, albeit sometimes implicitly.

As is widely known, urbanization in Latin America is a relatively recent process dating from the 1940s and 1950s. It unfolded over a very short time period, driven mainly by rapid mass migration from rural areas to the big metropolises in the wealthiest parts of the largest countries (Martine & Diniz 1997). The differentials in living conditions and opportunities between rural and urban areas generated internal flows of migrants to cities during the periods of rapid capitalist modernization that shaped the region from the 1930s onward (Gugler & Gilbert 1982). These flows were only partially absorbed by urban markets and the industrial sector. Consequently, unemployment and precarious work (the informal economy) became prevalent in these cities, together with a pattern of space production in poor areas that was marked by inequalities and precariousness. All these processes were intensely discussed by the literature since the 1970s, mobilizing at least three distinct explanations.

On one hand, various economists explained migration as an outcome of wage differences between rural and urban jobs and unemployment as the product of a mismatch between rates of urbanization and the pace of industrialization. Precarious jobs were seen to result from the low qualifications of the migrant labor force—at once a cause and a consequence of the economy's low productivity. In their view, these problems would be solved over time since the number of people able to migrate would decline, reducing wage differentials. Consequently, urban wages would also rise, increasing the pressure for improvements to economic productivity that would in turn reduce labor costs. Poverty in rural areas would thus decline through a reduction in the rural population; at the same time as urban poverty would "naturally" fall with the increase in economic productivity (Costa Pinto 1967). Convergence would be the overall result at international level.

These ideas were backed and paralleled by the application of modernization theories to development, especially in Latin America. Modernization theorists suggested that development follows capitalist modernization (Rostow 1960). The prevalence of underdevelopment during early stages of this process was taken to be caused, therefore, by "accommodation effects" that would fade away with time. Intensive modernization brought people with rural behaviors to the cities, detaching them from their rural origins, traditional relationships of authority and familiar economic activities. They were also removed from social contexts with few social connections but strong and primary ties and reinserted in a new urban and modern order. In response, they developed anomic, provincial, insubordinate and lazy behavior, ending up as "urban marginals."[4] Although this argument was broader in scope and in fact used to design (and legitimize) US foreign policy worldwide, it was also extensively employed to explain the prevalence of poverty and underdevelopment in Latin America, where capitalist modernization had already been in place for some decades.

Development theory was intensely criticized both by ECLAC economic theory (Furtado 1964) and later by dependence theory (Cardoso & Faletto 1977). In discussions of urban poverty in Latin America, authors developed two complementary critiques of the urban modernization and marginality debates. A first group of studies turned to ethnographic analyses, showing that the ideas and values of the poor were no different from mainstream society. They were in fact organized around progress, individual work and effort and family sacrifice and savings, pursuing objectives similar to those of other social groups, albeit with different strategies because of their more scarce resources and narrower life perspectives (Durham 1988, Lomnitz 1975, Perlman 1977).

These macro narratives contended that the region's countries and cities could be explained by the roles assigned to them in general theories of development, underdevelopment and dependency. Development theory emphasized the importance of differences between each country's level of modernization in explaining why certain countries had not (yet) converged. Dependency theory, meanwhile, appealed to the different positions of countries in the international division of labor to make sense of features such as unemployment, informal labor and poverty. In both cases, political processes, institutions, political actors and their strategies and choices and the state were left out of the analysis or were treated as products of macroeconomic dynamics. One important consequence of such approaches, however, is that they fail to capture the role of national and local processes or to understand country and city variations, taking these to be deviations from a general law rather than multiple forms produced by the interconnected historical processes common to the region.

Pursuing a complementary line of argument, other authors set out from Marxist structural analysis to insist that supposedly "marginal" populations were in fact a functional element of the peripheral capitalist economies of these countries (Kowarick 1979). The contribution of these countries to the world capitalist division of labor was to provide low-paid and poorly regulated labor forces. This was only made possible by the presence of a large and diversified informal economy that kept (alive) a large reserve industrial army, ready for mobilization at all times, pushing down wages in a sustainable way. Helping maintain this situation were the authoritarian political regimes that held power in the region between the 1960s and the 1980s (Kowarick 1979). Even during the periods of strong economic growth (or exactly because of it), therefore, poverty was widespread: Growth and poverty were two sides of the same coin (Camargo 1976), and people symbolized their lives similarly to mainstream society (Durham 1988, Perlman 1977). This literature dialogued (from afar) with French urban sociology but was produced independently of the latter.

Since then, the fragmentation of subjects and themes has become a trend, as rightly criticized by Rodgers et al. (2011). The region was rarely a topic at comparative level with the exception of empirical and descriptive works (Gilbert 1996, UN 2012) or studies that implicitly mobilized the aforementioned macronarratives, echoing the analyses of the 1970s (Fernandez-Maldonado 2001, Gugler & Gilbert 1982, Roberts 2005). The only exceptions have been the use of Latin American cities as examples in new macronarratives that oversimplify empirical realities, such as generic references to neoliberalism (Goldfrank & Schrank 2009), global cities (Taylor et al. 2010), precarious housing (Davis 2006), or violence and advanced marginality (Wacquant 2008). As in the proceeding macronarratives, local elements, actors, conflicts, institutions and struggles are all treated as peripheral details, leading to conclusions about the inevitability of processes and leaving no room for politics.

It is nonetheless true that Latin American cities share many common features. They generally display strong segregation with richer social groups located in central areas (where the scarce urban equipment and policies are concentrated), while the poor and recently migrated population lives in vast, homogenous, unserved and segregated peripheries (Duerau & Vanegas 2000, Joseph 2009, Kaztman & Retamoso 2005, Marques & Torres 2005, Preteceille & Cardoso 2008, Sabatini et al. 2005). The poor live in irregular settlements (Bonduki & Rolnik 1982) on the peripheries or in favelas, forming poverty enclaves in more central areas.[5] The houses in these areas are typically self-built, usually by collective and sometimes communitarian processes of mutual help. Instead of regulating land and combatting segregation, the state has reinforced the process through its construction of large-scale housing developments in outlying peripheries (Maricato 1987, Sabatini et al. 2005).

This description of urbanization in Latin America as a form of metropolitanization and/or peripheralization would become the paradigm for studying cities in the region. But although it may have accurately depicted the general features of Latin American cities in the 1970s, this model failed to account for the substantial variations present in many other aspects between and within these same urban landscapes. Moreover, the description is outdated (and in part misleading), given the recent transformations in the region, at least in São Paulo. In fact, the contemporary processes of social and spatial change cannot be analyzed by reapplying structuralist models of the 1960s nor by using interpretative frameworks based on dual, polar and fragmented visions of the city. In the end, these interpretations reproduce—even if only implicitly—the same oppositions of modern/tradition and developed/underdeveloped already heavily criticized in the literature. Within the cities, the center/periphery model of urban structure reproduced a similar duality, also curbing our comprehension of their diversity and producing an oversimplification of the heterogeneity of the processes, relations and features present in contemporary metropolises.

The development of urban comparisons that take into account local variations, heterogeneities and politics, and avoid over-imposing economic and global processes, depends on an appraisal of the historical processes responsible for forging these cities. At the same time, the historical formation of Latin American countries and cities presents both similarities and differences, each nested within each other.

To discuss this issue, I set out from a bold statement: There is no Latin America, and thus no Latin American cities, understood as a homogeneous region.[6] There are similarities and differences constructed through parallel historical processes, which at the same time produced a variety of historical, political and geographical legacies. Some of these processes and events are common to groups of countries and cities, while others are present in different countries and cities. Sometimes, even apparent similarities nest important differentiations. These countries and cities become a region only if we depart from the intertwined historical processes that constructed their societies, states and territories (and still reconstructed them at present) but not as a set of static features. This leads us to an interplay between theories (generality) and cases (historical specificities) at different levels of analysis—or between individualizing, variation-finding, encompassing (Tilly 1984) and incorporated (McMichael 1990) comparative strategies. So how were these similarities and differences historically produced in the region? Given my previous focus on economic issues, here we shall concentrate mainly on the historical and political dimensions.

Giving a Historical Background

The urbanization process in the region usually referred to as Latin America began in colonial times since earlier indigenous occupation did not lead to urban agglomerations with lasting effects on urbanization processes, with the exception of the capitals of the Aztec and Inca empires in Mexico City and Cusco, respectively. During the ensuing centuries, two colonial projects mainly acted over this vast territory, involving two different languages (not considering the indigenous languages, which in Brazil alone today number more than 250) and several ethnic and cultural heritages distributed over a vast geographical region. These colonial projects involved different urbanization strategies with different economic goals, which Holanda (1995) captures through the metaphors of the sower and the tile layer. Portugal built towns and cities located mainly on the coast of present-day Brazil, constructed with few regulatory controls, although in some cases with urban planning projects (Reis Filho 2012). In the interior, cities sprang up in scattered fashion, located mainly around mineral resources or along the roads and rivers used for transportation. Spain, by contrast, had a clear policy of territorial occupation through cities, usually planned and located both on the coast and in the continental interior, although not always locally following the rigid rules of the so-called Philippine ordinances (Reis Filho 2012).

Within each colonial project, however, the differences were considerable. In the case of the Portuguese historical legacy, Salvador (prior to the 1770s) and Rio (thereafter) concentrated resources and people along with the most important connections with the metropolis and administrative centers of the colonial government. Another important city was Belém do Pará, established as a Portuguese stronghold (and also Spanish, since the two kingdoms were unified at that time) at the mouth of the Amazon in 1616 to expel the French military forces attacking from Northern Brazil. São Paulo and Belo Horizonte, on the other hand, had almost no importance at the time. Until the end of the 1700s, São Paulo was no more than a regional commercial center. Belo Horizonte was a secondary city, located in a region made extremely wealthy by the discovery of gold and diamonds in Ouro Preto and Diamantina.

This heterogeneity was no less pronounced when it came to the Spanish colonies. Originally, this diversity was linked to the history of the creation of the vice kingdoms, each with its own importance and economic specialization: "New Spain" in 1535 (in Mexico Teochtitlan, later Mexico City); "de Peru" in 1543 (in Lima); "De la Nueva Granada" in 1550 (in Bogotá); and "De la Plata" in 1776 (in Buenos Aires). Buenos Aires formed part of the late Spanish strategy of occupying its southern territory and preventing Portugal from expanding its share of the continent. For those who may doubt the importance of this long-term legacy, it is enough to observe that the four largest metropolises existing in the region today outside Brazil are the four capitals of the Spanish vice kingdoms.

The region also included very different areas in geographical terms: the Caribbean, the Andean Highlands and the Lowlands, all of them large and heterogeneous. Obviously, several microgeographical and topographic elements have also played key roles in the development of cities, including the confinement of Lima and Santiago by the Cordillera de los Andes and the relationship between the sea and the local river system in Rio de Janeiro and Buenos Aires, respectively.

Another great source of heterogeneity has been ethnicity, associated with the different relationships between each state, its indigenous populations and other immigrants arriving over later centuries. Family structures vary according to these differences with consequences for housing units, settlements, community organization, sociability and local politics. This is a key issue when it comes to describing cities such as La Paz, Mexico City and Quito, for example. Very often, ethnic frontiers overlap with social class divisions. This may occur even where the indigenous presence is not very numerous, as in Argentina, but where a substantial part of the poor population has indigenous origins.

Different economic cycles were later associated with slavery or international migration. The presence of slavery influenced the region's countries and cities differently in economic, political, ethnic and cultural terms (Cardoso & Brignoli 1979). Cities such as Salvador, Rio de Janeiro and Bogotá have been profoundly shaped both politically and culturally by Afro-descendants. The region's countries have also received intense international migration since the end of the 19th century, especially agricultural migrants, vividly marking some countries and cities such as Buenos Aires and São Paulo. New waves of international migrants have also begun to leave poorer countries in the region like Bolivia, Peru, Guatemala, El Salvador (all of which have been hit too by civil wars) and more recently Haiti to live in cities such as São Paulo, Buenos Aires and Mexico City (Baeninger 2011).

Different countries also created very diverse urban networks and urban scales. The region contains 6 of the 29 cities expected to be world megacities by 2025, although with decreasing population growth rates. The largest cities tend to be in Brazil, the only country with numerous cities possessing more than 2 million inhabitants, 12 in total, compared to 4 in Mexico, 3 in Argentina and 3 in Colombia (UN 2009). Brazil also has the largest city (São Paulo with 20 million) and the fourth largest (Rio de Janeiro with 12 million). At the same time, urban primacy is smaller in Brazil than in the other countries (Cerrutti & Bertoncello 2006): 10 percent for São Paulo, which is not the capital, compared to 32 percent for Buenos Aires in Argentina, 18 percent for Bogotá in Colombia and 17 percent for Mexico City in Mexico (UN 2009). Various countries in the region are home to very large cities, therefore, usually with high urban primacy or a small number of large cities per country, while Brazil concentrates an urban network with many large cities and low primacy.[7]

The processes of institutional building and politics in the region can be divided into three key historical conjunctures, each of them creating similarities and differences among countries and cities. The first moment includes the transitions from colonial rule to independence. Although many historical differences existed, independence resulted from the incapacity of the metropolises to maintain their colonies after Napoleon's expansion through Europe. The Spanish colonies transformed into a set of independent republics, some of which were later subdivided (such as Colombia, Venezuela, Ecuador and Panama, which split some decades after independence). These processes unfolded with relatively little spread of liberal ideas among the local elites and the strong political influence of rural landlords, which heavily shaped the formation of the nation-state in several countries. The Spanish colonies became independent in the period between 1810 and 1830.[8] Brazil acquired independence around the same time, following the same historical trigger—the Napoleonic Wars—but with different results. The Portuguese royal family crossed the Atlantic in 1808, turning Brazil into the only known example of a colony that became the colonial metropolis from one day to the next. The importance of this different path is considerable since this halted the installation of a republic but played a substantial role in preventing the breakup of the vast territory claimed by the Portuguese colony.

The presence of the royal family also postponed independence itself for some years. In 1822, however, the Portuguese courts challenged the king, negotiating the end to the monarch's absolute rule. This led to the separation of the kingdom and the creation of the Brazilian empire in 1822, with the son of the Portuguese king becoming the first emperor. The latter ruled absolute until 1832, when constitutional power was introduced in Brazil. Even after this change, however, the emperor retained the power to review all laws and decisions made by the prime minister and the legislature. The republic would arrive only in 1889 (after the end of slavery in 1888), again with little input from liberal ideas and the strong political influence of landowners. Obviously, all these elements shaped political and social rights, as well as citizenship, in the country.

The second and crucial moment involved economic modernization and state formation in the first decades of the 20th century. Several cities had "modernized" their territories at the end of the 19th century through bourgeois urban reforms, following the examples of Haussman's Paris and Wagner's Vienna (Romero 2004). But although these reforms substantially changed the urban tissue of cities like Rio de Janeiro, Buenos Aires and Montevideo, they were linked more to the image that urban elites wished to project than to economic modernization per se.

Industrialization only arrived in very embryonic forms until World War I and the 1929 Wall Street Crash, which weakened and reduced both the capitalists and the working class. Rural elites, by contrast, were among the most important economic and political actors, and only rarely (e.g., during the Mexico Revolution) did peasants became politically significant. Economic modernization began in the 1930s and 1940s with the strong presence of the state as a producer of intermediary goods (oil and gas, steel, energy and cement) and infrastructures but also as the political guide of the process. In all cases, states implemented industrialization strategies based on import substitution, leading in the most successful cases (Brazil, Argentina and Mexico) to the creation of relatively diversified industrial sectors and relatively capable state structures. Even in these countries, however, the political strength of the rural elites sometimes made industrialization incomplete and less generalized, such as in Argentina (Sikkink 1993), especially during the military period (Torrado 2010). In other cases, rural elites were included peripherally, allowing industrialization and capitalist modernization but maintaining certain parts of the country under old forms of political control and economic development, as in the case of Brazil (Draibe 1985, Souza 1976).

In some countries, social policies and rights were granted by the state even under authoritarian regimes. The most important examples were Brazil under Getúlio Vargas (1930–1945), Mexico under Lazaro Cardenas (1934–1940) and Argentina under Juan Perón (1940–1955), although with more universal application in the Southern Cone of the continent (Franzoni 2008). This shaped the civil societies, polities and social protection systems of these countries, influencing political, civil and social rights in their cities, just as in European cities (Lehto 2000). The cases of Mexico, Argentina and Brazil involved the formation of state corporatist structures, although in Mexico these were developed in close association with the hegemonic party, with consequences for urban associations (Davis 1994) and for the control of civil society by the party and the state (Gurza La Valle & Bueno 2011). In Argentina, the corporatist system marked the party system itself and still today structures the most important splits between Peronistas and anti-Peronistas (Mcguire 1995). In the Brazilian case, the most important legacies of the period were associated with state design and administrative capacities (Nunes 1997, Sikkink 1993) and a set of social rights granted according to participation in the labor market, conceptualized by Santos (1979) as regulated citizenship. This occurred before the full acquisition of civil and political rights, inverting the classical order proposed by Marshall (1950) and leading to a kind of "stateship" instead of citizenship (Carvalho 2001).

The third and most recent moment of parallelism concerns the formation of authoritarian governments and the return to democracy. Many of the region's countries were ruled by authoritarian regimes between the 1960s and 1980s.[9] Some of these governments—Brazil and Mexico being the most prominent—intensified their import substitution policies and conservative modernization. In Argentina and Chile, the strength of the rural elites reduced the focus on industrialization, weakening the formation of a fully developed and interconnected industrial sector. During this period, urbanization and metropolitanization reached their peak, creating the metropolises we see today.

The large majority of the countries also returned to democracy in the 1980s and 1990s, introducing elections and new social actors, making redistribution more complex and inclusive. Several transformations were introduced to the region's social protection systems with different degrees of decentralization, participation (including institutionalized participation), privatization and the growth of the third sector. The different combinations of these elements among countries, however, are very important in terms of understanding what has happened in relation to the state provision of welfare. In some countries, the reforms of the 1980s and 1990s had clear neoliberal designs, the most prominent case being Chile under the Pinochet regime. Peru, Bolivia and Argentina, especially under Menen, also introduced privatization and neoliberal economic instruments, particularly in their pension systems (Mesa-Lago 2000). Brazil went in the opposite direction, as we shall see in Chapter 1, strengthening many of its health and education systems at federal level and reforming its pension system only "parametrically." At the same time, major demographic changes occurred after the 1980s, including a significant drop in migration, fertility rates and demographic growth, accompanied by increases in life expectancy, leading several of the region's countries and cities to undergo clear demographic transitions (Cerrutti & Bertoncello 2006).

These historical processes created legacies that shaped the general features of the economies, states and societies in the region. The legacy of the construction of peripheral capitalism generated intense migration from the rural world, rapid urban growth followed by metropolitan growth, low salaries and pauperization. State construction in the region, on the other hand, led to intense concentrations of authority at the federal level, feeble local governments and local political elites always dependent on the national state, weak state-society connections within authoritarian polities and state-driven citizenships with fragmented social policies. Territorially, the relative scarcity of infrastructure led the central and better-equipped regions to become occupied by the elites, leaving the external and unequipped peripheries, as well as the interstices of the urban fabric, to be inhabited by the poor migrants, thereby producing the peripheralization model typical to the region.

These general historical trends mingled with local processes in specific states and cities based on the presence and strategies of political actors (social movements, specific economic actors and political elites), political institutions (the pace and intensity of authoritarian governments, the presence or absence of federalism and the types of party systems and degrees of electoral competition) and the policies that national and local states produced and delivered (especially infrastructure, planning and social policies), leading to the distinct cities we know today. Chapter 1 will present these elements for the case of São Paulo.

As remarked earlier, the last few decades have brought intense transformations in economic, political and territorial terms, at least to São Paulo. The following section describes how the chapters of this book will tackle the different facets of these changes.

The Main Transformations in São Paulo

The investigation of such a broad set of transformations can only be achieved through a convergence of viewpoints, derived from the various existing thematic debates and deploying a variety of methods and techniques but working toward a common analytic aim. This is the strategy adopted in the following chapters: Each takes the debates on a specific topic as its starting point but converges toward a shared panoramic view of the changes occurring to (and within) the metropolitan area. This convergence has emerged from the intense dialogue between the authors in the various seminars held at the CEM to discuss preliminary versions of the chapters, following the CEM tradition of producing collective books rather than collections of articles. Another crucial point of this inquiry has been the exploration of a common diagnosis (and mapping) of social structure through which the specific processes described in the particular chapters have been analyzed.

Chapter 1 presents the city of São Paulo, its historical construction and the main features of the Brazilian institutions and polity in which the metropolis is embedded. It begins with a discussion of the most important historical processes and legacies in its formation as a metropolis. Next, the chapter describes the main features of the local administrations over the last 30 years as well as the electoral and political processes surrounding them. The chapter also presents the most important institutional, political and policy characteristics of the Brazilian federation that have framed and influenced the development of the metropolis through time, with special interest in the recent democratic period.

This chapter is followed by the first part of the book, dedicated to the processes of economic transformation and social structure. Chapter 2 thus discusses the most relevant socioeconomic dynamics framing the transformations analyzed in the rest of the book. Eduardo Marques, Rogério Barbosa and Ian Prates examine the profound productive and economic changes experienced by the São Paulo metropolis over the last two decades. Overall, significant economic growth occurred in the service sector, especially in productive services and commerce. Contrary to what some analyses from the 1990s suggest, however, this did not mean that industry was pushed out. The São Paulo metropolis apparently experienced an overlapping of economic functions, concentrating command capacities without completely losing its industrial production. The 1990s and 2000s showed opposite trends in relation to employment and poverty. In the 1990s, after a short burst of improvement in 1994 with the stabilization of the economy, unemployment, informal work and poverty all started to rise again. In the 2000s these vectors were reversed with a decline in unemployment and poverty and an increase in formal jobs. The general outcome of the past two decades indicates an overall reduction in poverty and inequalities, as measured by income, along with a fall in unemployment and growth in formal, paid work.

The effects of these kinds of economic transformations on social structure have already been discussed at length. Much of the national debate throughout the 1990s focused critically on processes of social polarization, which in analytic terms closely associated the two dualisms discussed earlier. In international terms, while some suggested the presence of occupational polarization, leading to social, spatial and income polarizations, other authors preferred to emphasize the professionalization apparent in the occupational structure, leading not only to growth but also to a transformation in relation to income distribution. To analyze these transformations in São Paulo's social structure, Marques, Barbosa and Prates constructed social classes on the basis of occupations using one of the most widely used occupational classifications: EGP (the initials are taken from Erikson, Goldthorpe and Portocarrero, its proponents).

The information on São Paulo over the last decades suggests a slow but consistent pattern of transformation. No signs of polarization were found, since although the higher occupational categories linked to professional activities have grown and the manual working classes shrunk, the intermediary classes have also expanded in terms of relative presence. On the other hand, the qualified and unqualified manual classes remain predominant, confirming the previous hypothesis of an overlap of economic functions in the metropolis—with the growth of command activities but maintaining strongly Fordist industrial manufacturing activities. It is worth adding that average schooling rose in all classes, resulting in greater access to educational policies, especially for the younger sections of the population.

In summary, it cannot be asserted that São Paulo's social structure has undergone social polarization over the last 20 years. Although the professional classes have grown substantially over the same period, however, neither was professionalization observed, as exemplified by some large European metropolises, since a substantial portion of the social structure linked to factory and manual work was maintained.

These movements were accompanied by a strong entry of women into the labor market among almost all the classes but especially in professional occupations with higher schooling and income. This process led to a reduction in gender inequalities in income and occupations, although they still remain high. The same was not observed, however, in relation to race: Although the presence of self-declared non-whites has increased among all classes, there was no alteration in their relative presence in the higher classes, suggesting that racial inequalities remained virtually untouched over the decade.

As would be expected, all these changes had impacts on income inequalities in the labor market. These are analyzed by Rogério Barbosa and Ian Prates in Chapter 3. The analysis showed signs of social polarization among occupations in the 1990s, the moment when productive restructuring took place, but this was reversed in the following decade when the Brazilian economy started growing again in an environment of greater commercial opening. The overall result of the last two decades has been a reduction in inequalities provoked by various processes not always running in the same direction. Breaking down inequality into these social dimensions showed the causes or correlates behind these reductions. The exercise undertaken by Barbosa and Prates showed that inequality decreased both between classes and within classes in terms of job formalization and gender. On the other hand, inequalities tended to increase in relation to generations of workers (age) and educational levels, although these changes have been lower than those observed between classes. The impact of educational levels is especially interesting: Although the rise in average schooling levels has helped reduce inequalities at national levels, it has had the opposite effect at local levels in São Paulo, possibly due to the rise in the minimum requirements for more qualified new jobs, reflecting the evidence of professionalization already indicated. The overall result of the two decades, however, has been a reduction in inequalities.

The chapter concludes by analyzing the relationship between poverty and the labor market. The latter became more receptive to low-skilled workers in the 2000s compared to the previous decade, leading to a relative (and absolute) growth in income for this workforce. Additionally, the authors reaffirm the occurrence of bias toward informality in the Brazilian labor market in the 1990s, although this was reversed in the 2000s. Nonetheless, these dynamics were not sufficient to alter the labor market broadly.

The next chapter opens the second part of the book, analyzing the main transformations in demographics and segregation. In Chapter 4, José Marcos Cunha examines demographic growth and migration, including intraurban, in Brazilian metropolitan spaces, focusing particularly on São Paulo. The chapter begins with an examination of the dynamics of population growth in São Paulo within the wider context of metropolitanization in Brazil. It demonstrates the absence of deconcentration in medium-sized cities, or interiorization, although the metropolitan phenomenon did spread, and low primacy remains the main defining characteristic of the Brazilian urban network when compared with the rest of Latin America. The author also shows the continuation of growth in most of the metropolises. In São Paulo, the recent rates were small but above stagnant growth. Migration to São Paulo, for its part, has fallen continuously since the start of the 1990s, although the region continues to attract people from other states and the interior of São Paulo state itself. This flow was accompanied by an intense migration to the latter region, a dynamic that has remained significant even in recent years, suggesting that the interiorization thesis makes sense for São Paulo, albeit not for other metropolises and states. Large intraurban and intrametropolitan flows were also observed, with the largest and most important municipalities—São Paulo, Guarulhos, Osasco and the ABCD municipalities—[10]being important sources of migrants to the state interior and the rest of the region. These flows also include higher-income groups who are moving to closed condominiums in outlying areas. At the same time, other smaller municipalities are absorbing migrants from other states and the metropolis itself.

As in earlier decades, these demographic processes acquire specific features when analyzed at more detailed levels. This is the task undertaken in Chapter 5, dedicated to studying the demographic dynamics within the metropolis. Eduardo Marques and Carolina Requena reveal a continued reduction in the average growth rate of the metropolis as a whole, which in the 2000s reached the lowest rate since the start of the 20th century.

However, the authors also show that this reduction conceals other important transformations. In general terms it is possible to argue for a cooling of the demographic processes overall, both in growth areas and in areas in decline. At the same time, though, the association between demographic dynamics and the social characteristics of each space of the metropolis reduced very substantially. As the literature has already explored in depth, growth in the 1990s was strongly associated with the income of the populations living in each section of the metropolis—wealthier areas showing an absolute decline, with poorer and more peripheral areas displaying high growth rates. In the 2000s, this association was no longer observable, and growth was clearly associated with localized processes of spatial production. On one hand, some central parts of the metropolis continued to decline demographically, while others returned to smaller growth rates, and others still grew at higher rates. The resumption of growth in these areas was strongly associated with the real estate dynamics of the formal market with verticalization and a certain degree of elitization. This process, however, was not generalized, implying that it would be too hasty to claim that the metropolitan center has started to grow again as a whole. Heterogeneity in the peripheral areas was even greater: While some peripheries increased in demographic size considerably, in others the populations remained stable. In this case, the areas that grew more intensely continued to receive recent migrants, suggesting that the continuation of the classic process of peripheralization coexists with processes of consolidation in other parts of the peripheries.

The intense transformations over the decade had interesting effects on the patterns of residential segregation in the São Paulo metropolis, one of its strongest constitutive dimensions. Chapter 6 by Eduardo Marques shows a fairly high and relatively stable segregation structure at general levels. In overall terms, the classical model already widely described by the literature continues to apply, with wealthier central areas inhabited by higher social categories contrasting with outside areas inhabited by the poorer population of manual workers and their families. However, this general structure conceals various important dimensions, observable only when the different spaces of the social groups are observed in detail.

While the region inhabited by the elites is almost entirely exclusive, the peripheral areas are fairly heterogenic in social terms. The most segregated groups are precisely the higher classes. In addition, a pattern of avoidance between social classes is clearly evident in this segregation, especially in terms of the elite classes. Hence, the levels of segregation are organized by each group in relation to all the others, with the levels increasing as we drop down the social structure. Over the decade, two processes classically considered by the literature as opposed could be observed. While the elite areas located in the inner region of the metropolis became more exclusive, the middle and peripheral areas became more heterogenic. The pattern of avoidance between classes also became clearer over the course of the decade.

This resulted from a growth in the presence of the professional classes in all the city spaces, even in the peripheries, albeit with higher growth in the elite areas. At the same time, the manual classes tended to shrink in all the spaces too but this time more emphatically in the peripheral areas. The historical center of São Paulo, on the other hand, became more popular over the course of the decade. West of the metropolis, closed medium-high and high level condominiums spread with resulting impacts on local sociability.[11] The processes therefore pointed to greater homogeneity in the elite areas and greater heterogeneity in the peripheral areas, which is incompatible with the idea of spatial polarization or with dual representations of the metropolis.

The chapter concludes with an assessment of urban conditions over the decade. A significant proportion of infrastructural services became increasingly universalized, even in the area of sewage treatment, which remains at a much lower level. The urban condition indicators, however, suggest the persistence of deep inequalities, still associated with the socioeconomic conditions of residents.

Contrary to a substantial portion of the local debates, Chapter 7 by Danilo França eloquently demonstrates the presence of high racial segregation, which combines with class in the constitution of residential segregation in the São Paulo metropolis. This does not appear in the general data—for example, when we examine the indices of dissimilarity between the white and black populations. However, when these data are disaggregated into income and race, higher segregation by race and income is found in the upper-income groups, with much lower segregation in the lower-income groups. In addition, there is a clear pattern of avoidance by skin color, especially among the rich white population. Although race and class combine to explain the segregation pattern—dissimilarity data show that rich white residents have less segregation than middle-income white and rich black residents and only more than poor white residents—the levels of segregation are much higher vis-à-vis black people, separating a rich white elite relatively closer to middle-income white residents than the rest of the population.

This racial dimension of segregation cogently reappears in França's analysis of spatial correlations by race and class. Groups with lower income have less racial segregation than higher-income groups. Within the black population, segregation is slight but is still much higher between them and white people of various income levels. In racial terms, therefore, the most highly segregated groups displaying clear socio-racial avoidance are the white elites. In fact the segregation of these elites increased over the decade, which is consistent with the findings already mentioned previously concerning segregation by class.

Chapter 8 begins the third part of the book, dedicated to the discussion of housing in the metropolis. The city of São Paulo has historically contained a large contingent of residents living in precarious housing conditions. During the most intense period of metropolitanization, in the 1960s and 1970s, clandestine and irregular settlements predominated, but gradually the favelas became integrated into the city's urban fabric. Camila Saraiva provides a detailed analysis of this form of precarious housing in Chapter 8. Her analysis shows that favelas expanded little during the decade, indeed less than the overall population of the metropolis. The author compares the conditions of the favelas, their surrounding areas and the urbanized favelas, showing that the latter are situated in an intermediary position. At the same time, the social conditions in São Paulo's favelas continued to improve over the last decade, even indicating a convergence between the average characteristics of the favelas located in the region's different municipalities when the results are compared with the findings of earlier studies. Nevertheless, favelas continue to be marked by intense heterogeneity in terms of social makeup and infrastructural conditions. When the present-day social situation and infrastructure of the nuclei is compared with those found in 2000, however, we observe less heterogeneity and an improvement in average terms, despite the persistence of a set of favelas with fairly precarious conditions. This group mainly does not include recent nuclei, suggesting the existence of a set of favelas with very poor and stable conditions coexisting with an improvement in conditions in most of the other favelas.

Housing policy has transformed considerably over recent decades. Private and public production have converged significantly through the expansion of private housing production to middle-low income bands, the result of both recent improvements in income and changes in federal regulations and through the forms of implementation chosen for the My House My Life (*Minha Casa Minha Vida*) Program, the main initiative in the public housing sector. Chapters 9 and 10 analyze these two areas of housing developments in the São Paulo Metropolitan Region (SPMR) showing a degree of complementarity.

In Chapter 9, Eduardo Marques and Leandro Rodrigues analyze the implementation of the My House My Life Program in the metropolitan area. Confirming the critical analyses of the program already existing at national level and in other cities, the São Paulo program appears to have eased the housing shortfall more strongly in the higher income bands than the lower, where most of the deficits are actually located. The spatialization of housing developments for each of the income bands, on the other hand, confirmed the existing view that the program's implantation shows a peripheral pattern, even more pronounced for the lowest income band. However, when compared with the earlier public housing programs run by the state and municipality of São Paulo (by COHAB and CHDU, respectively), we find evidence that these criticisms of the program need to be nuanced. The housing developments for the lowest income band (0 to 3 minimum salaries) effectively presented a pattern of localization similar to the previous local public housing developments, but the localization of housing for the higher bands clearly has a less peripheral pattern than existing developments. Here what we need to observe is that earlier housing developments in Brazil were not aimed at the lowest income group but mainly the second band of the My

House My Life Program. Compared with equivalent housing in the past, therefore, the program reveals less peripheral developments, although still relatively distant from centers and amenities. Although the program can be said to be missing the chance to have a greater impact on segregation in the metropolis, therefore, including through the lowest income band housing developments, it would be incorrect to describe its implementation as equal to earlier programs, at least in terms of the metropolitan region of São Paulo.

The formal housing developments built by the private sector were traditionally aimed at high and medium-high income groups. Although this tendency remains dominant, at least some of the recent private-sector developments have converged significantly with public projects, meaning that these forms of housing provision are often adjacent and sometimes overlapping. The market-derived housing production is analyzed in detail by Telma Hoyler in Chapter 10. Development production has shown a clear, three-phase cycle since the mid-1980s, each with distinct characteristics. While the first two phases were almost completely devoted to producing housing for high-income groups in elite spaces, the last phase (from 2005 to 2013) also included the more diverse popular market with territorially broader localizations and less concentration in the central areas. Finally the analysis suggests that over these cycles, the market became more "organized" or perhaps more consolidated, making it easier to predict what will be built where since there is an increasing association between the social makeup of the spaces (as measured by resident income) and the average prices of the housing developments.

Finally, Chapter 11 by Carolina Requena closes the book by analyzing one of the crucial dimensions of sociability and metropolitan life: mobility. Despite its huge importance, the theme has remained virtually unexplored by the social sciences and urban studies. Based on information from the Subway Company survey (which covers all dislocations—*Origem e Destino da Companhia do Metropolitano de São Paulo*), cross-referenced with census data, the author explores mobility in the metropolis over the last 20 years. The chapter reveals that mobility follows a highly consolidated structure in which around a third of journeys are made on foot, road transportation predominates, and rail transport is proportionally low. This structure has changed little over the last two decades. Buses are the most important form of public transport, accounting for a quarter of journeys, a relatively similar amount to journeys made using individual transportation. The data indicate, however, a strong association between the modes used by different social groups as well as the spaces inhabited by them. Groups with higher income and education living in more central areas walk less and use cars much more frequently, while the use of buses is more socially widespread. Finally, journey times also indicate clear social differences, with public transportation by bus presenting substantially longer journey times.

What, then, is the overall picture resulting from these processes of transformation? At risk of simplification, São Paulo has become a more heterogenic city in productive, social and spatial terms. In various aspects, it has also become a less unequal city in terms of income, inclusion in the labor market and living conditions, even in its precarious spaces. The processes involved in producing each of its spaces (and the plural is ever more important) are increasingly defining their respective patterns of growth, social conditions, forms of housing production and urban precariousness. In other aspects, though, patterns of inequality remain strongly present. Some precarious areas have improved little, while patterns of urban mobility tend to be stable and marked by strong social inequalities. From the viewpoint of its urban spaces, the metropolis remains heavily segregated in terms of race and class, forming a clearly hierarchical structure, as we shall see. Simultaneously, though, the city is experiencing processes usually considered to be dissociated, if not antagonistic: the popularization of its historic center and even more exclusive elite areas but with even more socially mixed intermediary and peripheral regions.

The recent processes suggest the need to avoid dualistic interpretations, allowing room for the existence of diverse types of intermediary spaces (and social groups) within the metropolis. This does not mean the complete disappearance of a radial and concentric structure at more general levels, much less the vanishing of the socio-spatial inequalities that so strongly characterize São Paulo, but rather its recomposition into more complex and continuous patterns. On one hand, some specific, precarious spaces still show little improvement in terms of urban conditions. On the other, the social homogenization of wealthy regions has occurred in parallel with a growing heterogeneity in mixed and peripheral spaces. In certain aspects, some of the city's intense inequalities have tended to reduce, but they remain a huge challenge to be overcome in building a fairer and more pleasant city in which to live.

Notes

1. Incidentally, I must add that the specificities of a third large research field—urban politics and policies—remains basically untouched and are still to be explored.
2. Just to continue with my previous example, although the same can be sustained for the discussion of labor markets, the state, and political institutions, among other subjects.
3. There are also some legal forms of land property associated with state concessions. They tend to be residual, however, and present importance mainly as recent strategies of land regularization of favelas and irregular settlements.
4. For an excellent critique of marginality theory, see Perlman (1977). It is also interesting to note the similarities between this culturalist (and behaviorist) explanations of urban poverty and the "culture of poverty debate" led internationally (and in the US especially) by Charles Murray's reading of Oscar Lewis: the "blame the victim" analytic strategy.

5. According to UN estimates, 23.5 percent of the region's population in 2010 was living in irregular or precarious settlements (a lower figure than the average for developing regions: 32.7 percent). This figure is declining—it was 29.2 percent in 2000 and 34 percent in 1990 (United Nations 2009) and tends to vary substantially. In Brazil, for example, while the most famous precarious areas are located in Rio de Janeiro and the largest precarious population lives in São Paulo, the highest relative levels of precarity are found in the North and Northeast of the country: Fortaleza, Belém do Pará, and Recife.
6. Obviously the same statement can be made even more emphatically about the global South as a whole.
7. This appears in several other dimensions of the urban networks. Ordoñez & García (2010), for example, show that the major cities in Brazil concentrate lower proportions of airplane mobility than in the rest of the region, with a pattern closer to the US than to the rest of the region.
8. Independence came to Argentina in 1816 (Saint Martin); Chile in 1818 (O'Higgins e San Martin); Colombia/Venezuela/Ecuador/Panamá in 1819 (Venezuela and Ecuador became separate countries in 1830, with Bolivar's death); Peru in 1820; Bolivia in 1809, but consolidated in 1825; Mexico in 1821; Paraguay in 1811; Uruguay in 1810 (from Spain) and 1828 (from Brazil and Argentina).
9. The list of coups d'état is long: Brazil (1930, 1937, almost in 1954, almost again in 1963, and finally in 1964), Argentina (1930, 1943, 1955, 1962, 1966, 1970, and 1976), Uruguay (1933 and 1973), Chile (1932 and 1973), Peru (1929, 1948, 1968, and 1975), Paraguay (1954, with Stroessner remaining president until 1989), Bolivia (1970 and again 1980), Venezuela (1945 and 1992), and Ecuador (1963 and 1976). The only large country with no coup d'état—Mexico—experienced the longest de facto authoritarian regime (from the 1920s to the 1990s). The choice of the PRI's candidate, made within the organization itself—the "destape"—was the only really important political competition for 70 years.
10. The ABCD region is the most important industrial region in the country, including the municipalities of Santo André, São Bernardo, and São Caetano e Diadema.
11. The advertising material from one developer announces as an advantage that "There no strange people enter."

Bibliography

Baeninger, R. (2011). Crescimento da População: desconstruindo mitos do século 20. In: Kowarick, L. and Marques, E. (eds.) *São Paulo: Olhares cruzados—Sociedade, Economia e Política*. São Paulo: Ed Loyola, p. 34.

Baltrusis, N. (2009). Mercado Informal de Tierras e Vivendas in São Paulo. *Bitacora Urbano Territorial*, 15, pp. 53–78.

Bonduki, N. and Rolnik, R. (1982). Periferia da Grande São Paulo: reprodução do espaço como expediente de reprodução da força de trabalho. In: Maricato, E. (ed.) *A Produção Capitalista da Casa e da cidade do Brasil*. São Paulo: Alfaômega, pp. 117–154.

Caldeira, T. (2000). *City of walls*. Los Angeles: University of California Press.

Camargo, P. (ed.) (1976). *São Paulo, 1975—Crescimento e pobreza*. São Paulo: Ed. Loyola.

Campolina Diniz, C. and Campolina, B. (2007). A região metropolitana de São Paulo: reestruturação, re-espacialização e novas funções. *Revista Eure*, XXXIII(98), pp. 27–43.

Canevacci, M. (1993). *A cidade polifônica*. São Paulo: Edusp.
Cardoso, C. and Brignoli, H. (1979). *História económica de América Latina*. Mexico City: Ed. Crítica.
Cardoso, F. and Faletto, E. (1977). *Dependency and development in Latin America*. Los Angeles: University of California Press.
Carvalho, J. (2001). *Cidadania no Brasil: o longo caminho*. Rio de Janeiro: Civilização Brasileira.
Cerrutti, M. and Bertoncello, R. (2006). Urbanization and internal migration patterns in Latin America. In: Tienda, M., Findley, S.E., Tollman, S., and Preston-Whyte, E. (eds.) *Africa on the move: Africa migration and urbanization in comparative perspective*. South Africa: Wits University Press, pp. 127–148.
Costa Pinto, L. (1967). Modernização e desenvolvimento. In: Costa Pinto, L. (ed.) *Teoria do desenvolvimento*. Rio de Janeiro: Zahar, pp. 8–31.
Davis, D. (1994). *Urban leviathan*. Philadelphia: Temple University Press.
Davis, M. (2006). *Planet of slums*. New York: Verso.
Draibe, S. (1985). *Rumos e metamorfoses: Estado e industrialização no Brasil (1930/1960)*. Rio de Janeiro: Paz e Terra.
Duerau, F. and Vanegas, A. (2000). Las diferentes expresiones del proceso de segregación en Bogotá. In: Jaramillo, S. (ed.) *Bogotá, en el cambio de siglo: promesas y realidades*. Quito: Olachi, pp. 195–220.
Duren, N. (2006). Planning à la Carte: The location patterns of gated communities around Buenos Aires in a decentralized planning context. *International Journal of Urban and Regional Research*, 30(2), pp. 308–327.
Durham, E. (1988). A sociedade vista da periferia. In: Kowarick, L. (ed.) *Lutas sociais e a cidade*. Rio de Janeiro: Paz e Terra, pp. 169–181.
Edensor, T. and Jayne, M. (2012). Introduction: Urban theory beyond the West. In: Edensor, T. and Jayne, M. (eds.) *Urban theory beyond the West: A world of cities*. London: Routledge, pp. 1–28.
Feltran, G. (2011). *Fronteiras de tensão*. São Paulo: Ed. Unesp/CEM.
Fernandez-Maldonado, A. (2001). Changing spatial logics in Latin American metropolises. In: Carmona, M. and Schoonraad, M. (eds.) *Globalization, urban form and governance*. Delft: DUP, pp. 267–284.
Franzoni, J. (2008). Welfare regimes in Latin America: Capturing constellations of markets, families, and policies. *Latin American Politics and Society*, 50(2), pp. 67–100.
Furtado, C. (1964). *Development and underdevelopment*. Los Angeles: University of California Press.
Gilbert, A. (ed.) (1996). *The mega-city in Latin America*. New York: United Nations University.
Goldfrank, B. and Schrank, A. (2009). Municipal neoliberalism and municipal socialism: Urban political economy in Latin America. *International Journal of Urban and Regional Research*, 33(2), pp. 443–462.
Granovetter, M. (1985). Economic action and social structure: The problem of embeddedness. *American Journal of Sociology*, 91(3), pp. 481–510.
Griffin, E. and Ford, L. (1980). A model of Latin American city structure. *Geographical Review*, 70(4), pp. 397–422.
Gugler, J. (2004). Introduction. In: Gluger, J. (ed.) *World cities beyond the West: Globalization, development and inequality*. Cambridge: Cambridge University Press, pp. 1–26.

Gugler, J. and Gilbert, A. (1982). *Cities, poverty, and development: Urbanization in the third world*. Oxford: Oxford University Press.

Gurza Lavalle, A. and Bueno, N. (2011). Waves of change within civil society in Latin America: Mexico City and Sao Paulo. *Politics & Society*, 39, pp. 415–450.

Gurza Lavalle, A. and Castello, G. (2004). Benesses desse mundo: associativismo religioso e inclusão socioeconômica. *Novos Estudos Cebrap*, 68, pp. 73–93.

Guzmán, J. (2006). The demography of Latin America and the Caribbean since 1950. *Population*, 61(5/6), pp. 519–576.

Hart, G. (2004). Geography and development: Critical ethnographies. *Progresse in Human Geography*, 28(1), pp. 91–100.

Holanda, S. (1995 [1936]). *Raízes do Brasil*. Rio de Janeiro: Nova Fronteira.

Joseph, J. (2009). Lima: Descentralización, democratización y desarrollo. In: Centeno, P. (ed.) *Lima, diversidade y fragmentación de una metrópole emergente*. Quito: Ollachi, pp. 283–324.

Kantor, P. and Savitch, H. (2005). How to study comparative urban development politics: A research note. *International Journal of Urban and Regional Research*, 29(1), pp. 135–151.

Kaztman, R. and Retamoso, A. (2005). Spatial segregation, employment and poverty in Montevideo. *Cepal Review*, 85, pp. 125–142.

Kowarick, L. (2009). *Viver em risco: sobre a vulnerabilidade socioeconômica e civil*. São Paulo: Ed. 34.

Kowarick, L. (1979). *A espoliação urbana*. Rio de Janeiro: Paz e Terra.

Lehto, J. (2000). Different cities in different welfare states. In: Bagnasco, A. and Le Galés, P. (eds.) *Cities in contemporary Europe*. Cambridge: Cambridge University Press, pp. 112–130.

Lomnitz, L. (1975). *Como sobreviven los marginados*. Ciudad de Mexico: Siglo Veintiuno.

Maricato, E. (1987). *Política habitacional no regime militar*. Rio de Janeiro: Paz e Terra.

Marques, E. (2012). *Opportunities and deprivation in the Global South: Poverty, segregation and social networks in São Paulo*. Londres: Ashgate Pub.

Marques, E. and Torres, H. (2005). *São Paulo: segregação, pobreza e desigualdades sociais*. São Paulo, Ed. Senac.

Marshall, T. (1950). *Citizenship and social class and other essays*. Cambridge: Cambridge University Press.

Martine, G. and Campolina Diniz, C. (1997). Economic and demographic concentration in Brazil: Recent inversion of historical patterns. In: *Urbanization in large developing countries: China, Indonesia, Brazil and India*. Oxford: Oxford University Press.

Massey, D. (2005). *For space*. London: Sage, pp. 205–227.

McCann, E. and Ward, K. (2010). Relationality/territoriality: Toward a conceptualization of cities in the world. *Geoforum*, 41, pp. 175–184.

Mcfarlane, C. (2010). The comparative city: Knowledge, learning, urbanism. *International Journal of Urban and Regional Research*, 34(4), pp. 725–742.

Mcguire, J. (1995). Political parties and democracy in Argentina. In: Mainwaring, S. and Scully, T. (eds.) *Building democratic institutions—party systems in Latin America*. Stanford: Stanford University Press, pp. 200–248.

Mcmichael, P. (1990). Incorporating comparison within a world-historical perspective: An alternative comparative method. *American Sociological Review*, 55(3), pp. 385–397.

Mesa-Lago, C. (2000). *Desarollo social, reforma del Estado y de la seguridad social, al umbral del siglo XXI*. Santiago: Eclac, Serie Politicas Sociales, No 36.
Nijman, J. (2007). Introduction – comparative urbanism. *Urban Geography*, 28(1), pp. 1–6.
Nunes, E. (1997). *A gramática política do Brasil: Clientelismo e Insulamento burocrático*. Rio de Janeiro: Jorge Zahar/Enap.
Oliveira, F. (1982). O Estado e o urbano no Brasil. *Revista Espaço and Debates*, 6, pp. 43–57.
Ordoñez, J. and García, C. (2010). Latin American cities and globalization: Change and permanency in the context of development expectations. *Urban Studies*, 47(9), pp. 2003–2021.
Perlman, J. (1977). *The myth of marginality*. Los Angeles: University of California.
Perlman, J. (2004). Marginality: from myth to reality in the favelas in Rio de Janeiro 1969-2002). In: Roy, A. and Alsayyad, N. (eds.) *Urban informality: Transnational perspectives from Middle East, Latin America and South Asia*. Lanham: Lexington Books, pp. 105–146.
Pickvance, C. (1986). Comparative urban analysis and assumptions about causality. *International Journal of Urban and Regional Research*, 10(2), pp. 162–184.
Portes, A. and Roberts, B. (2005). The free-market city: Latin American urbanization in the years of the neoliberal experiment. *Studies in Comparative International Development*, 40(1), pp. 43–82.
Preteceille, E. and Cardoso, A. (2008). Rio de Janeiro y São Paulo: ciudades duales? Comparación con Paris. *Ciudad y Territòrio*, XL(158), pp. 617–640.
Ragin, C. (1987). *The comparative method: Moving beyond qualitative and quantitative strategies*. Berkeley: University of California Press.
Reis Filho, N. (2012). Sobre o semeador e o ladrilheiro. In: Marras, S. (ed.) *Atualidade de Sérgio Buarque de Holanda*. São Paulo: Edusp/IEB, pp. 41–50.
Rihoux, B. and Ragin, C. (eds.) (2009). *Configurational Comparative Methods*. Thousand Oaks: Sage.
Roberts, B. (2005). Globalization and Latin American cities. *International Journal of Urban and Regional Research*, 29(1), pp. 110–123.
Robinson, J. (2014). Introduction to a virtual issue on comparative urbanism. *International Journal of Urban and Regional Research*, Virtual Issue. http://onlinelibrary.wiley.com/doi/10.1111/1468-2427.12171/epdf
Robinson, J. (2011). Cities in a world of cities: The comparative gesture. *International Journal of Urban and Regional Research*, 35(1), pp. 1–23.
Robinson, J. (2006). *Ordinary cities: Between modernity and development*. New York: Routledge.
Rodgers, D., Beall, J. and Kanbur, R. (2011). Latin American urban development into the twenty-first century: Towards a renewed perspective on the city. *European Journal of Development Research*, 23, pp. 550–568.
Romero, J. (2004). *América Latina: as cidades e as idéias*. Rio de Janeiro: Ed. UFRJ.
Rostow, W. (1960). The five stages of growth—A summary. In: Rostow, W. (ed.) *The stages of economic growth: A non-communist manifesto*. Cambridge: Cambridge University Press, pp. 4–18.
Roy, A. (2015). Who is afraid of postcolonial urban theory? *International Journal of Urban and Regional Research*, Virtual Issue[0]. Available at: *http://onlinelibrary.wiley.com/journal/10.1111/%28ISSN%291468-2427/earlyview*.
Roy, A. (2011). Slumdog cities: Rethinking subaltern urbanism. *International Journal of Urban and Regional Research*, 35(2), pp. 223–238.

Roy, A. (2009). The 21st-century metropolis: New geographies of theory. *Regional Studies*, 43(6), pp. 819–830.

Roy, A. and Alsayyad, N. (2004). *Urban informality: Transnational perspectives from Middle East, Latin America and South Asia*. Lanham: Lexington Books.

Sabatini, F., Cáceres, G. and Cerda, J. (2005). *Residential segregation pattern changes in main Chilean cities: Scale shifts and increasing malignancy*. Boston: Lincoln Institute of Land Policy.

Salcedo, R., Wormald, G. and Cáceres, G. (2008). *Tendencias de la segregación en las principales ciudades chilenas*. Santiago: INE.

Santos, C. (1982). *Processo de crescimento e ocupação da periferia*. Rio de Janeiro: IBAM/CPU.

Santos, W. (1979). *Cidadania e justiça*. Rio de Janeiro: Ed. Campus.

Savitch, I. (1988). *Post industrial cities: Politics and planning in New York, Paris and London*. Princeton: Princeton University Press.

Scott, A. and Storper, M. (2015). The nature of cities: The scope and limits of urban theory. *International Journal of Urban and Regional Research*, 39(1), pp. 1–15.

Sellers, J. (2005). Re-placing the nation: An agenda for comparative urban politics. *Urban Affairs Review*, 40, pp. 419–445.

Sikkink, K. (1993). Las capacidades y la autonomía del Estado em Brasil e Argentina. Un enfoque neoinstitucionalista. *Desarrollo Economico*, 32(128), pp. 543–574.

Souza, M. (1976). *Estado e partidos políticos no Brasil (1930 a 1964)*. São Paulo: Ed. Alfa-Ômega.

Taylor, P., Ni, P., Derudder, B., Hoyler, M., Huang, J. and Witlox, F. (eds.) (2010). *Global urban analysis: A survey of cities in globalization*. London: Routledge.

Telles, V. (2010). *A cidade nas fronteiras do legal e ilegal*. Belo Horizonte: Argvmentvm.

Tilly, C. (1984). *Big structures, large processes huge comparisons*. New York: Russell Sage Foundation.

Torrado, S. (2010). Modelos de acumulación, regímenes de gobierno y estrutura social. In: Torrado, S. (ed.) *El costo social del ajuste: Argentina 1976–2002*, Tomo I. Buenos Aires: Edhasa, pp. 21–62.

United Nations. (2012). *The state of Latin American and Caribbean cities 2012: Towards a new urban transition*. Washington, DC: United Nations.

United Nations. (2009). *World urbanization prospects*. New York: United Nations Press.

Wacquant, L. (2008). The militarization of urban marginality: Lessons from the Brazilian metropolis. *International Political Sociology*, 2, pp. 56–74.

Ward, K. (2010). Towards a relational comparative approach to the study of cities. *Progress in Human Geography*, 34(4), pp. 471–787.

Zaluar, A. (2010). Turfwar in Rio de Janeiro: Youth, drug traffic and hyper-masculinity. *Vibrant*, 2, pp. 7–27.

1 São Paulo Histories, Institutions and Legacies

Eduardo Cesar Leão Marques

This chapter presents the main institutional and political features of Brazil that have worked to shape the city of São Paulo, narrating the historical formation of the most important characteristics of this metropolis. The chapter's main objective is to help situate the foreign reader in relation to São Paulo's most important elements. In so doing, the chapter analytically reconstructs the interpretation of Brazilian cities prevalent until the 1980s and that still informs international debates about Latin American cities. The transformations of the last 20 years discussed in the following chapters have worked precisely to change the city described through this interpretation.

We can begin with some general geographical features of the metropolis. The metropolitan region of São Paulo is composed of 39 municipalities distributed across a total area of 7,947.28 km² of which 2,209.00 km² is urbanized. The most important municipality is São Paulo, which is the capital of the state (with the same name). Occupation unfolded along the basins of two large rivers, the Tietê, which runs from east to west, and the Pinheiros, which runs from south to north (see Figure 2 in the introduction). The latter flows from two large artificial lakes constructed at the beginning of the 20th century to provide water to the city. In the middle of this region lies the historical center, located near the hill that marks the site of the first settlement in the 16th century. This is surrounded by the so-called expanded center, delimited to the north and the west by the two main rivers and to the east and the south by large avenues. This region included most of the urban fabric until the 1940s and circumscribed the areas occupied by the São Paulo elite until the 1960s. A third region of interest is the important sub-centrality formed by the ABC Paulista, situated to the southeast, where the majority of the region's industrial activities are located, in addition to the municipalities of Guarulhos in the northeast and Osasco to the west. Urbanization sprawled across this vast urban fabric throughout the history of the city, with intense precariousness and social vulnerability to the north and in the East Zone as well as to the south around the lakes.

This chapter is divided into four sections, each organized chronologically. The first section discusses the main legacies from the colonial period to the so-called First Republic, ending in the late 1920s. The second section starts with the discussion of the impact of modernization processes promoted after 1930 and centered on state formation and industrialization in Brazil, with profound impacts on the city during the period of intense metropolitanization that began after the 1940s. The third section discusses the local and national transformations that occurred during the military dictatorship from 1964 until the mid-1980s with the consolidation of urbanization by metropolitanization and peripheralization. The fourth and final section covers the more recent process of democratization. As the following chapters focus on the economic, social and spatial transformations occurring in the metropolis since the return to democracy, the final section of this chapter turns its attention to policies and politics, both national and in São Paulo.

From Colonial Legacies to the First Republic in the 1920s

São Paulo is one of the most important metropolises in the world at the beginning of the 21st century, but for centuries it remained a small and unimportant village. The city was officially founded by Jesuit priests in 1554 with the creation of a small school for the evangelization of the region's Amerindian populations. In 1560 the population of a nearby village was transferred to the site of the Jesuit school since it presented better defensive conditions. This was the start of the occupation. The city, however, would remain peripheral and unassuming over the following centuries, reflecting the project of territorial occupation pursued by the Portuguese crown, as discussed in the introduction: The largest cities were located along the coast and functioned as administrative centers and exportation ports connecting Brazil with Portugal (Oliveira 1982). Until the end of the 1700s, São Paulo was no more than a regional commercial center and the departure point for the Bandeiras, expeditions to the interior of the state and into the state of Minas Gerais in search of Indians to enslave, as well as for gold and precious stones—mostly diamonds and emeralds (Bruno 1991). The Portuguese king's arrival in 1808 and Brazil's declaration of independence in 1822 had little effect on the status of São Paulo, which continued to be a small, peripheral village throughout the bulk of the 19th century.

As in other Brazilian cities, living conditions were precarious, and the presence of the state in terms of the provision of services and policies was negligible. By the second half of the 19th century, however, urban services in Brazilian cities had started to become organized, largely in response to the chronic presence or epidemic outbreaks of typhoid fever, yellow fever, malaria, cholera and a host of other diseases (Andrade 1986, Costa 1989). Although the creation of these services paralleled their implementation in the major cities of the Global North, regulatory constraints on construction and occupation were far less common in Brazil. In São Paulo, the first substantial urban regulation had to wait for the Sanitary Code issued in

1886 (Ribeiro 1993), and there was almost no public control over building work or urban design. Private land itself did not exist before 1850, with all land prior to that date technically belonging to the king (Marx 1989). The poor for the most part lived in precarious tenements or in the periurban settlements found in all Brazilian cities. This situation did not change with the abolition of slavery in 1888 nor with the inauguration of the republic in 1889. The end of the empire in fact left social inequalities intact, with poor social groups having little or no access to rights, policies or services (Carvalho 2001).

Since state capacities were effectively absent, the predominant strategy employed by the local elites to provide services was to appoint experts to produce studies and hire private companies to build infrastructures or set up and run services. In the large majority of cases, small, private Brazilian companies were hired, though foreign private companies would frequently acquire these later. This was the case of sewage services in Rio de Janeiro in 1863 (Marques 1995) and water supply in 1857; sewage services in 1865 in Recife; sewage in Florianópolis in 1910 (Ramos 1986); water, sewage and drainage in Santos in 1880 (Andrade 1992); water in São Paulo in 1877 (Bueno 1993), horse-drawn trams in 1872 in São Paulo (Segatto 1989) followed by Rio de Janeiro in 1862 (Abreu 1987) and gas street lighting in Rio de Janeiro in 1854 (Abreu 1987) to cite just some examples. The most famous episodes in the history of private control over urban services occurred in São Paulo, beginning with the inauguration of electric trams in 1899 by the Canadian-owned firm Light and Power. This company would eventually monopolize the provision of almost all the infrastructural services in the city, becoming known popularly as the "octopus" due to its widespread presence during the first decades of the 20th century (Carone & Dér 1989, Segatto 1989).

By the end of the 19th century, São Paulo had become an important commercial and economic center, mainly due to the flourishing of coffee plantations in the interior of the state from 1870 onward. Although the coffee economy was scattered throughout the interior of the state, São Paulo was the hub of an intense flow of workers and products along railway networks financed by the "coffee barons" (Sorocabana and São Paulo Railway) and built to connect their plantations to the global market via São Paulo and Santos, the city port located some 100 kilometers away on the coast. These plantations used immigrant labor brought to Brazil through institutional agreements with foreign governments, especially from Italy and Japan. Indeed, while the municipality of São Paulo had just 2,459 foreign inhabitants in 1872, this figure reached around 207,000 by 1920—36 percent of the population—which explains the importance of immigrant culture in the city even today.[1] At the same time, the absence of slave labor in the coffee economy also explains the lower black population in São Paulo when compared to cities like Rio de Janeiro, Salvador and Belo Horizonte.

By the end of the 19th century São Paulo had acquired several new neighborhoods, built to host the city mansions of the rural elites, such as Campos Elísios (1878), Higienópolis (1895) and Paulista Avenue (1891), located to the west and south of the historical center (Toledo 2004). This created new needs in terms of urban services and planning, leading to the development of new public agencies (Simões 1991) as well as generating a construction market for Brazilian engineers and companies (Silva 1994).

São Paulo grew in importance and size, reaching 240,000 inhabitants by 1900.[2] A significant proportion of the state's agricultural surplus was reinvested in urban activities. By the first decades of the new century, this had led to the development of industrial sectors engaged in traditional industries, including textiles, furniture and construction materials (Cano 1990). This first wave of import substitution was strongly reinforced by World War I and the Great Depression, which reduced the availability of imported products (Rangel 1987).

The first decades of the new century were also marked by important urban reforms, aiming to replace the colonial urban fabric with a more functional and infrastructured urban design, which at the same time would Europeanize the country's most important cities. To carry through these transformations, local governments hired foreign urban planners to redesign the central areas of the cities of São Paulo (Antoine Bouvard), Rio de Janeiro (Alfred Agache) and Recife (Abreu 1987, Leme 1999, SMU 2008, Zancheti 1991). Several public works were constructed in this effort to "embellish" the cities, including the construction of iconic public buildings such as the opera houses (locally called municipal theaters) in Rio de Janeiro (1909) and São Paulo (1911) and even in Manaus (1896), deep within the Amazon rainforest, in the latter case financed by rubber plantation barons.

In São Paulo, the central area of the city—what is now the historical center—was transformed at the turn of the century by several public works. The construction of a bridge over the Anhangabaú valley in 1892 connected the two sides of the valley (and the two main sectors of the historical center). This was later complemented by the Santa Efigência Viaduct, an iron bridge imported from Belgium in 1913. Both sides of the valley were transformed by a new garden, the opera house, several private constructions (such as the Palacetes Prates, built between 1908 and 1912) and later the city's first skyscraper: the Martinelli, built in 1929 (with the impressive height of 12 floors). Modern commercial activities also appeared, such as the first department store, the British-owned Mappin, opened in 1913.

At the same time, though, the burgeoning industrial working classes and the poor, many of them international migrants, were living in very precarious conditions. They produced important social mobilizations in the 1920s, mainly propelled by anarchist associations and immigrant leaders (Fausto 1983), inaugurated by the 1917 strikes, the first large-scale labor confrontations in Brazilian history. A few of these workers lived in company housing projects (Rago 1985), but the large majority inhabited tenements with very poor sanitary and housing conditions, known as the cortiços (Kowarick & Ant 1988). Still existing today, these are collectively occupied houses, originally old colonial houses, where each family occupies a single room, with the collective use of bathrooms, kitchens and laundry areas. The majority of these tenements were located in the industrial quarters of the city, east of the historical center. The city already had a clear pattern of segregation, albeit with small distances considering the small area covered by the city at the time. The poor social groups lived in company housing projects and precarious tenements to the east, while wealthier social groups inhabited private developments to the west and south.

The 1930s: Industrialization, State Capacities and Social Policies

When we consider economic modernization and federal regulation in Brazil, however, the 1930s are the real landmark. This decade represented a period of intense construction of the state apparatus, the formation of a national labor market and the development of a capitalist economy with a strong state presence. The process began with the 1930 revolution, when Getúlio Vargas seized power, interrupting a decades-long period of control of national policies by rural (and local) oligarchies. The Vargas government implemented a wide-ranging project of conservative modernization, centering around the construction of state capacities and an import substitution strategy that led Brazil to its second industrial revolution. This project involved a nationalist ideology that set the "construction of the nation" as its goal: The advance of territorial occupation into the interior and the west would be combined with substantial political and economic centralization. The political regime was based on an authoritarian form of corporatism, inspired by Italian fascism, and introduced a broad system of labor and capital organizations kept under close government control (Nunes 1997, Sikkink 1993). São Paulo was among the most important opponents of this national project (even rising in arms against the regime in 1932) since the Paulista elites faced a loss of power and the coffee economy was declining in importance. However, in the long run, São Paulo would be one of the cities to most benefit from the changes, considering the surge in industrialization that placed São Paulo as its epicenter over the following decades.

This was also the moment when the first national social policies were established in Brazil. The first national pension system was created, run by new state agencies called Pension and Retirement Institutes (IAP) and organized according to economic sectors (industrial, banking, ports and civil servants). These were also the conditions that enabled the first national health policies, social assistance policies (in association with the Catholic Church) and housing and sanitation policies, beginning in 1937.

In all these cases, the state granted rights to some social sectors based on their centrality in the economic development strategies, a regime that Santos (1979) called regulated citizenship. This left the vast majority of the population (e.g., rural laborers, informal urban workers and domestic employees) completely unprotected. This system has important parallels with what Esping-Andersen (1990) classified as the corporatist or conservative type of welfare state: rights granted by the state in authoritarian political structures, based on the person's occupation; intense presence of the family and the church in welfare; and benefits concentrated on the male role as breadwinner (Draibe 1989). This led to an unequal, incomplete and highly fragmented social protection system, similar to what happened in southern European countries (Mingione 2005). Although this system helped reduce poverty, it also reproduced and in some cases reinforced the social and racial inequalities that had become characteristic of Brazilian society.

In the case of São Paulo, the decades between the 1930s and the military coup of 1964 were marked by the construction of two opposite and complementary characteristics of the metropolis, starting a process that would be consolidated in the decades to come as the era of metropolitanization and peripheralization. On one hand, the central areas of the city continued to be equipped and serviced in what would later be called the expanded center. Several urban plans were produced, in particular the Avenues Plan, designed by Ulhoa Cintra and Prestes Maia in 1930. This sought to prepare the city's infrastructure for the new transportation technology based on the individual automobile (Leme 1999, Toledo 1996). Private constructors built new, large-scale housing developments for the elites in central regions of the city and in the neighborhoods located in the first ring around it, west and south of the historical center. The most important of these firms was the Companhia City, a British company that created several garden city neighborhoods, starting in 1915 with Jardim América, designed by Raymond Unwin and Barry Parker, and followed later by Pacaembu in 1925, Alto da Lapa in 1929 and Alto de Pinheiros in 1937 (Leme 1999, Simões Jr. 1991). Zoning policies also began to be implemented around this time, for the most part reserving central areas with better infrastructure and environmental conditions for occupation by the urban elites. This territorial strategy received a new momentum with the creation of the Secretary of Municipal Works and Services in 1945 and the São Paulo Municipality Department of Urbanism in 1947. Also in 1947, the city saw the promulgation of its first Land Use Law (Feldman 2005).

The other side of this process was the construction of vast peripheries with very low access to urban services. These became the home for the large and impoverished internal migrant population arriving in the city at this time, which set out from the poorer rural northeastern states of Brazil in search of better jobs and living conditions (Kowarick 1979). This process not only happened in São Paulo but also in several other Brazilian metropolises. In fact, from 1940 to 1960, the Brazilian urban population jumped from 12.9 to 31.3 million inhabitants (Baeninger 2011), with almost no public policies for providing housing to this influx of poor migrants into the largest cities.

Basically, the poor in Brazil had used three precarious housing solutions since the end of the 19th century: tenements, favelas and irregular settlements. As already mentioned, tenements (or *cortiços* in Portuguese) involve rented rooms in collective buildings with communal kitchens, bathrooms and laundry areas. Favelas are occupied areas that usually lack basic urban infrastructure and exhibit irregular patterns of physical occupation. What defines the favelas, however, is the absence of land ownership. Finally, irregular and clandestine settlements are built by private entrepreneurs who fail to comply with the due legalization, despite the weakness of state regulation: the first federal law establishing patterns for parceling dates from 1979. This hampered the legal division of plots and the issuing of separate land titles for each family, regardless of whether they had paid for them. While tenements (*cortiços*) tend to be centrally located, the irregular and clandestine settlements and the majority of the favelas are usually situated out in the peripheries of the metropolis. Today these precarious solutions are sometimes mixed.[3]

During the metropolitan expansion of São Paulo in the 1940s and 1950s, tenements were surpassed numerically by irregular and clandestine peripheral settlements as the housing solution most widely used by the poor, although tenements continue to exist even today. In other large Brazilian cities such as Rio de Janeiro, Salvador and Belo Horizonte, favelas became the most widespread low-income housing solution around this time, but in São Paulo favelas only became really important in the 1980s, when the territorial scale of the metropolis made the distances involved with further horizontal expansion almost unviable.

The expansion of irregular settlements in São Paulo from the 1940s onward was enabled by the substitution of trains and trams (predominant in the 1920s) by the bus as the main form of public transportation for the poor. As is widely known, track-based transportation systems induce urbanization patterns around their axes, creating concentric occupation spots around their stations. Buses, by contrast, move much more easily in all directions, opening up a wide and continuous territory for the expansion of the metropolitan area. In 1947, Light and Power's monopoly over public transportation expired, and the municipality created the Municipal Collective Transportation Company (CMTC), which would operate trams and buses. CMTC coexisted in the following decades with a continually expanding private bus fleet, responsible for a substantial part of the territorial sprawl from the 1950s (Henry & Zioni 1995). Although housing developments and bus companies were in the hands of private companies, the state strongly induced the urban form of the metropolitan region by planning and building large avenues, highways, bridges and other road transportation infrastructures.

During these decades, São Paulo's metropolitan region expanded from 1.6 million inhabitants in 1940 to 4.8 million in 1960 (Baeninger 2011). The resulting urban structure was marked by intense segregation between the wealthier social groups located in central (and equipped) areas and vast poor peripheries located on the city outskirts. This radial and concentric structure, which would be consolidated during the military years, became the predominant narrative about Brazilian (and Latin American) metropolises.

The Military Coup and Authoritarian Modernization

In 1964, the military ceased power, breaking the first experience of mass democracy in Brazil that had started in 1945. The process of state building that started in the 1930s was given a new impetus with the creation of various agencies and federal police forces. Wide-ranging policy reforms were introduced involving centralization, the closure of decision-making processes, now held under strict technocratic control, and the formation of federative financial arrangements based on economic returns and the absence of any kind of subsidies. The actual implementation of these reforms would later tend to be quite different with widespread corruption, mis-targeting and patronage schemes (Draibe 1989), basically following the same logic that had been cited as the motive for the coup d'état, but now with no accountability whatsoever.

In consonance with this technocratic and authoritarian surge in state building, several local administrative capacities were created in São Paulo during the same period. In 1971 and 1972 the city received a new master plan and a new zoning Law, which reinforced the tendency to secure the more central areas for the elite population to live in lower-density green neighborhoods while leaving the peripheries with very few regulations. In 1979 a federal law was introduced regulating settlement construction for the first time—the so-called 6766/79, establishing standards for their regularization. The law aimed to reduce the presence of irregular settlements, but the rapid impoverishment of the working classes caused by the military governments (Camargo 1976) meant that the law indirectly encouraged their expansion since the poor were unable to afford well-built settlements with urban infrastructure. A similar scenario unfolded in the southern part of the SPMR with the creation of new environmental legislation in 1975 and 1976 to protect the two large river dams used to supply water (Figure 1). The minimum standards established by the law were so high, increasing land prices as a consequence, that the private developers found no demand for regular settlements. In the following decades, the region became one of the most important locations for irregular settlements and favelas in the metropolis (Bueno 2000).

Several local agencies were also created and restructured during this period. In 1966, the municipal government created the subway company. This was complemented by the creation of the Transportation Municipal

Secretary (SMT) and the Street System Department (DSV), both in 1972, and the Traffic Engineering Company (CET) in 1976, an agency with greater technical and administrative autonomy.[4] Given the historical hegemony of private transportation in the city—as in the large majority of Brazilian cities—this company concentrated much more power than the public transportation authorities, implementing a mobility paradigm based on private vehicle use (Requena 2015).

Public transportation, on the other hand, had been controlled by CMTC since 1947, although private bus companies had gradually become predominant: In 1948 CMTC had 687 buses or trams, while private companies had just 173, but in 1970 the public company had only 1,189, while private providers had 4,939 (Henry & Zioni 1995). This difference continued to grow until 1989, when the municipal government under the left-wing Workers' Party (PT) tried to restructure and strengthen the public company but with ephemeral results. In the following administration, the company was transformed into a sector regulator—SP Transportes—responsible for regulating the private provision of transportation services. Most of the equipment and personnel were sold, rented or transferred to the private companies. Over the last two decades, however, the most important issue concerning this policy has been who pays for the system and what amount of public subsidy is embedded in the bus fare.

Buses are thus the most important public transportation solution in São Paulo (Chapter 11), but the subway is also present. The subway company was created in 1968, although the first line started to run only in 1974. The late entrance of the subway, along with its slow pace of expansion, is among the main reasons for the chaotic traffic in the city. In 2010 the metropolitan region had just 74.3 kilometers of track and 64 subway stations, compared to 201 kilometers and 175 stations in Mexico City, home to the same size of population, or London and Paris with almost half São Paulo's population but 402 kilometers and 270 stations and 214 kilometers and 301 stations, respectively.

In the area of public works and road building, several agencies were also reorganized. In 1972, the municipality created the Municipal Urbanization Company (EMURB) to be in charge of large public works in the city. In 1975, the Public Works Office was divided into Services and Works Office (SSO) and the Public Routes Office (SVP). The former was responsible mainly for garbage collection and public buildings, while the latter was responsible for the construction of bridges, tunnels, roads and large drainage works in the city. For the next two decades, SVP became the most powerful agency in the city, considering both its share of the municipal investment budget and the consequences of its policies for the territorial organization of the metropolis (Marques 2003). The importance of these agencies expresses the hegemony of road building over planning, present ever since the Prestes Maia Plan in 1930, at the same time as it reinforces the car's hegemony over public transportation.

In terms of social policies, local actions directly mirrored transformations at the federal level. The military governments reorganized several policy sectors, creating and implementing federal systems for pension and retirement schemes, medical care and social assistance. In these cases, the government created federal institutions, financial systems and state-level executive offices that expanded the number of beneficiaries but maintained the same general logic of regulated citizenship. Once again, rural, domestic and informal workers were omitted from the scope of these policies, although rural workers began to receive some more restricted benefits in 1972.

In housing and sanitation, the military government's policy involved the creation of a national financial system, a major funding source—a federal bank—and 27 state-level public housing companies responsible for producing housing developments (Maricato 1987). This was the first example of mass housing production in the country. The policy produced 4.5 million units between 1964 and 1986, when the bank was closed. The policy delivered just one single product for low-income housing: new units in large-scale housing projects on the outskirts of the cities for long-term financed sale. This policy generated substantial mis-targeting since the really poor had no demand even for financed sale: just 33.1 percent or 1.5 million units reached low-income buyers (Royer 2014). Additionally, the policy produced endemic corruption with the private builders hired for project construction. Finally, the policy delivered very low quality in construction and architectural terms and strongly reinforced the already high patterns of residential segregation. More importantly, regardless of its scale, the policy failed to confront the challenge posed by mass migration and high fertility rates: Between 1964 and 1986, 15 million new housing units were built in the country (1.5 million of them state provided), while the Brazilian urban population leapt from 31 million inhabitants in 1960 to 80 million in 1980 (Baeninger 2011). The SPMR population jumped from 4.8 to 12.6 million inhabitants in the same period.

The following map presents the expansion of the metropolitan tissue since 1882. The sprawl of the metropolis is indeed astonishing, especially after 1930 and between 1950s and the 1970s.

The expansion of the city corresponded in large part to the construction and consolidation of the processes of metropolitanization and peripheralization of previous decades, with radial and concentric segregation patterns and the poor living in precarious and irregular settlements in unequipped peripheries (Bonduki & Rolnik 1982) as well as favelas. All these forms of housing were self-built in collective processes by the inhabitants themselves during their free time. This urbanization pattern submitted the working population to a kind of exploitation derived from urban space or what Kowarick (1979) called "urban spoliation." The state classically reinforced segregation by constructing large-scale housing projects in outlying peripheries (Maricato 1987), some of them today with more than 200,000 inhabitants.

São Paulo Histories, Institutions and Legacies 41

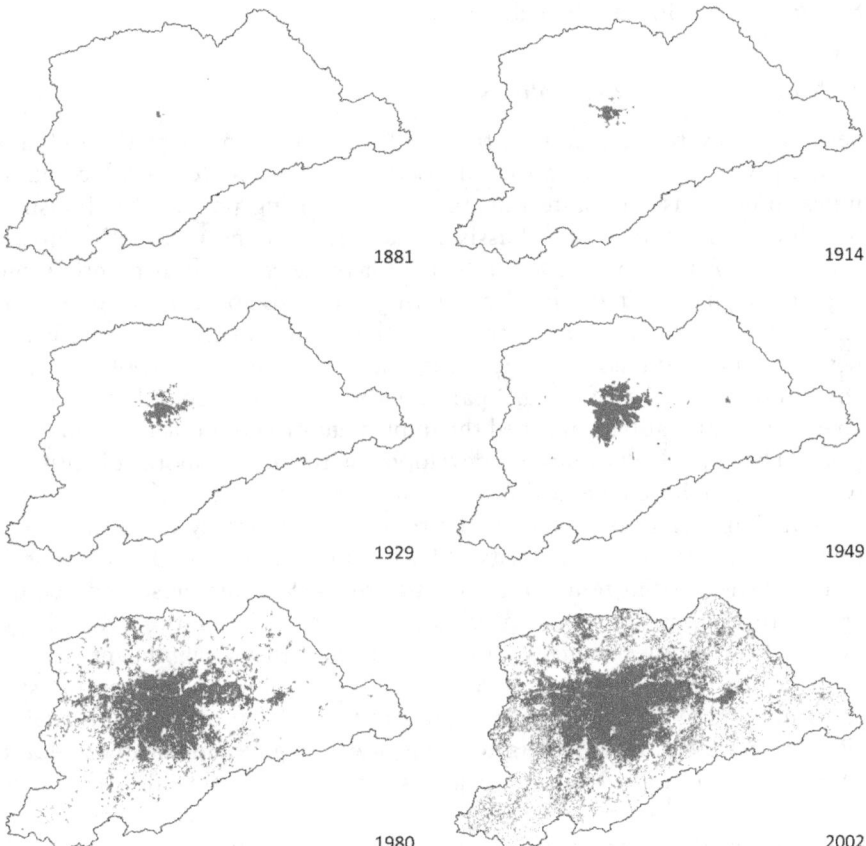

Figure 1.1 Expansion of the SPMR, 1881 to 2002.
Source: CEM based on original cartographies by Emplasa.

It is important to add that social movements in the region strongly opposed this urbanization pattern. In the 1970s and 1980s, they were very important actors during the transition from the military regime to democracy (Sader 1988). They were also at the origin of important changes in the Brazilian party system brought about by the growth of the PT, as we shall see.

The Recent Democratic Period

Recent decades have seen intense changes in political, economic and social processes at different scales in Brazil. Since we shall be discussing the most important urban changes in detail throughout the rest of the book, this last section focuses its attention on policies and politics at the national and local levels, presenting the processes that have surrounded and impacted São Paulo over the last three decades.

1. National Politics and Policies

Several policy reforms were introduced after the demise of the military regime, with the participation of social movements, technical communities, politicians and state bureaucrats in drafting policies for housing, health care, sanitation, social assistance, education and many other areas. The 1988 constitution was a landmark for those reforms, dismantling the logic of regulated citizenship by granting access to social policies regardless of the individual's participation in the labor market, although it left pending important issues concerning the financing of the policies. The constitution also had strongly participatory and municipal-based input, characteristics that have marked the implementation of policy reforms ever since. The model of economic development through import substitution was substantially changed (Portes & Roberts 2005), therefore, the path of Brazilian social policies since the return to democracy has gone in the opposite direction to the majority of Latin America. In several Latin American countries, social policy reform since the 1990s has presented neoliberal features aimed at reducing program costs and eligibilities (Mesa-Lago 2000). Among other changes, Brazil has strengthened a significant portion of its health and education federal systems while reforming its pension system only "parametrically." It is important to add that although the PSDB (Partido da Social Democracia Brasileira) was in government in 1994 and 1998 with Fernando Henrique Cardoso, and PT (Partido dos Trabalhadores) in the following four elections with Luis Inácio Lula da Silva and Dilma Rousseff, there has been a considerable continuity in policy at federal level associated with learning processes involved in the reforms to each social policy area (Arretche 2002). The result has been the production of relatively coherent policies over the years, at least by Brazilian standards, with positive effects in terms of the impact on social conditions (Anderson 2011, Roberts 2012).

Although the process is policy specific, especially in terms of the pace and resulting design of policies (Arretche 2002), in almost all cases there was more than just decentralization. The reforms constructed federalist policy systems, with the federal government retaining policy formulation capacities and granting financial resources and local governments mostly responsible for implementation (Arretche 2012). In several cases, participatory arenas were created and institutionalized within the policy sectors at local and federal levels (Heller & Evans 2010). Due to these reforms, access to policies is increasing relatively quickly, even for the very poor. In some cases, such as water supply, electricity and basic education, the services are almost universalized (Figueiredo et al. 2006, Perlman 2004). As a whole, poverty and inequalities have been declining in urban areas continuously and monotonically for the last 15 years (Anderson 2011, Barros et al. 2006), as will be discussed comparatively in Chapter 2. It is also true, however, that while the massification of services has solved a substantial part of the quantitative problem, it has created and magnified problems (and differences) in relation to service quality. It is fair to say that the next challenge—quality—seems set to pose even greater difficulties since it involves the betterment of urban equipment, staff training and the transformation of the technical cultures of several professional communities.

One social process that has shown a clear and alarming negative increase, however, is urban violence (Feltran 2012, Misse 2007 and 2011, Perlman 2004), with important consequences for urban segregation (Caldeira 2000). Organized crime around the drugs and firearms markets has expanded hugely since the return to democracy at the same time as several types of crime have become much more prevalent in almost all Brazilian metropolises. Homicides skyrocketed in the 1990s, though they have shown a downward trend in the last few years (Peres et al. 2011). While some authors see this fall as an outcome of state-level public security policies (Nadanovsky 2009), others argue that the reduction has at least in part been produced by the opposite: an increasing control over everyday sociability in the urban peripheries by the PCC (Primeiro Comando da Capital), an almost monopolistic criminal organization, at least in São Paulo (Biondi 2008, Feltran 2009 and 2012). It is important to add that public security is one policy sector that has passed through the recent decades unreformed, maintaining the same structure it had during the military period.

In any case, the reforms of the 1990s and 2000s changed policy provision in Brazil in several sectors, regardless of the unresolved problems in underfunding. Public education reform (FUNDEF) extended the federal government's capacity to formulate policy and led to the expansion of primary education schools run by states and municipalities, substantially reducing the number of children left outside the system, a reality that still affected the country in the mid-1990s. In the 2000s, this reform was extended to include high school education (FUNDEB). In the health sector, a national noncontributory and universal system (SUS) was implemented through the reorganization of the powers and responsibilities of the three levels of government and the development of local capacities for primary care, although hired private capacities were maintained in hospital services (Menicucci 2007). Social assistance has been intensively reorganized through the creation of the Bolsa Família Program, today the largest CCT (Conditional Cash Transference) program in the world, as well as the implementing of a federal system of social assistance (SUAS) and a network of social assistance facilities at local level, although the latter is still in its initial phase (Bichir 2010). These reforms have helped make basic services universally available, though differences in quality still create incentives for the elite population to remain outside the systems, whether choosing private schools for their children or purchasing private health care plans.

These policy reforms also substantially enhanced social participation in policy-making processes through the introduction of Policy Councils and Conferences (Tatagiba 2011). These new institutionalized arenas for policy discussion became widespread. The councils spread through local governments during the 1990s, reaching the federal level under the Cardoso administrations, and have been enforced locally by federal policies ever since. More recently, the Lula administrations held several national conferences by policy sector.

At the same time, however, the traditional involvement of social movements in rallies and protest activities has declined, following what some analysts have described as a transition from "active centrality" to "passive centrality" (Gurza Lavalle et al. 2008). Urban social activism has also become more heterogeneous since the 1990s in part due to the presence of other channels for participation and political action under democracy, including nongovernmental organizations (NGOs) and involvement in delivering public policy. The recent period also saw the dissemination of identity-based social and cultural movements, not only the Afro-Brazilian movement but also underground literature and rap music produced in the urban peripheries. Overall, these transformations in both associativism and public policy deliberation and implementation have substantially changed the role of civil society in the workings of democracy in recent Brazil (Gurza Lavalle & Bueno 2011).

In terms of urban policies, the federal government has almost entirely vanished from the scene since the decline of federal housing policy in the 1980s. Over the next 30 years, lacking any federal housing policy, the urban population would leap again from 80 million in 1980 to 161 million in 2010.

Contradictorily, the absence of federal resources and policies allowed the creation and dissemination of alternative initiatives designed and implemented at local level as part of a broad process of policy innovation. Among these new policies we may cite participatory councils, new financial arrangements, redistributive zoning, social rent and tenement renovation but especially slum upgrading, regularization of irregular settlements and self-help housing construction associated with the state. These initiatives started a learning process within the urban policy community that was key to the constitution of the Ministry of Cities in 2003, important in terms of institutional building, albeit with very little insulation from political interests (Rolink 2011). These initiatives included the Council and the Conferences of the Cities, national funds for popular housing and national plans for housing, sanitation, transportation and solid waste management. At the end of the 2000s, the federal government returned to financing urban policies with programs such as the Growth Acceleration Program (Programa de Aceleração do Crescimento [PAC]) and the My House My Life Program (Minha Casa Minha Vida [MCMV]). In the case of the PAC, local governments are responsible for implementing public works, including slum upgrading, transportation and major infrastructural works. In the case of the MCMV program, however, the implementation arrangement transferred responsibility directly to private builders to ensure quick results (Shimbo 2012), as we shall see later in Chapter 9. One indirect outcome of this program was that, because of its sheer scale, it ended up blocking local policies, leading the large majority of municipalities to simply reach agreements with the federal government and provide land for projects financed and produced via the program. On the other hand, it has reduced the possibilities for corruption at the local level since contracts are centralized (and heavily regulated) by a federal bank, the CEF.

Therefore, we can summarize the legacy of policy responsibilities over urban policies during the 2010s as follows. Brazil is organized institutionally as a federation with three tiers of government: federal government, states, and municipalities. Municipalities have political autonomy to elaborate and deliver several types of policies. The present division of tasks within Brazilian federalism includes municipal responsibility for land use, urban planning, housing, urban infrastructure, garbage collection and transportation (buses). Sanitation, public security (the police), the environment (licensing and enforcement of environmental laws) and public transportation by rail (trains and the subway) are state-level services (state organizations are sometimes also involved in road transportation). The subway is usually a state-level service, although in some cases (and during certain periods), municipal governments also assume part of its financing. Several of these are partially financed with federal resources, which provide the federal government with significant induction capacities. Health, education and social assistance are concurrent responsibilities, although the federal systems concentrate the largest responsibility for policy formulation at the federal level and implementation at the local level.

Metropolitan government has never really existed, although agencies were created in the 1970s and later dismantled. Today there are some formal councils that should theoretically deliberate on services of common interest. The state of São Paulo is traditionally stronger than the municipal government in financial, political and administrative terms (when compared to Rio de Janeiro, e.g., where the opposite occurs).

2. Local Politics and Policies

The period since the return to democracy has also brought many changes in the way local politics has unfolded since the 1960s, with important consequences for cities. From 1968 on, only two parties were allowed to exist in the country: Arena, the party of the regime, and MDB (Movimento Democrático Brasileiro), the tolerated opposition. Between 1968 and 1985, the mayors of state capitals, as well as those from cities classified as important to "national security" (those located on the national borders but also those with large infrastructures, such as large airports and oil refineries) were appointed by the governors, but aldermen continued to be directly elected as well as federal and state representatives. Governors, for their part, were elected indirectly by state assemblies whose representatives were elected. Various restrictions on political participation and voting existed, therefore, elections continued to be part of the political process in Brazil in the 1960s and 1970s.

Although the metropolitan region of São Paulo includes 39 municipalities, the municipality of São Paulo is by far the largest and most important in political, economic and administrative terms. Other important municipalities of the metropolis include the ABCD municipalities—Santo André, São Bernardo and São Caetano and Diadema as well as Osasco and Guarulhos. The first group was very important historically since it housed the so-called new labor movement, which contributed to the decline of the military regime and is tied to the birth of the PT. The main local electoral disputes in the 1970s, however, were concentrated in the municipality of São Paulo. In that decade, electoral results in São Paulo favored the opposition, especially center-left political groups. These, for example, elected 16 of the 21 aldermen in the 1976 election, even in the face of various maneuvers from the regime (Lamournier 1980). In 1980, the military government implemented electoral reform, extinguishing the two-party system and clearing the way for new parties—in fact another institutional maneuver aimed at splitting the opposition (Lima Jr. 1993). This gave rise to the present party system, although in the following decades several changes contributed to its consolidation (Meneguello 1998).

With the return to mayoral elections in 1985, the center-left opposition was certain that they would win the municipality of São Paulo since they had won the first direct election for state governor in 1982. The elected governor had appointed the engineer and center-left federal representative Mario Covas as mayor of São Paulo from 1982 to 1984. However, the election result favored Jânio Quadros from the PTB (Partido Trabalhista Brasileiro) over senator and PMDB (Partido do Movimento democrático Brasileiro) candidate Fernando Henrique Cardoso, who would become president of the republic in 1994 (Lamournier 1980). Quadros was a right-wing politician who had governed the city in the 1950s and became Brazilian president in 1961 for a short period, before resigning after seven months (Lamournier 1985, Sadek 1985). His administration focused on the construction of several large public works, redevelopment and various urban renovation policies. One important innovation for the city was the creation of the first Operações Interligadas (Interconnected Operations), a specific zoning instrument that allowed additional potential building plots to be purchased from the municipality (above the limits set for the rest of the city) in certain areas under renovation.

In 1988, the PT won the next local election with Luiza Erundina, a former social worker and alderwoman with strong ties to social movements.

During this period, the metropolis hosted a number of important movements and associations, mainly organized around health, sanitation and housing demands (Jacobi 1989). These movements forced increases in service delivery but also had a more diffuse effect associated with a shift of the local agenda toward distributive policies.

At this time PT was situated on the far left of the political spectrum and was clearly a minority party in local electoral terms, electing only 16 of the 53 aldermen. The victory in the mayoral election was mainly due to the electoral rule at the time specifying one single electoral round, irrespective of the results: This allowed Erundina to win with just 29.8 percent of the vote, compared to 24.5 percent for Paulo Maluf, the second-place contender and a right-wing former mayor and governor during the military period. The Erundina administration introduced many innovative and redistributive policies in close association with sector-based social movements. Among the innovative policies created were slum upgrading projects, restructuring of the transportation system, large self-build housing programs, educational reform and the regularization of irregular settlements and favelas as well as the implementation of sweeping fiscal reform of urban taxation (including strong redistributive features) and the production of the first master plan since the 1970s, both rejected by the legislature. Indeed, the government was marked by intense conflicts with the local legislature due to PT's minority status as well as by fights within the party itself (Couto 1994).

In 1992, the same right-wing political group that controlled the local government with Jânio Quadros returned to power with Paulo Maluf of the PPB, beating the PT candidate Eduardo Suplicy. The continuity between the administrations of the different right-wing political parties is also confirmed by the occupants of the most important positions in municipal departments and agencies, which show a remarkable continuity. The large majority of individuals had circulated among agencies and administrations since the 1970s during the governments of Reynaldo de Barros, Salim Curiati, Jânio Quadros, Paulo Maluf and Celso Pitta, the exceptions being the left-wing Mario Covas and Luisa Erundina governments (Marques 2003).

The Maluf administration dismantled the transportation reform and housing policies of the previous government and established as its main priority a major urban plan of road building (including tunnels under the city's largest park and under the Pinheiros river) as well as large-scale renovations of business districts. Changes in regulations transformed the Interconnected Operations into Urban Operations, the format that all major renovations in the city (and in other Brazilian cities) would assume in the future (Bonduki 2010). The most significant changes affected the Faria Lima/Águas Espraiadas/Berrini region in the southeast of the city, including a renovation project that consumed US$4.2 billion and evicted 10,000 poor people from central and wealthy areas (Fix 2001, Marques 2003). In 1996, the same mayor succeeded in electing his successor—Celso Pita of the PPB (his finance secretary)—who beat the PT candidate and former mayor Luíza Erundina. The policies implemented during Celso Pitta's government largely continued those begun during the administration of his predecessor and mentor, albeit with a declining capacity for investment. In fact, the costs of the constructed public works created a major financial crisis in the city in the 2000s. Several corruption scandals also marked his term of office.

The 2000 election registered a number of important shifts. On one hand, the election was won by Marta Suplicy from PT, with a large majority of 58.5 percent of the valid votes won in the second round. At the same time, the PSDB (a center party) appeared competitively for the first time, losing the chance to go into the second round to Paulo Maluf by just 0.1 percent of the vote. In fact, this election marked a transition: From this moment on the main political opposition would be between PT, now located on the center-left of the political spectrum, and the PSDB, which came from the center-left but captured the conservative vote in the city.

Marta Suplicy reorganized local policies along redistributive lines. Her government implemented slum upgrading, self-build housing programs, planning (the first master plan since the 1970s was approved by the legislature in 2002), garbage recycling (with the participation of waste-picker associations) and administrative decentralization through the creation of the sub-municipalities (Alves 2004). The most important projects, however, included a major reorganization of public transportation with the creation of an integrated bus system, which allows multiple trips with one single ticket (the Bilhete Único), and a large-scale program for building schools and culture or leisure centers in the peripheries (Centros educacionais unificados [CEU]) with the idea of integrating these facilities into their neighborhoods. Elsewhere the administration continued to renovate the Faria Lima/Águas Espraiadas/Berrini region and created an important policy instrument for the financialization of Urban Operations. The CEPACS are financial titles sold on the stock market that allow additional building potential within the limits of the Urban Operation. This instrument completed the process of transforming land into a financial asset, with obvious consequences in terms of the fluidity of the transactions as well as their speculative retention (Royer 2014). This model was exported to several other cities and especially to the Porto Maravilha project in Rio de Janeiro, the first mega urban project in Brazil, made possible by a broad coalition of interests, including the federal government, brought together by the plans for the 2014 World Cup and the 2016 Olympics (Saruê 2015).

Although her government had quite high acceptance rates, Marta Suplicy lost the following election for mayor in 2004 to the PSDB candidate José Serra, who gained 55 percent of the votes in the second round. The winner was a senator, a former minister of health in the Fernando Cardoso administration and the presidential candidate for the PSDB defeated by Luis Inácio Lula da Silva of PT in 2002. The Serra government represented a center-right administration, with an agenda mainly associated with balancing the municipal budget and reviewing contracts. The two most important urban projects were the expansion of the Bilhete Único (Single Ticket) system to include the subway and the formulation of the Nova Luz project, an initiative for renovating a severely degraded central area through an explicit process of gentrification. This project prompted many local forms of resistance from both poor tenement movements and from the area's commercial sector. In fact, it was never fully implemented due to this opposition and to legal problems in the courts (Souza 2011). Serra resigned less than two years later to run for state governor, leaving his vice mayor, Gilberto Kassab, in power. Kassab was a federal representative of the PFL and the DEM (the same right-wing party, which has been renamed) who had previously been planning secretary during the Celso Pitta administration. He represented the connection between the center and the right-wing political fields in the city. In 2008, the mayor was reelected with 61 percent of the vote, beating Marta Suplicy. The two Kassab administrations were to a large extent a continuation of the first years of his first term, including the unsuccessful implementation of the Nova Luz project, the design and initial implementation of a bicycle lane network, and the construction of more schools and cultural or leisure centers in the peripheries, although less open to the local neighborhoods. The main landmark of this administration, however, was its approval of stricter regulations on outdoor advertising—the Cidade Limpa (Clean City) project, aimed at reducing visual pollution in the city. In terms of housing, the municipality produced a large number of dwellings associated with the federal Minha Casa Minha Vida program, a topic discussed in Chapter 9.

In 2012, PT returned to power with Fernando Haddad, ex-minister of education in the Lula government, who beat former mayor and PSDB candidate José Serra with 55 percent of the votes in the second round. Haddad's administration focused on completing the reorganization of the transportation system, including the construction of 400 kilometers of dedicated bus lanes, the production of a new master plan (approved in 2014), the creation of new schools and culture or leisure centers on the periphery, and the expansion and consolidation of the bicycle lane network begun under the previous administration. His government halted the Nova Luz project but planned to start a very ambitious renovation project for a large area near the Tietê river—the Arco do Tietê. However, this did not reach implementation stage due to a lack of funds.

The local literature has already intensely discussed the region's electoral dynamic. From the military period until the end of the 1990s, local politics in São Paulo was controlled by right-wing political parties, with the exceptions of two left-wing mayors (1982–1985, appointed by the governor, and 1988–1992, elected), over a 36-year period (Marques 2003). Before 2000, the most important local political cleavage in São Paulo opposed the PT from the left to the political right, although this occupied different parties that changed their names and were subdivided or fused (Limongi & Mesquita 2011).

According to Pierucci and Lima (1993), the right returned to power—in 1985 and again in 1992—mainly due to the floating conservative vote. Others authors, however, have suggested that these results merely show a stable conservative advantage in local politics in São Paulo, with very stable spatial patterns (Limongi & Mesquita 2011). The victories of the left (which controls between 25 and 30 percent of local votes) represents moments during which the right (holding around 40 percent of the vote) cannot capture the center (representing between 30 and 40 percent). In this sense, it is the left-wing victories that need to be explained, not the contrary.

In geographical terms, the winner until 2000 tended to win in all regions of the city, although by larger margins in his or her own strongholds. Since then, this polarization has divided the municipal territory into electoral regions, with PT enjoying hegemony in the peripheries and PSDB holding a majority in the expanded center and in middle-class areas toward the north and east (Limongi & Mesquita 2011).

One important factor to bear in mind is that this party opposition also structures Brazilian electoral politics at the national level. At the federal level, PT has been hegemonic over the last four elections, winning power since 2002 (Limongi & Cortez 2010), with the PSDB capturing the federal government in 1994 and 1998 and running second ever since. At state level, the history is quite different, and the center has controlled the state government since 1982, although with two different party labels (first the PMDB and since 1994 the PSDB, which was formed by a dissident group from the former). For authors like Limongi and Cortez (2010), the repetition of federal disputes between the PSDB and PT in the six elections since 1994 has worked to stabilize and align the party system. The presence of the same electoral split in a very competitive local environment has created the conditions for the already mentioned expansion and diversification in policy over time.

In fact, increasing participation, together with the return to electoral politics, has reinforced the effects of the federal social policy reforms already mentioned, increasing service delivery to the poor. Investments in the peripheries and the reduction of inequalities in access were issues that used to oppose left- and right-wing governments until the 1990s. Today, though, all governments express the desire to effect such changes (although not necessarily doing so). The same can be said about slum upgrading policies, first launched during left-wing administrations but later spreading to all governments, even if sometimes only at the level of political discourse. This shift in the political agenda from the 1980s to the 2000s is probably an effect of left-wing governments, electoral competition and social activism (Marques & Bichir 2003), first at municipal level and later nationally. The 2010s already show some signs of a reversion to less redistributive agendas, although it is too early to confirm this as a trend.

Notes

1. See http://smdu.prefeitura.sp.gov.br/historico_demografico.
2. See http://smdu.prefeitura.sp.gov.br/historico_demografico.
3. For a recent and excellent ethnographic survey of living conditions in each of these precarious solutions in present-day São Paulo, see Kowarick (2009).
4. The author thanks Marcos Campos for correcting the dates of this chronology in a previous version of this chapter.

Bibliography

Abreu, M. (1987). *A evolução urbana do Rio de Janeiro*. Rio de Janeiro: Zahar/IplanRio.

Alves, M. (2004). São Paulo: The political and socioeconomic transformations wrought by the New Labour movement in the city and beyond. In: Gluger, J. (ed.) *World cities beyond the west: Globalization, development and inequality*. Cambridge: Cambridge University Press, pp. 299–327.

Anderson, P. (2011). Lula's Brazil. *London Review of Books*, 33(7), pp. 3–12.

Andrade, C. (1992). *A peste e o plano: o urbanismo sanitarista do engenheiro Saturnino de Britto*. FUA, USP: Unpublished MA dissertation.

Andrade, G. (1986). *A cólera-morbo: momento crítico da história da medicina em Pernambuco*. Recife: Fund. José Bonifácio.

Arretche, M. (2012). *Democracia, federalismo e centralização no Brasil*. Rio de Janeiro: Ed. FGV/Ed. Fiocruz/CEM.

Arretche, M. (2002). Federalismo e relações intergovernamentais no Brasil: A reforma de programas sociais. *Revista Dados*, 45(3), pp. 431–458.

Baeninger, R. (2011). Crescimento da população da região metropolitana de São Paulo: desconstruindo mitos do século XX. In: Kowarick, L. and Marques, E. (eds.) *São Paulo: novos percursos e atores*. São Paulo: Ed. 34, pp. 305–342.

Barros, R., Carvalho, M., Franco, S. and Mendonça, R. (2006). A queda recente da Desigualdade de Renda no Brasil. In: Barros, R., Foguel, M., and Ulyssea, G. (eds.) *Desigualdade de Renda no Brasil: uma análise da queda recente*. Brasília: IPEA, pp. 305–342.

Bichir, R. (2010). O Bolsa família na berlinda? *Novos Estudos Cebrap*, 87, pp. 115–129.

Biondi, K. (2008). *Junto e misturado: uma etnografia do PCC*. São Paulo: Ed. Terceiro Nome.

Bonduki, N. (2010). *Gestão, organização e financiamento do solo urbano*. Unpublished paper. Available at: http://www.cedeplar.ufmg.br/pesquisas/pis/Estudo%2028.pdf, April 2012.

Bonduki, N. and Rolnik, R. (1982). Periferia da Grande São Paulo: reprodução do espaço como expediente de reprodução da força de trabalho. In: Maricato, E. (ed.) *A Produção Capitalista da Casa (e da cidade) do Brasil Industrial*. São Paulo: Alfa-ômega, pp. 117–154.

Bruno, E. (1991). *Histórias e tradições da cidade de São Paulo*. São Paulo: Ed. Hucitec.

Buarque, S. (1998 [1934]). *Raízes do Brasil*. São Paulo: Companhia das Letras.

Bueno, L. (2000). *Projeto e favela: metodologia para projetos de urbanização*. São Paulo: FAU/USP, Unpublished PhD thesis.

Bueno, L. (1993). *O saneamento na urbanização de São Paulo*. São Paulo: FAU/USP, MA dissertation.

Caldeira, T. (2000). *The city of walls*. Los Angeles: University of California Press.

Camargo, C. (ed.) (1976). *São Paulo, 1975—Crescimento e pobreza*. São Paulo: Ed. Loyola.
Cano, W. (1990). *Raízes da concentração industrial em São Paulo*. São Paulo: Hucitec.
Carone, E. and Dér, R. (1989). Light versus Guinle. In: Eletropaulo (ed.) *Memória da Eletropaulo*, São Paulo: Eletropaulo, p. 113.
Carvalho, J. (2001). *Cidadania no Brasil: o longo caminho*. Rio de Janeiro: Civilização Brasileira.
Costa, J. (1989). *Ordem Médica e Norma Familiar*. Rio de Janeiro: Ed Graal.
Couto, C. (1994). Mudança e crise: o PT no governo em São Paulo. *Lua Nova*, 33, pp. 145–190.
Draibe, S. (1989). As políticas sociais brasileiras: diagnósticos e perspectivas. In: IPEA (ed.) *Para a década de 90: prioridades e perspectivas de Políticas públicas*. Ipea: Políticas sociais e Organização do Trabalho No. 4. Brasilia: IPEA/Plan, pp. 1–66.
Esping-Anderson, G. (1990). *The three worlds of welfare capitalism*. Princeton: Princeton University Press.
Fausto, B. (1983). *Trabalho Urbano e Conflito Social*. São Paulo: Difel.
Feldman, S. (2005). *Planejamento e zoneamento. São Paulo: (1947–1972)*. São Paulo: Edusp/Fapesp.
Feltran, G. (2012). *Fronteiras de tensão*. São Paulo: Ed. Unesp/CEM.
Feltran, G. (2010). The management of violence in the São Paulo periphery. The repertoire of normative apparatus in the PCC era. *Vibrant*, 7(2), pp. 109–134.
Feltran, G. (2009). Notes sur les 'débats' du 'monde du crime'. In: Cabanes, R. and Georges, I. (eds.) *São Paulo: la ville d'enbas*. Paris: L´Harmattan, pp. 183–192.
Figueiredo, A., Torres, H. and Bichir, R. (2006). A conjuntura social brasileira revisitada. *Novos Estudos Cebrap*, 75, pp. 173–183.
Fix, M. (2001). *Parceiros da Exclusão*. São Paulo: Boitempo.
Gurza Lavalle, A. and Bueno, N. (2011). Waves of change within civil society in Latin America: Mexico City and Sao Paulo. *Politics & Society*, 39, pp. 415–450.
Gurza Lavalle, A., Castello, G. and Bichir, R. (2008). *The backstage of civil society: Protagonisms, networks, and affinities between civil organizations in São Paulo*. Brighton: IDS.
Heller, P. and Evans, P. (2010). Taking Tilly south: Durable inequalities, democratic contestation, and citizenship in the Southern Metropolis. *Theory and Society*, 39(3–4), pp. 433–450.
Henry, E. and Zioni, S. (1995). Ônibus na metrópole: As articulações entre iniciativa privada e intervenção pública em São Paulo. In: Brasileiro, A., Henry, E. and Turma (eds.) *Viação ilimitada. Ônibus nas cidades brasileiras*. São Paulo: Cultura Ed. Ass, pp. 119–186.
Jacobi, P. (1989). *Movimentos sociais e políticas públicas*. São Paulo: Ed. Cortez.
Kowarick, L. (2010). *Viver em risco*. São Paulo: Ed. 34.
Kowarick, L. (1979). *A espoliação urbana*. São Paulo: Paz e Terra.
Kowarick, L. and Ant, C. (1988). Cem anos de promiscuidade em São Paulo. In: Kowarick, L. (ed.) *As lutas sociais e a cidade*. São Paulo: Paz e Terra, pp. 49–74.
Lamournier, B. (1985). A eleição de Jânio Quadros. In: Lamournier, B. (ed.) *1985: O voto em São Paulo*. São Paulo: Idesp, pp. 75–98.
Lamournier, B. (1980). O voto em São Paulo (1970–78). In: Lamounier, B. (ed.) *Voto de desconfiança: eleições e mudança política no Brasil (1970–1979)*. São Paulo: Vozes, pp. 1–34.

Leme, M. (ed.) (1999). *Urbanismo no Brasil (1895/1965)*. São Paulo: Nobel.
Lima Jr, O. (1993). *Democracia e instituições políticas no Brasil dos anos 80*. São Paulo: Loyola.
Limongi, F. and Cortez, R. (2010). As Eleições de 2010 e o Quadro Partidário. *Novos Estudos Cebrap*, 88, pp. 21–37.
Limongi, F. and Mesquita, L. (2011). Estratégia Partidária e Clivagens Eleitorais: As Eleições Municipais pós redemocratização. In: Kowarick, L. and Marques, E. (eds.) *Caminhos cruzados: sociedade, política, cultura*. São Paulo: Ed. 34, pp. 207–232.
Maricato, E. (1987). *Política habitacional no regime militar*. Petrópolis: Vozes.
Marques, E. (2003). *Redes sociais, Instituições e Atores Políticos no governo da cidade de São Paulo*. São Paulo: Ed. Annablume/Fapesp.
Marques, E. (1995). Da higiene à construção da cidade: A constituição do setor saneamento no Rio de Janeiro. *Revista Manguinhos: História, Ciência e Saúde*, 23, pp. 51–67.
Marques, E. and Bichir, R. (2003). Public policies, political cleavages and urban space: State infrastructure policies in São Paulo, Brazil—1975–2000. *International Journal of Urban and Regional Research*, 27(4), pp. 811–827.
Marx, M. (1989). *Nosso chão: do sagrado ao profano*. São Paulo: Ed. USP.
Meneguello, R. (1998). *Partidos e governos no Brasil contemporâneo (1985–1997)*. São Paulo: Paz e Terra.
Menicucci, T. (2007). *Público e privado na política de assistência à saúde no Brasil: atores, processes e trajetória*. Rio de Janeiro: Ed. Fiocruz.
Mesa-Lago, C. (2000). *Desarollo social, reforma del Estado y de la seguridad social, al umbral del siglo XXI*. Santiago: Eclac, Serie Politicas Sociales, No 36.
Mingione, E. (2005). Urban social change: A socio-historical framework of analysis. In: Kazepov, Y. (ed.) *Cities of Europe. Changing contexts, local arrangements, and the challenge to urban cohesion*. London: Blackwell, pp. 67–89.
Misse, M. (2011). *Crime urbano, sociabilidade violenta e ordem legítima. Comentário sobre as hipóteses de Machado da Silva*. Available at http://www.necvu.ifcs.ufrj.br/images/7Sobre%20a%20sociabilidade%20violenta%20de%20Machado.pdf, March 2011
Misse, M. (2007). Mercados ilegais, redes de proteção e organização local do crime no Rio de Janeiro. *Estudos Avançados*, 21(61), pp. 139–157.
Nadanovsky, P. (2009). O aumento no encarceramento e a redução nos homicídios em São Paulo, Brasil, entre 1996 e 2005. *Cad. Saúde Pública*, 25(8), pp. 1859–1864.
Nunes, E. (1997). *As gramáticas políticas do Brasil*. Rio de Janeiro: FGV.
Oliveira, F. (1982). O Estado e o urbano no Brasil. *Espaço and Debates*, no. 6, 43.
Peres, M., Vicentin, D., Nery, M., Lima, R., Souza, E., Cerda, M., Cardia, N. and Adorno, S. (2011). Queda dos homicídios em São Paulo, Brasil: uma análise descritiva. *Revista Panamericana de Salud Publica*, 29(1), pp. 17–26.
Perlman, J. (2004). Marginality: From myth to reality in the favelas in Rio de Janeiro 1969–2002. In: Roy, A. and Alsayyad, N. (eds.) *Urban informality: Transnational perspectives from Middle East, Latin America and South Asia*. Lanham: Lexington Books, pp. 105–146.
Pierucci, A. and Lima, M. (1993). São Paulo 92, a vitória da direita. *Novos Estudos Cebrap*, no. 35, pp. 94–99.
Portes, A. and Roberts, B. (2005). The free-market city: Latin American urbanization in the years of the neoliberal experiment. *Studies in Comparative International Development*, 40(1), pp. 43–82.

Rago, M. (1985). *Do cabaré ao bar: A utopia da cidade disciplinar—Brasil (1890–1930)*. Rio de Janeiro: Paz e Terra.

Ramos, Á. (1986). *Memórias do saneamento desterrense*. Florianópolis: Arquivo Público de Santa Catarina.

Rangel, I. (1987). O Papel dos Serviços de Utilidade Pública. In: CCJE/UFRJ (ed.) *Crise Urbana e Privatização dos Serviços Públicos*. Rio de Janeiro: UFRJ, pp. 1–24.

Requena, C. (2015). *O paradigma da fluidez do automóvel: burocracias estatais e mobilidade em São Paulo*. FFLCH/DCP, USP: Unpublished MA dissertation.

Ribeiro, M. A. (1993). *História sem fim. Inventário da saúde pública*. São Paulo: Ed UNESP.

Roberts, K. (2012). *The politics of inequality and redistribution in Latin America's post-adjustment era*. UN Working Paper No. 08.

Rolnik, R. (2011). Democracy on the edge: Limits and possibilities in the implementation of an urban reform agenda in Brazil. *International Journal of Urban and Regional Research*, 35(2), pp. 239–255.

Royer, L. (2014). *Financeirização da Política Habitacional: Limites e Perspectivas*. São Paulo: Ed. Annablume.

Sadek, T. (1985). A trajetória de Jânio Quadros. In: Lamournier, B. (ed.) *O voto em São Paulo*. São Paulo: Idesp, pp. 99–115.

Sader, E. (1988). *Quando novos personagens entram em cena*. São Paulo: Paz e Terra.

Santos, W. dos. (1979). *Cidadania e justiça*. Rio de Janeiro: Ed. Campus.

Saruê, B. (2015). *Grandes Projetos Urbanos e a Governança de Metrópoles: o caso do Porto Maravilha no Rio de Janeiro*. FFLCH/DCP, USP: Unpublished MA dissertation.

Segatto, J. (1989). A República e a Light. *Eletropaulo, Memória*, 2, pp. 145–167.

Shimbo, L. (2012). *Habitação social de mercado: A confluência entre Estado, empresas construtoras e capital financeiro*. Belo Horizonte: C/Arte.

Sikkink, K. (1993). Las capacidades y la autonomía del Estado em Brasil e Argentina. Un enfoque neoinstitucionalista. *Desarrollo Economico*, 32(128), pp. 543–574.

Silva, L. (1994). Os reformadores sociais na década de 1920: alguns aspectos da atuação dos engenheiros na cidade do Rio de Janeiro. Paper presented at the 3º Seminário de História da Cidade e do Urbanismo, São Carlos, USP/ANPUR.

Simões Jr., J. (1991). O setor de obras públicas e as origens do urbanismo moderno na cidade de São Paulo. *Espaço e Debates*, no. 34, p. 2037.

SMU. (2008). *Planos urbanos—Rio de Janeiro—o Século XIX*. Rio de Janeiro: Secretaria Municipal de Urbanismo/IPP.

Souza, F. (2011). *A batalha pelo Centro: Santa Efigênia, concessão urbanística e projeto Nova Luz*. São Paulo: Ed. Paulo.

Tatagiba, L. (2011). Relação entre movimentos sociais e instituições políticas na cidade de São Paulo. O caso do movimento de moradia. In: Kowarick, L. and Marques, E. (eds.) *Caminhos cruzados: sociedade, política, cultura*. São Paulo: Ed. 34, pp. 233–252.

Toledo, B. (1996). *Prestes Maia e as origens do urbanismo moderno em São Paulo*. São Paulo: Empresa das Artes.

Toledo, B. (2004). *São Paulo: Três cidades em um século*. São Paulo: Cosac Naif.

Zancheti, S. (1991). Formação e consolidação da Repartição de Obras Públicas de Pernambuco (1836–1844). *Espaço e Debates*, no 34, pp. 78–95.

Part I
Economic Processes and Social Structure

2 Socioeconomic Transformations and Social Structure

Eduardo Cesar Leão Marques, Rogério Jerônimo Barbosa and Ian Prates

The city of São Paulo presents a complex social structure associated with its diversified production base and rich migratory and demographic history. Analysis of its social groups and the territories associated with them has been undertaken ever since the social makeup of the peripheries became a theme in classic studies such as Kowarick (1979). Over recent decades, various studies have used census information to systematically analyze the formation of groups and classes, as well as their spatialization, both by studying socioeconomic variables (CEM 2004, Marques & Torres 2005) and by employing social classification methods based on occupation (Bógus & Taschner 2001, Marques et al. 2012, Preteceille & Cardoso 2008). However the 2000s brought intense social changes in terms of economic activities, employment and income (Comin 2010), as well as residents' access to services. The city's industrial sector shrank in relative terms, while tertiary sector activities and jobs expanded. Additionally the return to strong economic growth after 2003 was accompanied by a rise in formal employment and a fall in poverty as measured by income. Simultaneously, access to services continued to improve, as we discuss in later chapters. Taking all these transformations into account, a description of the social groups present in the São Paulo metropolis is essential to understanding the city. In this chapter we analyze the socioeconomic transformations and changes in social structure over time. This analysis is complemented later by the investigation in Chapter 6 of the distribution of social groups in space, exploring segregation patterns and their recent transformations.

To analyze the social structure of São Paulo's metropolitan region in this chapter, we use the EGP occupational groups (Erikson et al. 1979), a classification system widely used in the national and international debates on social stratification (Costa Ribeiro 2007, Erikson & Goldthorpe 1992, Marques & Scalon 2009a and 2009b).

The chapter is divided into three parts in addition to this introduction and a final summary. In the first, so as to better situate the observed transformations, we present the main points debated by the literature on the topic. Next we discuss the principal dynamics of economic activity, employment and poverty over the last decades. Finally we analyze the composition and transformation of social groups in the period from 1991 to 2010 using census data. For the purposes of this description, our interest resides in both the overall dynamics of the occupational classes and their composition in terms of gender, race, schooling and socio-occupational status (measured by ISEI[1]: see Ganzeboom et al. 1993).

The Literature on Social Structure and Recent Economic Transformations

The last few decades have seen intense transformations not only in Brazilian metropolises but throughout the world. In the Brazilian case, as well as the changes in state policies during the period after the country's return to democracy already discussed in the first chapter, other recent and important processes of transformation with a strong impact on cities have included population dynamics, such as a fall in migration and the advance of demographic transition and economic transformations caused by the economic opening of the 1990s.

The first broad set of transformations in Brazilian metropolises is related to demographic dynamics (Baeninger 2011, Cunha 2013), including the decline in fertility and migration rates, accompanied by reduced mortality and an increase in life expectancy, resulting in an overall aging of the population. Although these processes are found throughout the country, they affected the big metropolises especially strongly, São Paulo included. In part these processes are associated with the greater presence of women in the labor market, as we shall see later in this chapter. The reduction in poverty that took place in the 2000s is also related to these demographic transformations. In Chapter 5 we discuss the combined impacts of these dimensions on São Paulo's demographic growth.

The economic transformations of the 1990s are a topic already explored by the literature with respect to São Paulo and other Brazilian cities, interpreted as representing a moment of dissolution of the existing model of social integration, leading to a general increase in poverty, social fragmentation and a consequent shortening of social trajectories and horizons (Cabannes & George 2009, Ribeiro & Telles 2000). This diagnosis suggested very negative prospects in social and urban terms over the following decades. However, when the transformations occurring during the decade are placed in perspective, as in the brief description sketched in the next section, the need for a more nuanced interpretation becomes clear, especially due to the interweaving of global processes with local dynamics. This difference in interpretations is also encountered in the international debate.

Since the 1990s there has been an intense debate on the social and spatial effects of economic changes at a global level on the big cities. Generally speaking, this debate has adhered to the hypothesis advanced by Sassen (1991), who asserted that recent transformations in the dynamic of capitalism would concentrate the business world's command activities in the major cities. As a result, the secondary Fordist manufacturing activities that had already been leaving the biggest world metropolises since the 1970s would be replaced by the provision of services to companies and financial institutions, associated with highly specialized and very well paid jobs. The centrality of these cities and the growth in consumerism would lead to an expansion of commerce and a broad sector of low-skilled and poorly paid personal and domestic services.

In social terms this would lead to a polarization of occupational and income structures, with a growth in better-paid activities, including the emergence of a group of hyper-rich and poorer social groups, accompanied by an abrupt shrinking in the middle band of income distribution, associated with the decline in industrial work. In spatial terms, the command activities of business and finance, as well as the demand for luxury housing for professionals at the top of the productive service sector, would explain the upsurge in urban reform projects responsible for gentrifying large areas and affecting cities as a whole through a general rise in land values. The hypothesis was initially conceived for New York, London and Tokyo but later spread to many other cities (Knox & Taylor 1995).

Since then, these hypotheses have been subject to empirical testing in various cities around the world. In general, the various component parts of the argument have survived differently over the course of time. While some actors confirmed these trends (Burgers 1996, Walks 2001), others challenged them, especially the idea of social polarization, arguing for the importance of diverse mediations of global processes like welfare regimes, urban history and structures, local land markets, political processes and those linked to public policies (Baum 1999, Hamnett 1994, 1996a and 1996b, Maloutas 2007, Musterd & Murie 2002, Vaattovaara & Kortteinen 2003, Wessel 2000). According to these studies, rather than polarization, the recent dynamics have been marked by professionalization, associated with recent transformations in production. This led to a growth in professional occupations (in the sectors providing services to companies and to people) and a series of middle positions in the occupational structure (linked to commerce and the company service industry), which more than compensated for the reduction in middle-income positions based on Fordist mass production. Contrary to the scenario predicted by Sassen (1991), the result was a growth in middle and high-middle job positions and incomes. Even the growth in income inequality, these studies argue, was not caused by an expansion in the top and bottom with the disappearance of middle-income groups but the emergence of a social group of superrich, pulling the top of the distribution upward. The list of cities is large and includes, among others, London, Paris, New York, Toronto, Singapore, Athens, Madrid, Oslo and Helsinki, strongly focused on the Global North. The hypotheses discussed in the international literature have also included trends toward spatial polarization, but these will be analyzed in Chapter 6.

The 1990s and 2000s in Brazil provide an excellent case for analyzing these dynamics, given that they represent a moment of concentrated transformation in economic and occupational structures. The following section presents evidence of such transformations, and the third section summarizes the transformations in social structure. At the end of the chapter we contrast the observed evidence with the main hypotheses established in the literature.

Economic Dynamics and Labor Market Situation in the Metropolis

As is widely known, the 1990s represented a moment of intense productive restructuring in São Paulo, driven primarily by the economic opening and accompanied by the sudden intensification of Brazil's participation in international trade. These transformations began during the Collor government (1990–1992) and increased in intensity during the presidency of Itamar Franco and the two mandates of Fernando Henrique Cardoso, by now with inflation under control and a foreign exchange policy favorable to imports. An avalanche in imports of manufactured goods was seen, precipitating the fall of industrial activity. In the industrial sector, this restructuring represented a reduction in costs through the implementation of automation processes, the incorporation of technologies, outsourcing and downsizing. The policies for privatizing state companies, especially in the sector of infrastructure and intermediate goods, was accompanied by mergers and acquisitions and by the entry of large-scale foreign capital in sectors like infrastructure, banking and retail—all employing substantial workforces. Although these processes occurred nationwide, they strongly affected greater São Paulo, the country's most important economic and business center.

While industry employed almost a third of employed workers in 1991, this share had fallen to less than a fifth by 2010. In the opposite direction, the service sector grew by almost 30 percent in the first decade and rose more gradually in the second. The same kind of result can be observed when we turn to production by economic sector, indicating that the result expresses a change in the presence of the sectors and not merely different growths in productivity of the sectors of the economy over time (Comin 2010).

It is worth adding that these relative changes do not represent deindustrialization in the strict sense, which classically describes situations in which production becomes less dynamic, leading to the migration of industrial activities to other areas of the country or even abroad. Although São Paulo's industrial workforce has indeed shrunk in absolute terms over the last decades, this shrinkage is substantially less than the decline observed relative to other sectors.[2] In fact various studies have shown that Brazil's industrial deconcentration occurred in a concentrated form, relocating or building new industrial plants at a small distance from the metropolitan region of São Paulo, within the so-called macro-metropolitan area that encompasses the adjoining regions of Campinas, São José dos Campos and others

(Campolina Diniz & Campolina 2007). The São Paulo metropolis, on the other hand, concentrated even more activities linked to producing innovations and coordinating these same activities, now relocated, boosting their dynamism (Campolina Diniz & Campolina 2007, Comin 2010). The situation is different, therefore, both to classic deindustrialization as occurred in Detroit, for example, and to the formation of dynamic command centers that do not directly coordinate industrial production, as in the global cities described by Sassen (1991). The outsourcing of the São Paulo economy did not represent the emergence of a tertiary city, as some have argued, but the development of new command, innovation and coordination functions closely associated with the secondary economic activities, overlapping secondary and tertiary centralities (Comin 2010).

This is confirmed if we disaggregate the information on jobs recently created in the service sector. Commercial and distribution activities increased substantially, adding around 600,000 jobs per decade between 1991 and 2010. Additionally, the sector of "productive services"—the services provided to companies—summed 200,000 and 550,000 new job positions per decade, respectively. In the 2000s, the subsector was responsible for generating almost 800,000 jobs, second only to the "commerce and distribution" sector.

These economic transformations were accompanied by profound social changes. The 1990s were characterized by worsening socioeconomic conditions in general, which only began to show signs of recovery in the mid-2000s. Unemployment rose almost continuously between 1989 and 2003 (except for the years after economic stabilization in 1994), a period marked by economic recession. Economic policy was focused on monetary stabilization through high interest rates and the abandonment of measures designed to boost aggregate demand. From 2004 onward, the unemployment rate began a downward and monotonic trend in a context of economic growth, driven by the expansion of a thriving service sector that was integrated at national level with the revival in industrial and export activity. In the SPMR, however, as we observed previously, relatively speaking, industrial employment did not recover. Total unemployment, however, remained slightly above the level recorded in the mid-1980s as well as operating in much more fluid conditions than in the past (Guimarães 2009). The level of formalization in the economy followed an opposite trend, falling continuously between 1990 and 2001 and recovering quickly ever since. Although the intensity of economic growth declined after 2010, with the worsening of the international crisis begun in 2008, the current levels of formalization were in 2014 the highest yet recorded by the employment survey conducted by Seade/Dieese in the SPMR.

As would be expected, the combined dynamics of the labor market had direct effects on poverty levels and on income inequality in the metropolitan region. The proportion of persons below the PL showed a significant decline between 1993 and 1995—from 27 to 16 percent—due to the economic stabilization achieved by the Plano Real. Thereafter, however, levels of poverty grew continuously until 2003, when the proportion achieved 28 percent, practically annulling the advances made previously, in large part as a result of the economic conjuncture already described. The SPMR, in fact, alongside Brasilia, showed the highest relative rise in poor people between the mid-1990s and the mid-2000s (Torres et al. 2006). From 2003, though, the proportions of poor people fell continuously until reaching 15 percent again in 2008, largely as a combined result of an economic growth cycle based on full employment boosting the domestic market and policies that increased the real value of the minimum wage and implemented various conditioned income transfer programs, especially the Bolsa Família, the largest conditional cash transference program in the world at the moment (Neri & Souza 2013). At the end of the period, the proportion of poor people had fallen back to roughly the same level reached after the Plano Real, the lowest point of the series. Poverty figures have stabilized since the 2008 global financial crisis and will possibly rise again with the 2015 crisis.

The Gini index for income followed similar trends. In 1992, the Gini index was 0.524 for the SPMR. It rose almost continuously until 2002, when it reached 0.572, declining monotonically thereafter, falling to 0.516 in 2008, the lowest point of the historical series.[3]

Social Structure in São Paulo

The recent changes in the labor market are associated with important demographic transformations. Some of the economic indicators shown here reveal more structural and perennial dimensions, such as sector reorganization (a growth in services and industrial shrinkage) and the decline in poverty and extreme poverty. However, the indicators more specifically linked to the labor market—like rates of unemployment and formalization—mainly concern conjunctural elements or those whose effects occur directly in the short term. Much of the recent discussion on the expansion of class C in Brazil is based on conjunctural dimensions such as income, which lose their explanatory potential as soon as the economic situation changes.

To understand how the dynamics of the labor market brought about deeper structural transformations to forms of employment and the life possibilities of the population, here we make use of a concept of social class based on occupational categories. From the sociological viewpoint, occupations provide a longer-term picture, allowing us to discern both the potential future income of individuals taking into account both conjunctural dimensions and the more structural aspects related to the division of labor and economic development, a form of analysis undertaken by other authors for other countries (Preteceille 1995).

Occupations are also effectively social institutions, defining spaces more or less open to worker turnover, flexibilization and specialization (Sorensen & Kalleberg 1979), organizing worldviews and giving meaning to social action (associations, unions, employer organizations and so on; see Grusky & Galescu 2005, Grusky & Sorensen 1998, Grusky & Weeden 2008, Weeden 2002) or even to habits and lifestyles (Bourdieu 2007, Weber 1999 [1922]). The sociological approach to class analysis seeks precisely to combine similar occupational categories with those characteristics already mentioned or other dimensions (Erikson & Goldthorpe 1992, Erikson et al. 1979, Goldthorpe 2000 and 2007, Wright 1997). In this way, although it sets out from occupational groupings—which are strongly linked to the labor market—the analysis of classes allows us to discern more structural elements of inequalities and social organization.

The EGP classes are founded on some basic distinctions: rural work versus urban work, manual versus nonmanual, routine versus nonroutine. In each of these dichotomies, the second term represents a higher socioeconomic and occupational status. The model also takes into account aspects linked to occupational position and hierarchy. It thus distinguishes between employed workers, supervisors, the self-employed and employers. In this chapter, we do not consider rural classes (employers, subsistence and farmworkers) since they comprise a residual group in the São Paulo metropolis.

The distribution of the employed population among the EGP classes from 1991 to 2010 is depicted in Figure 2.1, constructed using the methodological procedures set out in Barbosa & Marschner (2013). As can be seen, the most frequent classes are manual workers—both skilled and unskilled—followed by low and high-level, routine, nonmanual employees. Next, at a third level, come the high- and low-level professionals. The graph also provides us with important information concerning the dynamic over the two decades. As we can see, the proportion of professionals tends to increase, while the relative presence of skilled and unskilled manual workers has declined, although these two classes still easily predominate. High-level, routine, nonmanual employees

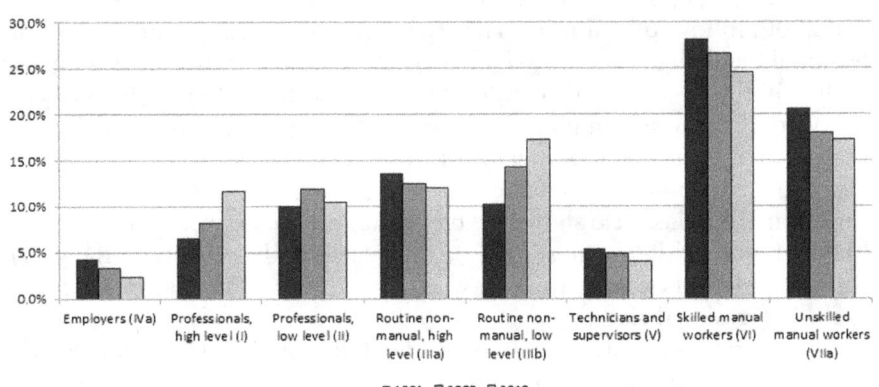

Figure 2.1 Distribution of EGP classes, SPMR, 1991, 2000 and 2010.

Source: IBGE censuses 1991, 2000 and 2010, authors' elaboration.

have tended to stay at the same level or fallen back very slightly, which may be due to sample variation. However low-level, routine nonmanual employees display a clear upward trend. In fact, by the end of the period, unskilled, manual workers and low-level, routine, nonmanual employees had an almost equal share of the labor market, which in a sense is emblematic of the transformations happening in the lower portion of the city's social structure. Employers seem to have declined in relative terms, but since the group size is very small, this result may simply be due to sample variation.

This overall result is contrary to what would be predicted by theories that associate productive restructuring processes with social polarization. Evidence of polarization would be encountered, for example, if the higher classes, especially proprietors and high-level professionals, had grown at the same time as skilled manual workers declined and unskilled manual workers rose. The transformations indicated in the graph are more compatible with the idea of professionalization provoked by productive restructuring. The topic of job polarization will be discussed in more detail in Chapter 3. However, the results presented in the graph already provide an indication that any diagnosis based on this hypothesis should be treated with caution.

But what important changes occurred in the social makeup of the classes? To provide a more detailed picture of these transformations, we analyzed class composition in terms of income, occupational status, education, gender and race. The following table shows the relative income and average ISEIs of the classes in 2000 and 2010. Based on income and ISEI, we analytically divided the classes into three strata, reorganizing them as upper, middle and lower. The information on relative income, dividing the class's average income by the average income of the metropolitan region as a whole, looks to ignore income variations between the two census periods since we are interested here merely in comparing the classes with each other.

In the case of relative income, the situation over the last decade shows little real change, though most categories register a small fall between 1991 and 2000, followed by a recovery between 2000 and 2010. High-level professionals and high- and low-level manual workers showed a systematic decline in their relative incomes, though the amount is small. The only category to show a substantial variation is the employer class, which grew very strongly and later declined. As observed earlier, though, this group has a small absolute size, and census data are highly susceptible to sample variation. This class also shows the biggest difference between remuneration (the highest) and ISEI (the second or third largest, depending on the year), consistent with the dissociation between earnings and education (in contrast to the professional classes).

The average ISEI also remained fairly stable, with a slight rise for the region as a whole and for most classes, as seen in Table 2.1. Small rises were observed among low-level, routine, nonmanual workers, low-level professionals and employers and a fall in the average ISEI for skilled and unskilled manual workers.

Socioeconomic Transformations and Social Structure 65

Table 2.1 Relative income and ISEI in the EGP classes, SPMR, 2000 and 2010.

	Average Income (R$ de 06/2012)			Relative Income			ISEI		
	1991	2000	2010	1991	2000	2010	1991	2000	2010
Upper Classes									
IVa—Employers	6,209.76	9,531.52	7,855.88	2.97	4.36	3.87	42.9	54.5	60.0
I. Professionals, high level	5,891.93	5,852.85	5,232.82	2.82	2.68	2.58	71.1	72.3	71.5
Middle Classes									
II. Professionals, low level	2,926.35	3,120.36	2,904.00	1.40	1.43	1.43	52.1	54.2	57.7
IIIa. Routine, nonmanual, high level	1,682.00	1,797.24	1,647.51	0.81	0.82	0.81	46.5	46,7	46.8
V. Technicians and supervisors	2,342.38	2,238.58	2,006.00	1.12	1.02	0.99	42.0	44.3	44.0
Lower Classes									
IIIb. Routine, nonmanual, low level	1,213.60	1,135.84	1,210.30	0.58	0.52	0.60	39.6	38.3	41.5
VI. Skilled manual workers	1,479.99	1,378.70	1,235.38	0.71	0.63	0.61	31.9	31.7	30.7
VIIa. Unskilled manual workers	1,084.31	838.05	819.07	0.52	0.38	0.40	24.6	21.3	20.0
Total	2,087.56	2,185.29	2,031.87	1.00	1.00	1.00	38.7	39.9	41.4

Source: IBGE censuses 1991, 2000 and 2010, authors' elaboration.

One important transformation concerns education. As is widely known, the average educational level of the population in general in Brazil has advanced rapidly over the last decades. In the specific case of the labor force in the São Paulo metropolis, the progress made in this area has been substantial. In Table 2.2 we compare educational level by class for the years from 1991 to 2010. We show the proportion of individuals for the completed three educational levels—primary, secondary and higher (omitting those without completed primary education).

The information should be read in two ways. First the table indicates the result of changes in the educational makeup of the labor supply. The advance in the coverage of the education system, especially public schooling, combined with policies to eliminate child labor and the income transfer policies conditional on school attendance, have increased the amount of time children and young people spend in the school system and lowered the rates of early entry into the labor market.

Table 2.2 Educational level by class, SPMR, 2000 and 2010 (%).

EGP Classes	1991			2000			2010		
	Primary	Secondary	Higher	Primary	Secondary	Higher	Primary	Secondary	Higher
I. Professionals, high level	6.2	23.5	60.7	7.7	26.2	62.0	5.6	23.2	65.0
II. Professionals, low level	15.2	32.1	19.0	21.5	37.6	26.7	10.5	36.6	44.8
IIIa. Routine, nonmanual, high level	24.5	41.3	13.2	21.6	50.5	17.2	15.4	44.2	30.4
IIIb. Routine, nonmanual, low level	24.9	15.7	2.5	32.5	33.2	3.1	24.6	46.9	6.5
IVa. Employers	10.6	28.7	25.3	20.8	31.8	36.7	10.0	31.2	46.2
V. Technicians and supervisors	19.5	29.0	5.9	29.4	40.3	7.8	18.8	47.2	13.6
VI. Skilled manual worker	14.1	7.1	1.4	33.8	15.5	0.9	23.9	29.2	2.3
VIIa. Unskilled manual workers	11.8	8.4	2.8	29.6	12.1	0.7	23.6	24.4	1.6
Total	15.9	18.7	10.5	27.0	27.0	12.8	18.9	34.0	19.5

Source: IBGE, 1991, 2000 and 2010 censuses, authors' elaboration.

Second, the result also reveals the changes in the demand for skilled labor, indicating an increase in the requirements set by the market for obtaining and maintaining jobs. So although the improvement in schooling has obvious positive dimensions, it also inevitably entails the market's adjustment to the supply of workers with educational qualifications, which can push down (and push out) individuals without them. As we shall see in Chapter 3, the last two decades were substantially different in relation to the labor market's receptiveness to the different educational strata.

As would be expected, the higher occupational classes present a much larger proportion of individuals with higher education degrees and far fewer with just primary and secondary education. As we descend to the classes lower in the structure, the percentages with just secondary and later primary-level education increase. In the classes located in the middle of the structure—low-level, nonmanual routine and technicians—schooling to complete secondary level (high school graduation) predominates. In the class of unskilled manual workers, even complete primary-level schooling is still relatively infrequent.

In addition, we can observe an increase in average schooling across all classes, although with emphases on different educational levels. Despite this overall trend, the classes presenting a greater relative increase are the low-level professionals (almost 26 percent of the increase in higher education), the high-level, nonmanual routine employees (almost 17 percent in higher education), low-level, nonmanual, routine employees (almost 31 percent secondary education) and skilled manual workers (around 22 percent in secondary education). Although there has been an overall increase in educational requirements in the labor market, therefore, this rise was more strongly concentrated in the middle occupational classes.

A more pronounced variation is observed when we examine the participation of women in these different classes. While in 1991 the economically active population (PEA) presented two men for each woman, in 2010 the composition was almost equal. The distribution of classes by gender also shifted significantly, with the relative presence of women increasing among virtually all the strata. In other words, there was a huge transformation in the degree to which men and women engage in the market, radically altering both the profile of this market and the strategies used by individuals and families to improve their lives by how they sell their labor force.

Of more interest, however, is the fact that among almost all the classes—with the exception of the high-level, nonmanual, routine workers, the technicians and supervisors and the skilled manual workers (the latter concentrating most of the industrial occupations)—the positive variation in women's participation between 1991 and 2010 is very similar, always slightly above 10.0 percent. What these data suggest, first of all, is that the mass entry of women into the labor market over the last 20 years did not occur asymmetrically. On the other hand, it is notable that women account for almost two-thirds of unskilled manual workers (explained in large part by the large contingent of domestic workers).

The breakdown of occupational class participation by skin color also reveals interesting data and, although indicating a degree of stability in terms of job inequalities, also shows an increase in black participation among all strata. In general terms, the first important evidence is the relatively small presence of non-white people in the employed population—just 31 and 32 percent in 1991 and 2000, although this rose to 39.1 percent in 2010. However, given the nature of the information (originated by self-declaration of the interviewees), it is impossible to tell whether this increase is simply due to the increased participation of non-white individuals in the labor market or whether it also expresses an increase in the number of people declaring themselves "black" or "brown," reflecting the activism of black identity-based social movements during this period.

In this case, the data suggest the maintenance of racial differences. The growth in the proportion of non-whites follows the general movement of racial reclassification of the population with no large transformations or redistribution between the classes. The concentration of non-white workers is consistently very high in manual activities. Also striking is the degree of underrepresentation of non-white people among employers and among high-level professionals. The situation alters only slightly among low-level, nonmanual, routine workers (who after 2000 began to concentrate a higher proportion of non-white workers than the proportion among the population as a whole) and among technicians and supervisors (where we can glimpse the same change occurring from 2010).

Final Considerations

The last two decades have seen intense transformations in production with effects on social structure, as would be expected. Intense restructuring is observable after the economic opening of the 1990s, which increased the relative presence of services, especially production related, and reduced the presence of industry. In social terms, these transformations led to an intense rise in unemployment, informality and poverty during the 1990s. These trends were reversed in the 2000s, but the overall result of the two decades is to some extent incongruous: clearly positive in terms of job formalization and poverty reduction but less clearly positive in terms of unemployment rates, which merely returned to the levels of the late 1980s.

Such a broad set of transformations cannot fail to have impacted strongly on social stratification in São Paulo. Observed globally, the base of the class structure was reduced with a decline in the relative participation of skilled and unskilled manual workers—a fact that in some ways reflects the transformations in the productive structure of the metropolis itself. On the other hand, we can observe a growth in the middle strata of nonmanual, routine employees—office workers being the clearest example—and high-level professionals, making evident the "corporate" and "professional" character of São Paulo. This evidence suggests the opposite dynamics to those expected in the social polarization hypothesis. At the same time, professionalization by itself cannot describe the situation since there has been a reduction in skilled manual workers, but their presence remains very high, probably due to the significant industrial activities that remain in the region even after productive restructuring. Apparently the SPMR experiences something that can be denominated professionalization, as argued by other authors vis-à-vis the metropolises from the Global North, but that has maintained a degree of centrality for the lower-skilled categories in its social structure, the result of an overlapping of functions that has marked the evolution of the metropolis over the last 20 years.

When we look to identify patterns specific to the internal composition of each of the classes, the recent transformations that most stand out relate to education and female participation. In terms of education, we can note the strong influence of the changes in the educational composition of the workforce, meaning that all the classes showed a gradual increase in people with more schooling. In terms of female participation, the growing inclusion of women in the labor market took place in a relatively uniform manner across the classes, making it difficult to assert either an increase or a decrease in inequality in terms of the relative positions of the sexes in the occupational structure. A similar dynamic is shown in relation to race, and—albeit in a less pronounced form than before—both women and non-whites continue to be more frequently present in occupations with lower pay, less schooling and less social prestige.

Notes

1. ISEI stands for International Socio-Economic Index of Occupational Status, which is derived from the occupational classes defined according to the international system (ISCO). It constitutes a continuous scale of socioeconomic status and is generally used in complementary form to categorical/discrete (class) groupings like the EGP scheme. Its values vary between 16 and 90. For more detailed information, see Ganzeboom et al. (1993)
2. In the municipality of São Paulo, for example, the decline in industrial employment was 18 percent between 1997 and 2007, while the decline in the industrial sector's relative share was 25 percent (Comin 2010).
3. Data taken from IETS by Sônia Rocha. See http://www.iets.org.br/article.php3?id_article=915.

Bibliography

Arretche, M. (2012). *Democracia, federalismo e centralização no Brasil*. Rio de Janeiro: Ed. FGV/Ed. Fiocruz/CEM.
Baeninger, R. (2011). Crescimento da população na região metropolitana de São Paulo: desconstruindo mitos do século XX. In: Kowarick, L. and Marques, E.

(eds.) *São Paulo: novos percursos e atores: sociedade, cultura e política*. São Paulo: Ed. 34/CEM, pp. 53–78.
Barbosa, R. and Marschner, M. (2013). *Uma proposta de padronização de classificações em pesquisas do IBGE (Censos 1960–2010) e PNADs (1981–2011): educação, setores de atividade econômica e ocupação (ISCO-88, EGP11 e ISEI)*. Working paper. São Paulo: CEM, Mimeo.
Baum, S. (1999). Social transformations in the global city: Singapore. *Urban Studies*, 36(7), pp. 1095–1117.
Bógus, L. and Taschner, S. (2001). São Paulo, o caleidoscópio urbano. *São Paulo em Perspectiva*, 15(1), pp. 31–44.
Bourdieu, P. (2007). *A distinção: crítica social do julgamento*. São Paulo: Edusp.
Breen, R. (2005). Foundations of a Neo-Weberian class analysis. In: E. Wright (ed.) *Approaches to class analysis*. Cambridge: Cambridge University Press, pp. 31–50.
Burgers, J. (1996). No polarization in Dutch cities? Inequality in a corporatist country, *Urban Studies*, 33(1), pp. 99–105.
Cabannes, R. and George, I. (eds.) (2009). *Sao Paulo, debut de siècle: la ville d'en bas*. Paris: Harmattan.
Campolina Diniz, C. and Campolina, B. (2007). A região metropolitana de São Paulo: reestruturação, re-espacialização e novas funções. *Revista Eure*, XXXIII(98), pp. 27–43.
CEM. (2004). *Mapa da Vulnerabilidade Social da População da Cidade de São Paulo*. São Paulo: CEM/Cebrap; SAS/PMSP.
Comin, A. (2010). Cidades-Regiões ou hiper-concentração do desenvolvimento? O debate visto do Sul. In: Kowarick, L. and Marques, E. (eds.) *São Paulo: novos percursos e atores: sociedade, cultura e política*. São Paulo: Ed. 34, pp. 157–178.
Cunha, J. (2013). Migrações. In: Arretche, M. (ed.) *Quanto o Brasil mudou nos últimos cinquenta anos*. São Paulo: CEM, pp. 279–309.
Erikson, R. and Goldthorpe, J. (1992). *The constant flux: A study of class mobility in industrial societies*. Oxford: Clarendon Press.
Erikson, R., Goldthorpe, J. and Portocarrero, L. (1979). Intergenerational class mobility in three western European societies. *British Journal of Sociology*, 30, pp. 415–441.
Ganzeboom, H., Treiman, D. and De Graaf, P. (1993). A standard international socio-economic index of occupational status. *Social Science Research*, 21, pp. 1–56.
Goldthorpe, J. (2007). *On sociology—Illustration and retrospect*. Stanford: Stanford University Press.
Goldthorpe, J. (2000). *On sociology: Numbers, narratives, and the integration of research and theory*. Oxford: Oxford University Press.
Grusky, D. and Galescu, G. (2005). Foundations of a neo-Durkheimmian class analysis. In: Wright, E. O. (ed.) *Approaches to class analysis*. Cambridge: Cambridge University Press, pp. 51–81.
Grusky, D. and Sorensen, J. (1998). Can class analysis be salvaged? *The American Journal of Sociology*, 103(5), pp. 1187–1234.
Grusky, D. and Weeden, K. (2008). Are there social classes? A framework for testing sociology's favorite concept. In: A. Lareau and D. Conley (eds.) *Social class. How does it work?* New York: Russel Sage Foundation, pp. 65–92.
Grusky, D. and Weeden, K. (2001). Decomposition without death: A research agenda for a new class analysis. *Acta Sociologica*, 44, pp. 203–218.

Guimarães, N. (2009). À procura de trabalho: instituições do mercado e redes. Belo Horizonte: Ed. Argumentun.
Hamnett, C. (1996a). Why Sassen is wrong: A response to Burgers. *Urban Studies*, 33(1), pp. 107–110.
Hamnett, C. (1996b). Social polarization, economic restructuring and welfare state regimes. *Urban Studies*, 33(8), pp. 1407–1430.
Hamnett, C. (1994). Social polarisation in global cities: Theory and evidence. *Urban Studies*, 31(3), pp. 401–424.
Kalleberg, A. and Sorensen, A. (1979). The sociology of labor markets. *Annual Review of Sociology*, 5, pp. 351–379.
Knox, P. and Taylor, P. (1995). *World cities in a world-system*. Cambridge: Cambridge University Press.
Kowarick, L. (1979). *Espoliação urbana*. Petrópolis: Paz e Terra.
Maloutas, T. (2007). Segregation, social polarization and immigration in Athens during the 1990's: Theoretical expectations and contextual difference. *International Journal of Urban and Regional Research*, 31(4), pp. 733–758.
Marques, E. (2013). Condições urbanas. In: Arretche, M. (ed.) *Quanto o Brasil mudou nos últimos cinquenta anos*. São Paulo: CEM, pp. 223–248.
Marques, E., Bichir, R. and Scalon, C. (2012). Residential segregation and social structure in São Paulo: Continuity and change since the 1990s. In: Maloutas, T. and Fujita, K. (eds.) *Residential segregation in comparative perspective*. London: Ashgate, pp. 135–152.
Marques, E. and Scalon, C. (2009a). A dinâmica dos grupos sociais em São Paulo na década de 1990. In: Scalon, C (ed.) *Ensaios de Estratificação*. Belo Horizonte: Ed. Argumentum, pp. 45–67.
Marques, E. and Scalon, C. (2009b). Comparando estruturas sociais no Rio de Janeiro e São Paulo. In: Scalon, C (ed.) *Ensaios de Estratificação*. Belo Horizonte: Ed. Argumentum, pp. 68–91.
Marques, E. and Torres, H. (2005). *São Paulo: segregação, pobreza e desigualdades sociais*. São Paulo: Ed. Senac.
Musterd, S. and Murie, A. (eds.) (2002). *The spatial dimensions of urban social exclusion and integration*. Amsterdam. Available at: www.frw.uva.nl/ame/urbex
Neri, M. and Souza, P. (2013). *A década inclusiva (2001–2011): Desigualdade, pobreza e políticas de renda*. Comunicados IPEA, 155. Brasília: IPEA.
Preteceille, E. (2006). La ségrégation sociale a-t-elle augmenté? La métropole parisiense entre polarization et mixité. *Societé Contemporaines*, 62, pp. 69–93.
Preteceille, E. (1995). Division sociale de l'espace et globalization. *Societé Contemporaines*, 22/23, pp. 33–67.
Preteceille, E. and Cardoso, A. (2008). Rio de Janeiro y São Paulo: ciudades duales? Comparación con Paris. *Ciudad y Territorio*, XL(158), pp. 617–640.
Ribeiro, C. (2007). *Estrutura de classe e mobilidade social no Brasil*. São Paulo: Edusc/Anpocs.
Ribeiro, L. and Telles, E. (2000). Rio de Janeiro: emerging dualization in a historically unequal city. In: Marcuse, P. and Kempen, R. (eds.) *Globalizing cities: A new spatial order?* Oxford: Blackwell, pp. 78–94.
Sassen, S. (1991). *The global city: New York, London, Tokyo*. Princeton: Princeton University Press.
Sorensen, A. (1996). The structural basis of social inequality. *American Journal of Sociology*, 101(5), pp. 1333–1365.

Torres, H., Pavez, T. and Bichir, R. (2006). Uma pobreza diferente? Mudanças no padrão de consumo da população de baixa renda. *Novos Estudos Cebrap*, 74, pp. 16–23.

Vaattovaara, M. and Kortteinen, M. (2003). Beyond polarization versus professionalization? A case study of the development of the Hensinki region, Finland. *Urban Studies*, 40(11), pp. 2127–2145.

Walks, R. (2001). The social ecology of the post-Fordist/global city? Economic restructuring and socio-spatial polarization in the Toronto Urban region. *Urban Studies*, 38(3), pp. 407–447.

Weber, M. (1999 [1922]). *Economia e sociedade: fundamentos da sociologia compreensiva*. São Paulo: UNB/Imprensa Oficial.

Weeden, K. (2002). Why do some occupations pay more than others? Social closure and earnings in equality in the United States. *American Journal of Sociology*, 108(1), pp. 55–101.

Wessel, T. (2000). Social polarization and socioeconomic segregation in a welfare state: The case of Oslo. *Urban Studies*, 37(11), pp. 1947–1967.

Wright, E. (1997). *Class counts: Comparative studies in class analysis*. Cambridge: Cambridge University Press.

3 Labor Market, Income Inequalities and Poverty

Rogério Jerônimo Barbosa and Ian Prates

The city of São Paulo and its surrounding municipalities have always played a paradigmatic role in Brazilian studies of the labor market. This centrality stems from its historical concentration of important economic and political functions since the mid-19th century and the coffee era. The SPMR represents around 10 percent of the country's population and 18 percent of its GDP. Precisely due to its centrality, the region experiences moments of crisis, stagnation and growth with similar intensity. For these reasons, the majority of studies on labor markets in Brazil have focused on the SPMR, the pioneer in so many processes: urbanization and industrialization (Singer 1973), class structure transformation (Fernandes 1965), informality (or "marginality"; Kowarick 1975, Nun 2003, Oliveira 2003), unionism (Rodrigues 2009), productive restructuring (Cardoso 2000), unemployment (Guimarães 2009a) and new forms of job searching (Guimarães 2009b).

In this chapter we analyze two dimensions related to the SPMR's labor market: income inequality and poverty. We observe how patterns of job creation institutional changes and alterations in the composition of the workforce have affected income distribution over a 30-year period, potentially amplifying or reducing wage dispersion and the level of welfare of individuals. Income inequality and poverty are distinct yet associated phenomena. However, we set out from the premise that this association is not necessarily linear and direct: It depends on characteristics of the context and institutions of the labor market. Under determined conditions, it is possible for inequality to grow without levels of poverty being affected and vice versa; on other occasions, though, the two indicators move in the same direction.

Our departure point is the contemporary debate on the labor market and income inequalities, then we show how this literature can contribute to studies of poverty. One of the key arguments is that patterns of job creation are fundamental to comprehending patterns of income distribution. Some authors have emphasized that a process of occupational polarization linked to the demand for skills and qualifications has systematically contributed to increasing inequality in some advanced national economies (Autor et al. 2003, Goos et al. 2007 and 2009). Others, however, have highlighted the fact that polarization processes are contingent on the existing institutional framework, referring to occupational structure (Mouw & Kalleberg 2010, Wright & Dwyer 2003) and especially to welfare systems (Fernandes-Macías 2012). We propose two forms of operationalizing the concept of polarization. The first will be directly functional, testing its potential impact on inequalities in earnings. The second will enable us to observe how the dynamics of occupational structure affect the temporal evolution of poverty.

After this introduction, the chapter is structured as follows: In the first section, we provide a brief historical panorama of the labor market, inequality and poverty in Brazil and in the SPMR, highlighting the relevant points to the debate. In the second section, we examine the main explanations advanced by the contemporary international literature when it comes to analyzing income inequalities and occupational polarization. In the third section we briefly present the data used and the methodology employed (further details can be found in the Statistical Appendix). In the fourth and fifth sections we present our findings and interpretations. In the last section we discuss the consequences and relevance of our findings and propose a number of final considerations.

Labor Market, Inequalities and Poverty in Brazil and the São Paulo Metropolitan Region—A Brief Historical Survey

Brazil is one of the most unequal countries in the world (Neri 2011). But why is such inequality found, especially in terms of earnings? There is no complete and unequivocal reply to this question—but all reasonable explanations recognize the fact that the contemporary asymmetries observed in the labor market are the result of both short- and long-term processes, sociopolitical factors that have historically established and delimited the rules of the game within the environment of labor supply and demand (as well as who can play). In this section we deal first with the general trends of inequality and poverty for Brazil to then focus more specifically on the SPMR.

Before the 1970s, income inequalities had yet to be rigorously measured. The works by Hoffman & Duarte (1972), Fishlow (1972) and Langoni (1973) marked a turning point in the empirical studies. These and other texts observed that, despite an average growth in GDP of almost 7.0 percent between 1960 and 1970, levels of inequality had grown alarmingly over the period—the Gini index rose from roughly 0.53 to 0.58. Diverse explanations were given for what became known as the controversy over income distribution and development (Tolipan & Tineli 1975): on one hand, explanations rooted in the idea of human capital, emphasizing a regrowth in demand for educational qualifications and, on the other, "political-institutional" explanations emphasizing the policies unfavorable to workers during the military regime, especially wage compression. In this context, poverty levels had remained more or less unaffected, with a slight drop from 58.0 to 55.0 percent, before declining strongly over the following decade (1970 to 1980), when they fell as low as 34.0 percent. Langoni (1973) argued that the increase in income inequality during economic growth did not necessarily imply a reduction in the population's well-being; on the contrary, access to consumption and income were on average growing (which partly explained the fall in poverty levels) but in fairly asymmetric and heterogenic form among different social groups.

Levels of labor regulation and formalization were always historically very low, while access to various social protection services (including health care and social security) had depended directly on the individual's participation in the labor market. The few urban workers properly registered were able to enjoy these rights—a system that Santos (1979) dubbed "regulated citizenship." To adopt the typology of Esping-Andersen (1990), this model reflected a conservative regime of social welfare, corporativist but highly exclusionary due to the narrow scope of the formal labor market, which provided the social basis for accessing rights.[1]

The rapid economic growth during the period 1968–1973 generated a huge expectation among much of the population for their inclusion in the formal market (Machado da Silva 1991). Despite some advances, though, the Brazilian state proved unable to establish an adequate institutional framework to enable and support this inclusion. Urban populations grew at a much faster pace than the labor markets. Categories like "marginality" and "informality" were formulated to describe the large contingent of workers located outside the formal protected sector (Kowarick 1975, Nun 2003, Oliveira 2003). The excluding nature of the labor market's institutional structure always brought along the phenomenon of poverty as its outer limit.

The 1980s showed diverse and in some ways contradictory tendencies. In terms of economic performance, the country from 1981 onward was hit by cycles of recession, stagnation and recovery—movements that led to this period being called the "lost decade." National indicators of income inequality had begun to fall between 1976 and 1979 (Soares 2006), but this trend was subsequently reversed, and rapid growth took place, meaning that by 1989, Brazil had the highest levels of income concentration on record. The process of workforce formalization and inclusion was also interrupted (Machado da Silva 1991).

However, the promulgation of the 1988 constitution after the country's return to democracy represented a regulatory and institutional turnaround that largely expanded social rights. This change signaled a new and inclusive pattern of association between the labor market and poverty, assuring access to minimum levels of welfare through nonmarket means and thus protection to the most vulnerable individuals. The state became responsible for guaranteeing universal access to health services as well as a profound reformulation of how welfare and labor rights functioned.[2]

Nonetheless, despite the expansion in social protection, the start of the 1990s was also marked by a strong restructuring of the economy as it went through a process of commercial opening. This situation was further exacerbated by the flexibilization of labor laws at various moments of President Fernando Henrique Cardoso's two terms of government (1995–1998 and 1999–2002). The national industries (specially their core, located in the SPMR) were forced to restructure their processes in response to growing international competition, adopting more intensive rather than extensive productivity mechanisms. This corporate restructuring—which ranged from the factory floor to management levels—involved the transfer of some peripheral production activities to contracted or "outsourced" companies (Comin & Amitrano 2003). This fragmentation in the contracting of services and staff worsened the disintegration of unions and consequently the capacity for workers to mobilize and collectively bargain (Rodrigues 2009).

The indicators for inequalities in earnings in the SPMR oscillated much more strongly than the national indicators. After the period of instability in the 1980s, it tended to decline until 1996 and increase from that year until around 2004. The distribution of income in the SPMR proved fairly sensitive to the intense transformations in the labor market. In the SPMR inequality only began to fall from 2005 and even so not measured in the same form by the different indices.

Here we shall investigate in more detail the impact of some of the factors involved in these scenarios of changes in inequality and poverty. First, it is important to question the consequences of informality and occupational restructuring. However, we also need to evaluate the canonical factors identified by the literature as responsible for the decline in inequalities at national level: namely, the transformations in the returns and composition by schooling, gender and age structure. In the next section we present some of the main explanatory hypotheses proposed in the international literature for the growth and decline in inequalities and relate them to the dimensions that we intend to explore here.

Inequalities and Polarization: Patterns of Employment Generation

Recently income inequality has grown in the majority of developed countries as well as other BRICS countries (Brazil, Russia, India, China, and South Africa). In the 2000s, Brazil in fact experienced an opposite trend. But while the rise in inequalities is a recent phenomenon for emerging countries, in some European nations and the United States, it has been underway since the mid-1970s. For some analysts, the main cause is the transition from the manufacturing model to the "service economy," accompanied by the growth in financial institutions, open markets, new technologies and the difficulties faced in adapting social protection systems to these new configurations.

The economic crises of the 1970s strongly curbed the demand for labor, just when the baby boomers and women began to enter the labor market, making the environment unfavorable for those who wanted (and needed) to sell their labor. This was a growth in the labor supply in a hostile environment—precisely as Brazil would experience decades later. The financial crisis led to a decline in company profits, which prompted them to try to reduce costs and increase productivity. This new configuration had direct impacts on less-skilled workers and on lower wages (the "working poor"), who had previously had the chance to work in sectors that provided stable, protected, long-term employment.

In the United States, the occupational structure adapted to the economic transformations through the creation of poorly paid jobs, minimizing the unemployment problem but simultaneously intensifying wage dispersion and inequality (Freeman & Katz 1995). In some European countries, the rigidity of the institutions regulating labor and the capillarity of social welfare meant that the wage structure and inequality altered little—at first—though less-skilled workers were seen to have become "redundant" in the face of the new productive context (Marx 2007).

In the debate on the "causes" behind the increase in inequality, some analysts argued that the technological evolution skewed demand in favor of better-skilled workers, unequally rewarding those at the top of the occupational hierarchy and minimizing demand at its base (Acemoglu 2002). This hypothesis is similar to that of Langoni (2005[1973]), who analyzed the Brazilian case. At the core of both explanations resided the premise that inequalities are driven by changes in the demand for labor and in the capacities (or the human capital) of individuals to supply them. A skill-biased technological change (SBTC) is seen to be occurring, leading to a continuous rise in the demand for skills.[3]

In later analyses, however, what was observed in the United States and in many European countries was not a slow upgrade of the occupational structure through the increase in demand *solely* for skilled work but the polarization of the occupational structure as a whole. Autor et al. (2003) proposed a nuanced version of the SBTC hypothesis. According to the authors, the automatization of tasks within firms had tended to replace routine jobs (clerical and manual) with mechanized processes. Since routine jobs were situated precisely in the middle of the wage and occupational distribution, their stripping away led to polarization. Simultaneously, "nonroutine cognitive" occupations at the top (liberal professionals, managers and creative workers) expanded along with "nonroutine, noncognitive" jobs at the base (waiters, cleaners, etc.). The "ALM hypothesis" (incorporating the authors' initials: Autor, Levy and Murnane) or the "routinization hypothesis" was reinforced by other studies, including analyses of Western European countries (Goos et al. 2007 and 2009).

However, the supply side—that is, the behavior of trends relating to the characteristics of individuals—also are a central part of this debate. Apropos the United States, Goldin and Katz (2008) argued that the equalization in educational composition maintained until the 1970s served to make wage distribution less unequal, meaning that the benefits of postwar economic growth were much better distributed within the labor market. From the mid-1970s, however, the process was reversed, and the disproportional returns on educational level grew. In other words, the authors attributed growth to inequalities in the pattern in which the educational supply evolved.

Pursuing another viewpoint, Wright and Dwyer (2003), who studied patterns of job creation in the United States from the 1960s to the 2000s, argued that Hispanic American immigration, a fundamental element in the composition of the local labor market, was central to promoting polarization. During the 1990s, the large majority of jobs created at the base of the occupational structure were linked to immigrants, while the top jobs were taken essentially by members of the native white population. In addition to changes in demand caused by routinization, therefore, discrimination mechanisms linked to ethnicity could also be observed. This situation was exacerbated by the fact that some immigrants were in the country illegally, leaving them unable to obtain better jobs in any case.

Looking to explore the theme beyond the supply–demand relationship, Kalleberg (2012 and 2013), along with Mouw and Kalleberg (2010), argues that the occupational dynamics also have an independent and specific impact on inequalities.[4] The authors point out that wage differences *between occupations* have grown considerably since the 1980s—in others words, the increase in inequalities since then has largely been due to structural changes in the labor market (i.e., the occupational structure) rather than changes in the composition and effect of individual characteristics (like age, gender and schooling). Kalleberg (2012) suggests that the institutional configuration of the US labor market (more specifically: the declining strength of the unions over the last 40 years, the decentralization of wage-setting institutions and the increased flexibilization of labor relations) has provided the institutional framework that enabled or facilitated the process of occupational polarization.[5]

Fernandez-Macías (2012) and Oesch and Menes (2010) also criticized the overemphasis on technological development and the scant importance attached to institutional aspects in explanations of inequalities and polarization—directly opposing the views of Autor et al. (2003 and 2006) and Goos et al. (2007 and 2009). Analyzing the labor market in diverse European countries, they show that the design of institutional, welfare and labor regulation frameworks has an independent impact on the forms taken by employment expansion—and can dampen or alter potential tendencies toward polarization.

Based on this debate, we can ask: To what extent does the notion of polarization explain the shifts in income inequality and poverty rates in the specific case of the SPMR? If Brazil in the 1990s shows similarities with the scenarios experienced by some developed countries in earlier decades, does the explanations of the dynamics in these countries also apply to the Brazilian context? This question is particularly interesting in the case of the São Paulo metropolis, a region that still comprises the most industrialized area of the country and where studies of labor have primarily focused their gaze.

During the periods when inequalities rose in the SPMR, was there also a polarization process? Did this possible polarization have any effect on the incidence of poverty?

To reply to these questions, it is important to refine this notion analytically. This will allow us to deal with two distinct notions of polarization. The first enables us to identify its potential effect on income inequality, while the second evaluates its effects on poverty rates.

In the first case, earnings are the main dimension through which we shall measure polarization. The poles are defined by the individuals located at either end of the income distribution. In the second case, polarization is related to two aspects: to the *stock* of workers in the labor market and to the *flow* of jobs—that is, to patterns of employment generation or reduction. In this sense, polarization may occur because: (1) existing jobs are pushed further apart on the income spectrum, becoming polarized, or (2) new jobs created during a particular period were only generated at either end of the income distribution, or (3) the jobs that once occupied the middle of the income distribution (as in office or industrial work, according to the ALM model) disappeared.

Conversely, setting out from the premise that polarization can help explain the sinuous movement of inequalities during the period under study, we can also ask whether the recent fall in income inequalities is linked to a "depolarization." It is also useful to explore the characteristics of the individuals and jobs that become polarized or "depolarized." In other words, by what means does polarization operate? Is it closely linked to educational components (i.e., workforce qualifications), as the SBTC and ALM hypotheses maintain? And finally, what role is played by institutions and the institutionalization of the labor markets (formalization or contractual relation)?

To observe how the dynamic of the labor market affected the incidence of poverty, we shall investigate the pattern of job creation. In the next section we present the methodology used for each one of the analyses.

Analytic Models and Data

Analysis of Inequalities in Earnings

To analyze income inequality, our analytic strategy is based on group decomposition methods. In this section we present the overall aim of these models. Detailed estimation statistics can found in the appendix.

The inequality indicator adopted here is the variance of the natural logarithm of earnings. Unlike the Gini index, which measures the concentration of income quantities among fractions of the population, the variance of the log, like the Theil index, is an indicator of entropy.[6] The use of the variance of the logarithm is subject to limitations and criticisms,[7] but it also allows the application of multivariate and sophisticated decomposition techniques, (Lemieux 2006, Mouw & Kalleberg 2010, Western & Bloome 2009).

Put simply, the dispersion of a continuous variable can be decomposed on the basis of groups of a categorical variable. The total variance is equal to the sum of the variance between and within groups.

Var [LN(income)][J] = *Between Groups* + *Within Groups*

In mathematical notation,

$$V = \sum_{j=1}^{J} \pi_j \left(\mu_j - \bar{\mu} \right)^2 + \sum_{j=1}^{J} \pi_j \sigma_j^2 \qquad (1)$$

The first expression on the right side of the equation represents the *between groups* component. A group (*j*) contributes to the overall inequality the more its mean (μ_j) moves away from the grand mean $\bar{\mu}$, and the importance of its contribution is proportional to the fraction it occupies in the population as a whole (π_j). However a group can also contribute to inequalities if it is itself internally unequal—that is, depending on its variance (σ_j^2). The contribution of this internal inequality is obviously proportional to the size of group (π_j). Hence the second term on the right side of the equation represents the *within groups* component.

Suppose a hypothetical distribution of income by groups of a categorical variable:

(1) *The groups can move apart from each other.* In other words, their means can become polarized. We call this the *mean effect* or simply the *between groups* component. This involves the growth of the expression ($\mu_j - \bar{\mu}$)^2 in Equation 1.
(2) Maintaining the means constant (i.e., maintaining the groups in their places), *an increase in the internal inequality of the groups can occur.* We call this the *variance effect* or the *within groups* component. This involves the growth of σ_j^2 in Equation 1.
(3) Maintaining the means and variances constant, groups that are *internally very unequal can increase in size.* In other words, unequal groups come to *compose* a greater fraction of the overall distribution. We call this the *within groups composition effect*.
(4) Maintaining the means and variances constant, groups that are already at opposite pools can increase in size (in other words, growth can take place in polarized form). We call this the *between groups composition effect*.

These are the components into which we divided up income inequality over the studied period, 1981 to 2011. Items 1 and 4 operationalize the effects of a potential polarization. Item 1 relates to the polarization of the *stock* of jobs—that is, the increase in the distance between groups, given that we maintain their sizes constant. Item 4, for its part, relates to the polarization produced through job *flow*—that is, through the creation or removal of jobs, maintaining the existing distances constant.

To begin we calculated the values for the components of Equation 1 for all the years between 1981 and 2011. Next we fixed each of the components at the values observed in 1981. This way, we were able to produce a series of counterfactual exercises that allowed us to distinguish how each of the four mechanisms acted. This is important for us to be able to answer, for example:

(1) What would income inequality be like in each of the years until 2011 were the *income difference between* the educational groups to have remained constant at 1981 values? The difference between the inequality effectively observed and the counterfactual value shows the degree to which changes in inequalities during the period was due to the *mean effect* related to education.

(2) What would income inequality be like in each of the years until 2011 were the *income variance within* the educational groups to have remained constant at 1981 values? The difference between observed and counterfactual values reveals the *variance effect* (within).

(3) What would income inequality be like in each of the years until 2011 were the *size* of the educational groups to have remained constant at 1981 values? The difference between observed and counterfactual values reveals the *composition effect*.[8]

The target *groups* in our analysis are defined by the following variables: the EGP occupational classes (eight categories—excluding the rural groups),[9] educational bands (six categories), the formal and informal sectors (two categories), gender groups (two categories) and age groups (five categories).[10] This gives us a total of 960 cells formed by the cross-classification between categories of these variables. Each cell has a mean log-income, an internal variance, and accounts for a certain proportion of the labor market. In Equation 1 each group (j) represents one of these cells.

Occupation (EGP) operationalizes institutional aspects of the labor market (Mouw & Kalleberg 2010). Education informs us about the importance of supply and demand for human capital and connects with the hypotheses formulated by economists. (In)formality[11] is directly related to the macro-institutional regulation of the labor market, linking with the hypothesis (Fernandes-Macías 2012).

We used the Pesquisa Nacional por Amostragem de Domicílios (PNAD, or National Household Sample Survey) from 1981 to 2011. We selected only those individuals who worked during the reference week, had an income above zero, were aged between 25 and 65, and lived in the SPMR. The income measure used is the monthly earnings from the person's main job. The logarithmic transformation means that the variance is not subject to deflationary or monetary conversion effects—hence, the decomposition analyses do not require adjustments to the income variable. Even so, to present descriptive data, we applied the deflators proposed by Corseuil and Foguel (2002).

Analysis of the Job Creation Patterns and the Evolution of Poverty

We apply a similar methodology to that used by Wright and Dwyer (2003), Goos et al. (2009) and Fernandez-Macías (2012), among others, to evaluate trends in the United States and Europe, and by Carvalhaes et al. (2012) and Comin et al. (2012) to study the case of Brazil. It involves a simple procedure for ranking occupations in a hierarchy and making them comparable over time.

Our data sources are the demographic censuses from 1991 to 2010. We selected just the cases of the SPMR and combined the three databases. Next, we converted the occupational codes of each census to the ISCO-88 system and the sector codes to ISIC-3. We then cross-classified the observations, creating cells of occupation-by-sector.[12] These cells were then organized in ascending order according to the average earnings and organized into five quintiles (i.e., groups aggregating approximately 20 percent of workers). This division is made in such a way that all the individuals of a cell of occupation-by-sector are uniquely classified in a single quintile. Consequently, the individuals from the cells located on the boundary between two different quintiles were moved to the category in which they had a majority.

As the unit of analysis is the occupation-by-sector, whose ranking is fixed over time (i.e., it always belongs to the same quintile, we can assess the balance (growth, maintenance or decline) of the quintiles over the two decades, which is the same as accompanying the number of workers in the same occupation over time. Since the quintiles are a measure of the quality of the job, the behavior and balance of these categories reveal transformations in the structure of the labor market and reveal patterns of job creation.

Fernandes-Macías (2012) and Comin et al. (2012) show that this methodology for analyzing job flow can be sensitive to alterations in the form of categorizing and grouping occupations and sectors as well as the selection of the study's target population.

Poverty will be treated here as a lack of income. It is assumed that a level of sufficient income exists to ensure a minimum level of welfare. Those located below this line are defined as living in poverty. Though aware of the debate on the multidimensionality of poverty, here we maintain our focus on income—which indirectly also brings evidence on other dimensions. In sum, it is a reasonable summary measure. We utilize the PLs calculated by IETS (Institute of Labor and Social Studies), which take into account diverse consumer and welfare needs, as well as the variation in the cost of living in different localities. The values of the PLs are available at http://www.iets.org.

Income Inequalities: Counterfactual Results and Trends

Using OLS and Gamma (GLM) regression models, we estimated the means and variance for each of the 960 cells formed by cross-classification of the explanatory variables (see Statistical Appendix). Through a descriptive analysis, we obtained the observed proportions. This procedure was repeated for all the years from 1981 to 2011. In this way we obtained the values for each of the components used to calculate the variance in accordance with Equation 1.

Counterfactual results are obtained by maintaining all the values constant at the period t = 1981, allowing just one of the components to vary over the years. In other words, to discover the temporal trends of the means effect, we maintained constant the proportions and variance of each cell as they were in 1981 and let just the difference between groups to vary. First, in Figure 3.1, we present the findings relating to education.

Taking the level of inequalities of 1981 as a base, the lines show how each of the components contributed to raise or lower this level. The sum of all the lines in a given year represents the cumulative effect of the variation of the characteristics linked to education until that point in time.

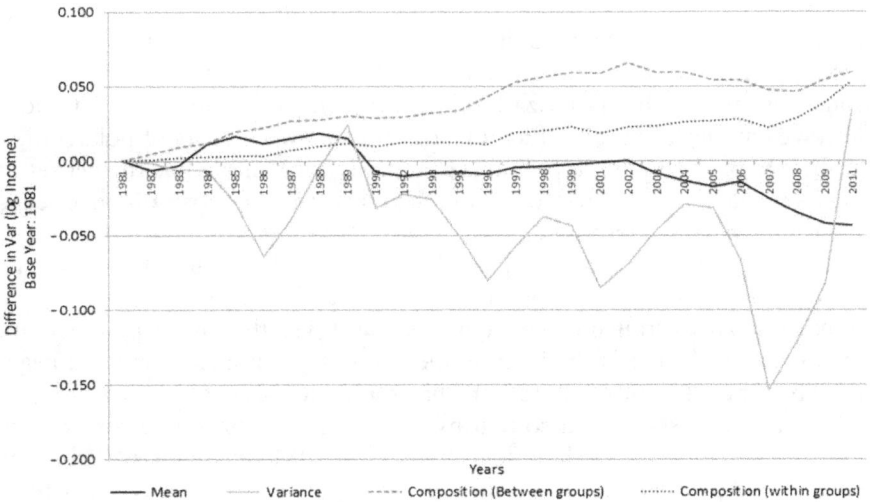

Figure 3.1 Counterfactual decomposition: effects of education.[13]

Source: Demographic censuses, IBGE, 1991–2010, authors' elaboration.

Observing the mean and composition effects, we can say that the education in the 1980s led to a slight polarization of the São Paulo labor market. This tendency was in part reversed between 1989 and 1990, when the mean component (distance between groups) underwent rapid decline. However, between 1990 and 2002 these components grew steadily—especially the composition effect. This means that the balance of jobs (*flow*) in the 1990s was polarized in educational terms and that the wage distance between those with the highest and lowest levels of schooling slightly increased (effect on the entire *stock*). This finding partly corroborates the expectations of the ALM hypothesis: In a context of intensifying competitiveness, the increase in productivity involves the demand for skilled workers (*skill-biased*), while routinization produces the replacement of routine jobs by technological processes. Here polarization comprises a high demand for skilled labor on one hand and a large supply of unskilled labor on the other.

However, we need to keep in mind that we are dealing with a fairly specific period. The micro-organizational restructuring that began at the end of the 1980s and continued throughout the 1990s led to a high number of redundancies that inflated unemployment rates. Consequently the polarized trend perhaps says less about a new type of "demand" for qualifications on the part of companies and more about the profile of the "survivors" of the crisis and restructuring. The idea that the polarization phenomenon may have been conjunctural is corroborated when we observe the data for 2002 and afterward. There is a clear and intense reversal of the means effects: In other words, the wage distance between educational groups starts to fall continuously. After 2002 we can also detect a reduction in polarization linked to the educational composition (*job flow*). The period of economic boom may have softened polarizing trends—or, in the 1990s, these movements were no more than conjunctural. We still lack sufficient elements to discard either of these two hypotheses. However, what we can say with some certainty is that polarization is not the only game in town. Additionally, we emphasize that the final outcome of the two vectors of polarization at the end of the analyzed period is practically zero, and while the net result of the mean effect is a reduction in inequality, the composition effect ends up in the opposite direction.

In terms of inequalities within the educational groups, there are two major movements. The first is the sinuous behavior of the variances, which traces out an overall movement of decline. Over the entire period (with the exception of 1989) the internal inequalities component remained negative. It is precisely for this reason that the major shift occurring between 2006 and 2007 stands out so that by 2011 it had become a vector producing an inequality higher than that observed in 1981. Inequalities within the educational groups increased sharply. This signifies uncertainty (or heterogeneity) in terms of the returns obtained from education. This may indicate a correlation between this fact and the expansion in higher education that occurred in the middle of the decade. The second movement linked to internal inequalities concerns the continuous trend toward growth of those groups that are already more internally unequal.

Although the overall indicator of inequality has fallen, we observed that the net effect education increased inequalities (at the end point, the sum of the components is positive). This was counterbalanced by the other variables, since the overall balance is a decline. In summary, the educational dynamics in the SPMR between 1981 and 2011 increased inequalities. The large turnaround in the variance component is the main factor responsible for this scenario. In other words, it is due to the uncertainty of educational returns—probably linked to a diversification in the quality of education on offer as well the entry of an increasingly diverse population into the education system.

We can turn now to the dynamics of the formal and informal sectors, which reveal aspects of institutional regulation (Figure 3.2). In the 1980s, we find a setting in which the behavior of the decomposed vectors is highly irregular, a phenomenon that may be explained by the extremely unstable economic environment. After 1989, though, there is an almost linear decline in inequalities within both the formal and informal groups. Interestingly this is precisely the period during which, between 1989 and 2001, there was a major downsizing of the formal sector in the metropolis (see Chapter 1). We can hypothesize that this reduction in internal inequalities is associated with (1) relative (and increasing) homogeneity in the profile of those surviving the wave of redundancies and reforms undertaken by or impacting on companies and (2) monetary stability, which ended the widespread practice

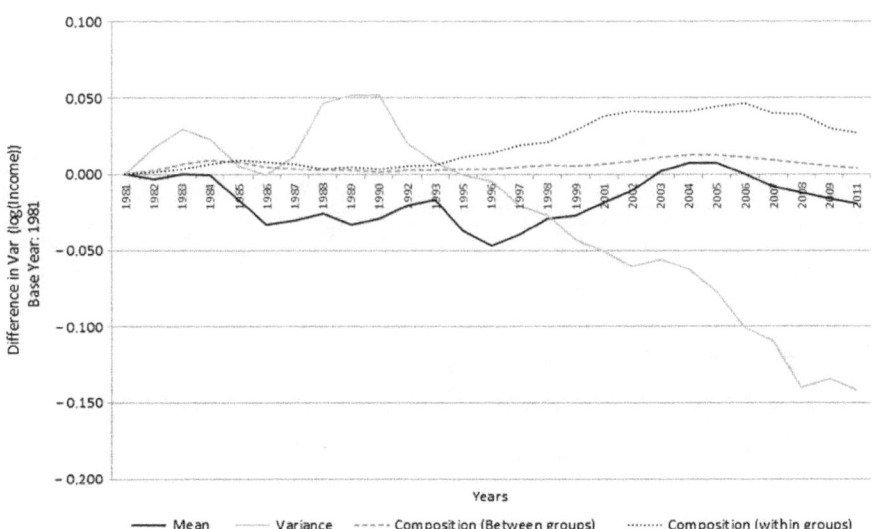

Figure 3.2 Counterfactual decomposition: (in)formality effects.

Source: Demographic censuses, IBGE, 1991–2010, authors' elaboration.

of wage adjustments (which were also unequally distributed). When job formalization returned from 2004 onward, the fall continued its course, probably pulled down now by the homogenization enabled by regulation policies, especially the minimum wage.

In the 1990s, the mean effect reveals an intense process of polarization between the formal and informal sectors: Wage differences between the groups increase. We therefore encounter a form of polarization that is not only linked to education or qualifications (and hence productivity), as the ALM hypothesis anticipates. In this case, this is due to the institutional dynamics of regulation and deregulation. In the 2005-to-2011 period, all the components show a systematic decline. Some authors (Baltar et al. 2010) have emphasized the impact caused by the expansion in the Ministry of Labor's monitoring of labor relations and the incentives given to formalization. By the end of the period, formalization is a vector in the fall in income inequality in the SPMR.

When we break down inequality in terms of EGP occupational classes, there are two main results. First, the fall in inequalities is basically due to the reduction in variance within the classes. From 1981 to 1992, there was a tendency for the variance component in income to increase. This trend was interrupted after 1994—and from this point to 1999, the distances between the earnings of individuals within the groups diminished. However, until 2011 the final trajectory once again resumed a sharp decline.

Second, mean differences declined following a sinuous path during the 1980s—but in the mid-1990s the distances between the classes in terms of income began to widen again (see Figure 3.3). This is a period during

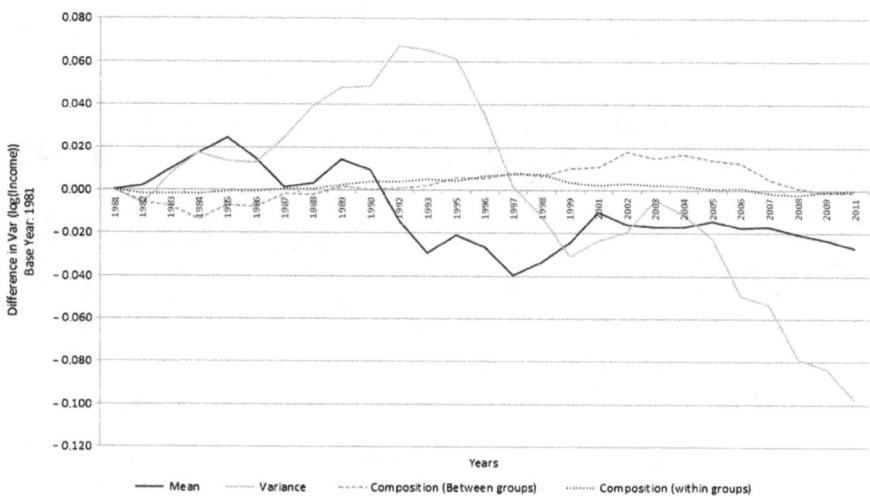

Figure 3.3 Counterfactual decomposition: class structure effects (EGP).

Source: Demographic censuses, IBGE, 1991–2010, authors' elaboration.

which a growth in the composition effect (between groups component) is also observed. In other words, our two measures show a slight degree of polarization that peaks in 2002. Thereafter, the situation begins to reverse, and all the components start to fall systematically. None of them registers a positive net balance by the end of the 30-year period under study. Hence, the widespread homogenization of incomes within the classes, combined with the slight reduction in the distances between them, ended up comprising the main factor in the fall in inequalities in the SPMR.

Labor Market Dynamics and Poverty in the Region

What results did all these changes in the composition of the job creation have over the levels of poverty present in the SPMR? Poverty in the region might have been produced by the levels of salaries and by unemployment but also by the dynamics of the creation of jobs in the region. Figure 3.4 presents the patterns of job creation across two decades (1991–2000 and 2000–2010), recalling that each of the quintiles represents a set of occupations-by-sectors ranked according to average earnings. They comprise an ordinal scale of job quality. Studying the patterns of the balances will reveal the patterns of employment generation (providing us with another angle from which to determine whether polarization occurred). Furthermore the analysis of the individuals occupying these jobs will enable us to assess how these balances can increase or reduce levels of poverty among the workers.

We can confirm the occurrence of polarized job creation in the 1990s and simultaneously suggest that the pattern observed in the 2000s effectively comprises an "de-polarization". This picture becomes even clearer when we add the balance of unemployed.

The 2000s saw a relative improvement in jobs. But the scenario is still far from representing a context of job upgrading or a transformation in the SPMR's occupational structure. We stress that this is a study of the *flow* of jobs—not the *stock*. The balances of the sector occupation quintiles reveal only the differentials arising from the dynamics over the decades in question.

From the outset we can note that the condition of poverty is strongly related to the ways in which individuals are absorbed into the labor market: A household whose individuals are unemployed or engage in poorly paid activities is more likely to have a per-capita income below the PL—given that income from work makes up the largest portion of household revenue. Consequently, a scenario of strong unemployment and low wages at the base of the structure will certainly tend to increase the potential number of poor people. In the 1990s, jobs created in the first quintile, were occupied by those still living below the PL. We define families as "extremely poor" when they have a per-capita income up to one-half the PL and as "poor" when they have an income between one-half and one PL.

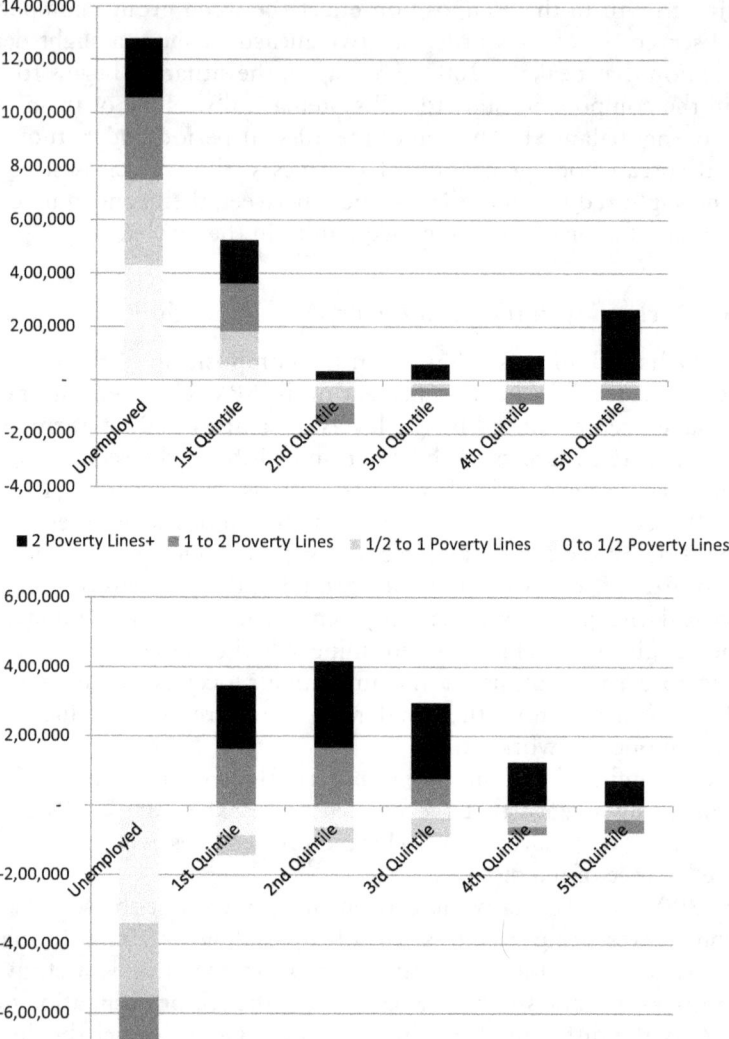

Figure 3.4 Employment generation and unemployment balance per household income. SPMR, 1991–2000 and 2000–2010.

Source: Demographic censuses, IBGE, 1991–2010, authors' elaboration.

This situation indicates that being employed does not guarantee minimum subsistence conditions. Moreover, much of the unemployment balance consists of individuals living in poverty or extreme poverty. In fact, 58.6 percent of the 1,277,296 newly unemployed were living in poverty in 2000.

The situation changes in the following decade: All the jobs created were occupied by individuals whose per-capita household income was located in the interval between one and two PLs. Simultaneously, most of the negative unemployment balance relates precisely to the poor population. The pattern of job creation established over the course of the decade was fundamental to reducing poverty.

However, while the analysis of job creation relates to the absorption of individuals into the market, the definition of poverty is related to the household, that is, to a collective. To evaluate these findings better, we need to describe the typical household composition of the different income bands. First, the poorest households contain a higher number of residents, many of whom are not yet at an economically active age (under 10 years old). Second, even among those who can sell their workforce in the market (the economically active population), a relatively small fraction actually does so (compared to the fraction observed in wealthier households). Finally, unemployment is higher among the poorest population. The condition of poverty implies an increasing selectivity, which begins in the conditions imposed before entering the labor market.

Returning to the analysis of the occupational structure, we need to explore the nature of the occupations characterizing the employment quintiles over the last two decades and how these relate to the structure of household income. Poverty is closely associated with manual work, a fact that has changed little over the years. However it is worth highlighting the behavior of some specific occupations. The first is the "domestic and manual workers" occupation group, which is widely present in the lowest income bands and remains frequent in the bands of two PLs or over. Second, the poor also show a predominance of manual work related to care and cleaning (also expressed by the occupation "cleaning and building maintenance work"). Third, work in civil construction is also prevalent ("builders and construction workers"). This occupation is also fairly typical in the bands up to two PLs but less so in the higher stratum. Cleaners and construction workers therefore illustrate the persistence of the occupational structure associated with poverty.

Over the decades analyzed, there was a growth in commercial "vendors and demonstrators"—that is, attendants in retail or wholesale establishments. On one hand, this reflects the growth in distribution services following the decline in industrial employment. On the other, it reveals a growth in salaried worker, even among the poorest income bands—in detriment of the self-employment (which in Brazil is largely a characteristic of the informal labor market).

In sum, this information gives us some idea of the considerable persistence and the small changes in the occupational structure that characterizes poverty.

The flow of job creation over a time span of one or two decades has had only a limited capacity to alter the occupational bases of the labor market. But even so, the place of poor people in the labor market has gradually altered.

This also becomes evident when we calculate the percentage of poor individuals in each occupation-by-sector. If the correlation between the percentage of the poor in the same occupations-by-sectors between two years remains stable, it means the places destined to the poor in the labor market didn't change. If the correlation declines, this means that the jobs typically occupied by the poorest are no longer the same.

Calculating the Pearson coefficient for the percentage of poor people in the occupations-by-sector in 1991 and 2000, we obtain the value 0.909—fairly high but already indicating that the jobs occupied by many poor people in 1991 were not exactly the same in 2000. Jumping forward another 10 years (i.e., comparing the positions in 1991 and 2010) this association falls to 0.782. There is a growing, albeit slow, tendency for diversification in the relation between occupational structure and poverty. The "occupational niches" in which the poor are allocated within the labor market slowly became more diverse. Obviously, distinct patterns favor the direction and speed of this trend to different degrees.

Discussion and Final Considerations

The SPMR experienced a fall in inequalities and poverty over the last years, as in the rest of Brazil. But many specific aspects are involved. First, it should be emphasized that the inequalities in the metropolitan region were much more susceptible to the economic cycles and labor market transformations that occurred over the studied interval of time. Second, the magnitude of the fall in inequality is smaller. And finally we have seen that the vectors are not the same as those operating at national level.

Explanations based on economic expectations, which focus mainly on the labor profile demanded by companies, seem to be of limited applicability in our case. A "skill-biased" polarization took place during the 1990s—something that had direct consequences for income distribution and was also expressed in the patterns of job creation. However this tendency was largely reversed during the 2000s.

In terms of income inequalities, we also find a polarization associated with factors other than skills. This was the case, for example, with the dynamics between formal and informal sectors. This result gives us the confidence to assert that the institutional action of the state on the labor market, including the removal or introduction of regulatory instruments, has the power to amplify or reduce asymmetries. We have evidence to think that this was the case, at least in the last two decades.

The dynamics of the occupational classes were precisely the components that played the most important role in reducing inequalities, closely followed by the process of formalizing the workforce. The occupational hierarchies express structured and systematic inequalities, founded both on the political protection of some occupations (associations, unions, professional regulations, etc.) and on more diffuse institutional structures, rooted in cultural representations of prestige and value and, obviously enough, on the position of the occupants in the productive structure (i.e., proprietors, employers, employees, etc.). In a study such as this, we do not intend to analyze which mechanisms produced the effects actually observed. It is interesting to note, however, that the main vector in decline is the one related to inequalities within the classes. One possible reading is that a class regime has become more cohesive after this process. In other words, with the inequalities between individuals declining within occupations, it is the inequality between occupations that for the most part remains—making this component of more explanatory importance in terms of the remainder. A somewhat similar result was obtained by Carvalhaes et al. (2012) in a study dedicated to occupational inequalities in Brazil over the last decade. However, the practical consequences of this greater clarity in the occupational divisions within the labor market are less clear—and indeed may not be correlated with other dimensions of the social stratification.

Our analysis of the SPMR case also shows evidence of behavior diverging from the national trends—in the case, for example, of education (which at the end of the period generated an increase in inequalities). These findings indicate the existence of specific processes, placing in suspension any possibility for easy generalization of the diagnoses. Furthermore, as we stated earlier, our study shows that even the pattern of polarization that was theoretically expected by economists has been more or less reversed in the SPMR over recent years. This fact raises a question about the strength of this process informed by the demand for skilled labor and about the conditions necessary for its occurrence.

The analysis of poverty dialogues closely with the analysis of income distribution. We emphasize from the outset that the condition of poverty is not produced solely by a different mode of incorporation into the labor market, but since this is the main locus of distribution of goods and assets, it becomes central to studying this interaction. We look to identify how patterns of job creation can alter the "occupational niche" reserved to the poor and how these patterns can also provide opportunities for them to escape poverty. There are, indeed, marked differences in the behavior of the labor market between the two decades, clearly visible in the patterns of job creation (*flow*).

As we have seen, the 1990s were marked by a form of "polarization" that amplified inequalities and contributed moreover to the rise in poverty between 1991 and 2000, not only because of the high unemployment rates over the decade but also due to how the occupations were created and how they absorbed different income groups. Here we should recall that the first quintile of the balance of jobs contained poor and extremely poor individuals (the working poor). This picture reveals that job creation and the labor market may not be effective in terms of redistribution. In the 2000s, growth took place within the occupational structure in an inverse form to polarization. Consequently, the reduction in poverty via the labor market took place due to (1) the fall in unemployment, and (2) the increase in the real value of the minimum wage, but also because (3) relatively better occupations were created within the occupational structure.

Analyzing the stock of workers and individuals living in poverty, however, we can observe that the occupations typically exercised by poor people became more diverse, albeit slowly. There is less segmentation in the labor market, but based on the present speed of this process, many more decades would be needed to alter significantly the list of jobs typically associated with poverty. We should also note that this alteration can end up including occupations in the set of those classed as "typically poor," as proved to be the case in the 1990s.

The analysis of occupations has revealed more enduring aspects of the organization of the labor market, which, at the macro-social level, inform the system of labor division and, at individual level, points to the prospects for income in the long-term and to future opportunities.

Statistical Appendix

The variance of the log-income can be decomposed as follows:

$$V = \sum_{j=1}^{J} \pi_j \left(\mu_j - \bar{\mu}\right)^2 + \sum_{j=1}^{J} \pi_j \sigma_j^2 \qquad (A.1)$$

Where:
  j = category or group
  μ_j = mean of the category
  $\bar{\mu}$ = overall mean of the income log
  π_j = proportion (from 0 to 1) of each category
  σ_j^2 = variance within each category

When the number of groups analyzed is very high, decomposition methods based on regressions are recommended. The basic model of Variance Function Regression (VFR) can be implemented in two steps (Western & Bloome 2009):

$$Y_i = \beta_0 + \sum_{k=1}^{K} \beta_k X_{ik} + \varepsilon_i \qquad (A.2)$$

$$\ln\left(\sigma_i^2\right) = \lambda_0 + \sum_{k=1}^{K} \lambda_k X_{ik} + \omega_i \qquad (A.3)$$

The Expression A.2 is an OLS regression. If these covariables were categorical, the predicted values would be the means of each of the groups formed by the intersections between the categories. The residuals of this regression would be precisely the portion of the variation not explained by these means, that is, the inequality between individuals within groups. Since all the residuals are centralized, the sum of the squared residuals indicates the variance within groups.

We assume heteroscedasticity and take the variables delimiting the groups as themselves the factor explaining the differences between the variances of the groups. Consequently, the second step is to take the residuals squared as a dependent variable in a Gamma regression model with a logarithmic link function (which allows for strictly positive and right skewed variables). To obtain non-biased estimates of the standard errors, an iterative method can be implemented in order to produce Maximum Likelihood estimates. The maximum likelihood function is given by:

$$L(\beta,\lambda;y_i) = -\frac{1}{2}\left[\log(\sigma_i^2) + (y_i - \hat{y}_i)/\sigma_i^2\right]$$
$$= -\frac{1}{2}\left[z_i'\lambda + d_i exp(z_i'\lambda)\right]$$
(A.4)

where d_i indicates the square of the residuals of the linear regression. Consequently the steps for the implementation are: (1) estimate a linear regression, saving the residuals; (2) estimate a Gamma regression for the residuals squared, saving the predicted values: $\sigma_i^2 = exp(z_i'\lambda)$; (3) estimate the linear regression again, using $1/\sigma_i^2$ as weights (*weighted least squares*); (4) repeat Steps 2 and 3 until the maximum likelihood function reaches convergence. The coefficients of the linear regression thus express the effect of the differences of means between groups, while the coefficients of the Gamma regression express the differences between the variances of the groups. The predicted values of the two regressions can substitute μ_j and σ_j^2, respectively, in Equation A.1.

We adjusted these models for all the years between 1981 and 2011. To estimate the counterfactual decomposition of the inequalities for each variable:

(1) We fixed the β coefficients of the linear regressions at the 1981 values and calculated the predicted values for each year. The differences between the inequality observed in a given year and the counterfactual inequality gives the mean effect.
(2) We fixed the λ coefficients of the Gamma regressions at 1981 and calculated the values of the variances within the groups. The difference between the inequality actually observed in a given year and the counterfactual gives the variance effect.
(3) Additional adjustments are necessary for the composition effect. The marginal proportions of the variable of interest in 1981 (p_{0c}), and the marginal proportions in a given year t of the series (p_{tc}) are calculated. By taking π_j as the proportion of the group j in the total of existing groups, it is possible to calculate an adjusted proportion $\tilde{\pi}_j$ which

fixes values based on the marginal distributions of 1981 based only on the variable of interest through the formula $\tilde{\pi}_j = (p_{0c} / p_{tc})\pi_j$.

(a) The composition effect (between groups factor) is calculated through the use of this adjusted proportion only on the first term of the variance decomposition Equation A.1.
(b) The composition effect (within groups factor) is calculated through the use of this adjusted proportion only on the second term of the variance decomposition Equation A.1.

Notes

1. Just to illustrate this point, in 1979 around 54 percent of wage-earning workers were formally employed. This percentage remained fairly stable throughout the 1980s before declining during the 1990s and rising again in the 2000s. In 2013, however, the proportion of workers formally employed was still less than 60 percent.
2. Among the legal frameworks established in the field of social protection after 1988, Draibe (1998) emphasizes: (1) less dependency on contribution payment as a structuring principle of the system, (2) the universalization of access and expansion of coverage, (3) the recuperation and redefinition of minimum levels of social benefits and (4) increased engagement from the State, increasing the provision of goods and social services. We can also cite the universalization of access to health care through the National Health Service (SUS) and the expansion of the education system. Cardoso (1999) highlights among the principal advances in labor legislation: the right to strike, the freedom to create unions without control by the state, direction negotiation between unions and employers, reduction of the working week to 44 hours, unemployment benefits and maternity/paternity leave.
3. "This conclusion is based on the sharp increase in overall inequality starting in the 1970s and on the fact that returns to schooling rose over the past thirty years despite the unusually rapid increase in the supply of educated workers" (Acemoglu 2002, p. 1266).
4. Among other things, the occupations represent institutional aspects of the labor market, given that they define the bases for unionization and for professional and employer associations and are subject to state regulations and interventions. Moreover, occupations are a good proxy for an individual's permanent income—they thus set limits and possibilities for consumer habits and lifestyles.
5. For a similar perspective, see DiPrete et al. (2005) and Mimieux (2007).
6. By way of example, if all the individuals possess the same income value, there would be no variance or dispersion of this variable; in other words, they would all be "equal." For a comparison of the measures for earnings inequality, see Cowell (1995).
7. The log is a nonlinear transformation and thus does not respect the "transfer principle" (cf. Cowell 1995). Consequently its sensitivity to the movement of inequality differs from the Theil index.
8. On distinguishing between and within composition through counterfactuals, see the Statistical Appendix.
9. High-level professionals; low-level professionals; high-level, nonmanual routine; low-level, nonmanual routine; employers (urban); technicians and supervisors; skilled manual workers and unskilled manual workers.

10. The variables in the years studied for the 1980s were standardized in line with the model proposed by Soares and Lima (2002). Next we compiled educational level categories for all the years analyzed: illiterate or without schooling, incomplete primary, complete primary or incomplete secondary (combined), complete secondary, incomplete higher and complete higher. We divided the age groups as follows: 25–34, 35–39, 40–44, 45–49, 50–54 and 55 and over. For variable standardization, we used the model proposed by Barbosa and Marschner (2013).
11. We considered formal employees: (1) workers of the private sector with a signed "carteira de trabalho" or employment record card (including domestic workers), (2) public-sector workers and military personnel, (3) self-employed and (4) employers who contribute to the social security system.
12. We used three-digit ISCO codes and two-digit ISIC codes. In total, 659 sector occupations were created.
13. In fact all the counterfactual decomposition graphs show values that are mobile means to smooth out the lines and make reading the results easier.

Bibliography

Acemoglu, D. (2002). Technical change, inequality and the labor market. *Journal of Economic Literature*, 40(1), pp. 7–72.

Autor, D., Katz, L. and Kearney, M. (2006). *The skill content of recent technological change: An empirical exploration*. National Bureau of Economic Research, Working Paper 11986. Available at: http://www.nber.org/papers/w11986

Autor, D., Levy, F. and Murnane, R. (2003). The skill content of recent technological change: An empirical exploration. *The Quarterly Journal of Economics*, 118(4), pp. 1279–1333.

Batar, P. E. A., Santos, A. L., Krein, J. D., Leone, E., Proni, M. W., Moretto, A., Maia, A. G., Salas, C. (2010). *Trabalho no governo Lula: uma reflexão sobre a experiência brasileira recente*. Geneva: Global Labor University Working Papers.

Barbosa, A. (2008). *A formação do mercado de trabalho no Brasil*. São Paulo: Alameda.

Barbosa, R. and Marschner, M. (2013). *Uma proposta de padronização de classificações em pesquisas do IBGE (Censos 1960–2010) e PNADs (1981–2011): educação, setores de atividade econômica e ocupação (ISCO-88, EGP11 e ISEI)*. Working paper. Mimeo.

Cardoso, A. (2000). *Trabalhar: verbo transitivo*. Rio de Janeiro: FGV.

Cardoso, A. (1999). *Sindicatos, trabalhadores e a coqueluche neoliberal*. Rio de Janeiro: FGV.

Carvalhaes, F., Barbosa, R., Souza, P. and Ribeiro, C. (2012). *Os impactos da geração de empregos e desigualdade de renda: uma análise da década de 2000*. Working Paper. Mimeo.

Comin, A. and Amitrano, C. (2003). Economia e emprego: A trajetória recente da Região Metropolitana de São Paulo. *Novos Estudos Cebrap*, 66, pp. 53–76.

Comin, Á., Barbosa, R. and Carvalhaes, F. (2012). *Manufacturing jobs. ESRC pathfinder programme on collaborative analysis of microdata resources: Brazil and India*. Working Paper.

Corseuil, C. and Foguel, M. (2002). *Uma sugestão de deflatores para rendas obtidas a partir de algumas pesquisas domiciliares do IBGE*. Rio de Janeiro: Ipea: Texto para Discussão, n. 897.

Cowell, F. (1995). *Measuring inequality*. Oxford: Philip Allan.

DiPrete, T., Goux, D., Maurin, E., and Quesnel-Vallee, A. (2005). *Work and pay in flexible and regulated labor markets: A generalized perspective on institutional evolution and inequality trends in Europe and the U.S.* Working paper. Available at: http://www.yale.edu/ciqle/CIQLEPAPERS/DiPrete,%20work%20and%20pay%20in%20flexible.pdf

Draibe, S. (2003). A política social no período FHC e o sistema de proteção social. *Revista Tempo Social*, 15(2), pp. 63–101.

Draibe, S. M. (1998). A Política Brasileira de Combate à Pobreza. In: Velloso, J. P. R. (org.). *O Brasil e o Mundo no Limiar do Novo Século*. Rio de Janeiro: José Olympio.

Draibe, S. (1988). *O welfare state no Brasil: Características e perspectivas* NEPP/UNICAMP [Caderno de Pesquisa n° 8]. Campinas.

Erikson, R., Goldthorpe, J. and Portocarrero, L. (1979). Intergenerational class mobility in three Western European societies. *British Journal of Sociology*, 30, pp. 415–441.

Esping-Andersen, G. (1999). *The social foundation of post industrial societies*. New York: Oxford University Press.

Esping-Andersen, G. (1990). *The three worlds of welfare capitalism*. Princeton: Princeton University Press.

Fernandes, F. (1965). *A integração do negro na sociedade de classes*. São Paulo: Dominus.

Fernandez-Macías, E. (2012). Job polarization in Europe? Changes in the employment structure and job quality, 1995–2007. *Work and Occupations*, 39, pp. 157–182.

Ferreira, F., Leite, P. and Litchfield, J. (2006). Ascensão e queda da desigualdade de renda no Brasil. *Econômica*, 8(1), pp. 147–169.

Fishlow, A. (1972). Brazilian size distribution of income. *American Economic Review*, 62(2), pp. 391–402.

Freeman, R. and Katz, L. (1995). *Differences and changes in wage inequality*. Chicago: Chicago University Press.

Goos, M. and Manning, A. (2007). Lousy and lovely jobs: The rising polarization of work in Britain. *The Review of Economics and Statistics*, 89(1), pp. 118–133.

Goos, M., Manning, A. and Salomons, A. (2009). Job polarization in Europe. *The American Economic Review*, 99(2), pp. 58–63.

Goldin, C. and Katz, L. (2008). *The race between education and technology*. Cambridge, MA: Harvard University Press.

Guimarães, N. (2009a). *Desemprego: uma construção social*. Belo Horizonte: Argumentvm.

Guimarães, N. (2009b). A sociologia dos mercados de trabalho: ontem e hoje. *Novos Estudos Cebrap*, 85, pp. 151–170.

Hoffmann, R. and Duarte, J. C. (1972). A distribuição da renda no Brasil. *Revista de Administração de Empresas*, 12(2), pp. 46–66.

Kalleberg, A. (2012). Job quality and precarious work: Clarifications, controversies and challenges. *Work and Occupations*, 39, pp. 427–448.

Kalleberg, A. (2013). *Good jobs, bad jobs: The Rise of Polarized and Precarious Employment Systems in the United States, 1970s to 2000s*. New York, Rusell Sage Foundation.

Kalleberg, A. and Sorensen, A. (1979). The sociology of labor markets. *Annual Review of Sociology*, 5, pp. 351–379.

Kowarick, L. (1975). *Capitalismo e Marginalidade na América Latina*. Rio de Janeiro: Paz e Terra

Langoni, C. (2005 [1973]). *Distribuição de renda e desenvolvimento econômico no Brasil*. Rio de Janeiro: FGV.
Lemieux, Thomas. (2006). Increasing residual wage inequality: Composition effects, noisy data, or rising demand for skill? *American Economic Review*, 96, pp. 461–498.
Machado da Silva, L. (1991). A (des)organização do trabalho no Brasil urbano. *São Paulo em Perspectiva*, IV(3/4), pp. 2–5.
Machado da Silva, L. (1971). *Mercados metropolitanos de trabalho manual e marginalidade*. PPGAS do Museu Nacional. UFRJ, Rio de Janeiro: MA dissertation.
Marx, I. (2007). *A new social question?* Amsterdam: Amsterdam University Press.
Mimieux, T. (2007). *The changing nature of wage inequality*. National Bureau of Economic Research, Working Paper 13523. Available at: http://www.nber.org/papers/w13523
Mouw, T. and Kalleberg, A. (2010). Occupations and the structure of wage inequality in the United States, 1980s to 2000s. *American Sociological Review*, 75(4), pp. 402–431.
Neri, M. (2011). *A nova classe média*. São Paulo: Editora Saraiva.
Nun, J. L. (2003). *Marginalidad y exclusion social*. Buenos Aires: Fondo de Cultura Económica.
Oesch, D. and Menes, R. (2012). Upgrading or polarization? Occupational change in Britain, Germany, Spain and Switzerland, 1990–2008. *Socio-Economic Review*, 9, pp. 503–532.
Oliveira, F. (2003). *Crítica à razão dualista; o ornitorrinco*. São Paulo: Boitempo.
Rodrigues, I. (2009). Estratégia operária e neocapitalismo. *Tempo Social*, 21, pp. 51–64.
Santos, W. G. (1979). *Cidadania e justiça*. Rio de Janeiro: Editora Campus.
Singer, P. (1973). *Economia política da urbanização*. São Paulo: Braziliense.
Soares, S. (2006). Brasil de 1976 a 2004 com Ênfase no Período Entre 2001 e 2004. *IPEA—Textos para discussão 1166*. Avaliable at: http://www.ipea.gov.br/portal/images/stories/PDFs/TDs/td_1166.pdf.
Soares, S. and Lima, A. (2002). A mensuração da educação nas Pnads da década de 1990. *IPEA—Texto para Discussão*, 928. Brasilia. Avaliabel at: http://reposito rio.ipea.gov.br/bitstream/11058/2826/1/TD_928.pdf.
Tolipan, R. and Tinelli. A. C. (1975). *A controvérsia sobre a distribuição de renda e desenvolvimento*. Rio de Janeiro: Zahar.
Western, B. and Bloome, D. (2009). Variance function regressions for studying inequality. *Sociological Methodology*, 39, pp. 293–326.
Wright, E. and Dwyer, R. (2003). The patterns of job expansions in the United States: A comparison of the 1960s and 1990s. *Socio-Economic Review*, 1, pp. 289–325.

Part II
Demographic Dynamics and Segregation

4 Population Dynamics and Migration 1991–2010

José Marcos Pinto da Cunha

The aim of this chapter is to describe some of the key aspects of the demographic dynamic of the SPMR from two different perspectives. The first seeks to relativize the idea that a process of metropolitan deconcentration is actually happening in Brazil—an idea that, through the repeated and very often superficial use of data, has become crystallized among some researchers and has led to claims in support of hypotheses such as "interiorization" and "de-metropolitanization" (Santos 2005). The second, linked to the first, looks to show that even with an increasingly slower rate of demographic growth, Brazilian metropolitan regions, especially the SPMR, continue to show a huge potential for territorial and intra-regional demographic expansion.

The question of deconcentration from metropolitan areas is a theme that has galvanized many scholars concerned with its conditioning factors and its consequences for the urban network of European countries (Champion 1998), Latin American nations (Lattes 1998, Rodriguez & Busso 2009) and the United States (Frey 2006, Gottdiener 1988). Indeed, while in the 1970s, especially, many countries showed clear signs that their major cities were declining in importance, principally in demographic terms,[1] some of these analyses, in particular the more recent (Champion 1998, Frey 2006), indicate that this deconcentration was relative and does not seem to have been sustained in the long term.

As Champion (1998) points out in relation to "developed countries," by the 1980s the expectation of deepening counter-urbanization had not materialized on a large scale. On the contrary, a degree of reversal toward reconcentration was observable. For the author, this indicated the collapse of a pattern and consequently greater heterogeneity compared to previous decades.

From the demographic viewpoint, the theses of deconcentration or even continuity have not proved sustainable, even in the case of Latin America, where the process began much later. According to Lattes (1998), by the 1990s the process was slowing down or even reversing in various countries, as in the cases of Mexico, Colombia, Uruguay and Chile in relation to the metropolitan regions containing their capitals.

In addition, the data show that, in economic terms, concentration is still evident in large urban agglomerations around the world. As Krätke (2007) argues, "The urban agglomerations and metropolitan regions function as the 'motors' of economic development in the EU and at the same time as the prime nodes of Europe's integration in the global economy" (2007, p. 1).

According to some of the authors cited here (Champion 1998, Krätke 2007), one of the main elements picked out to explain the deacceleration (or discontinuation) of deconcentration away from large cities are the transformations in production observed particularly in the 1990s. The emergence of the so-called information economy, the result of globalization and productive restructuring (Harvey 1991), had significant implications for the organization of the economy and the labor market (Castells 2009). Contrary to what might have been predicted, these processes not only reconfigured but also reinforced the role of cities, in particular the largest (Sassen 2006). It is also worth remembering that in the case of Latin American countries, the centralization of political and administrative structures in the major cities is a characteristic that typically favors the concentration of productive activities, in particular those linked to services (Lattes 1998).

In the case of the SPMR, the process of deconcentration from its principal city (the municipality of São Paulo) involved a movement toward the other cities of the metropolitan context or even to other parts of the surrounding region. However, this deconcentration, its dynamic, speed and above all sustainability were no different to those observed in various other countries, which means that this hypothesis should be rejected or at least relativized.

In this chapter, discussion of this argument is preceded by a brief overview of the demographic behavior of Brazil's metropolitan regions as a whole, not only to emphasize this behavior but also to provide a backdrop on which the patterns found in the SPMR can be more clearly discerned.

There is no doubt that one of the main features of the process of Brazilian urbanization, which gained impetus particularly in the 1970s, was the emergence of large urban agglomerations, particularly those of a metropolitan kind (Brito 2009, Farias 1991, Santos 2005). What could be called a "metropolitan phenomenon" thus coincides with the steady decline not only of the population living in rural areas but also those inhabiting the small cities of the country's interior, a process in which migration was the major factor.

However, it is interesting to note that although Brazilian urbanization undoubtedly led to demographic concentration (especially in coastal areas), the country's most singular characteristic, perhaps, was not exactly the speed with which the nation became urbanized but the fact that this process unfolded without recording a high degree of primacy between the cities and, above all, between the large urban agglomerations. When compared to other countries like Argentina, Chile and Uruguay, for example, Brazil may even be said to present a relatively balanced regional distribution of its population, at least in terms of demographic concentration in one or a few regions.

Hence, the term "concentrated deconcentration" (Rodriguez & Busso 2009)—which has been used to capture the trends toward demographic and economic expansion beyond metropolitan borders but within spatially limited radii—could, perhaps, also be used to understand the formation of the national urban network since much of its expansion occurs in a context of urban agglomerations—metropolitan or not. Martine (1987) at the end of the 1980s argued that very little remained of the demographic spatial redistribution trends that had led to their interiorization, a behavior that not only did not reverse but actually intensified. In fact, even the much vaunted "growth of medium-sized cities" succumbed to a more detailed analysis when contextualized in terms of where these cities are located in Brazil.

The argument explored here through a demographic analysis draws support from the ideas developed by Davidovich (2004):

> It seems sufficient to observe that since the end of the 1970s, the decline in industrial productivity had been affecting important centers of the United States and Europe, the so-called 'Fordist accumulation crisis'. Hence, pressures have increased for financial and economic changes and for productive restructuring. These changes have converged on the recentralization of wealth, which, according to Veltz (1996), lies at the base of the return of the metropolis. Urban concentration is thus reassuming the strategic role that it had played in attracting and fixing assets, i.e. the valorization of capital; the metropolis constituted through the support above all of the forces of agglomeration and economic growth ...
>
> It also needs to be observed that this perspective of the return of the metropolis was not confined to the more developed countries. On the urban policy agenda of the World Bank during the 1990s for countries like Brazil, the metropolis was focused on as a motor of economic growth, no longer stigmatized as the expression of urban pathology.
>
> (Davidovich 2004, pp. 200–201)

It should be recognized, however, that the "metropolitan question" is important not only because of the fact that the metropolitan regions have reestablished (or maybe maintained?) their hegemony in the national context. In fact, even if the phenomenon of deconcentration is an indisputable reality, we would still need to evaluate the implications of decades of concentration. In fact, there is even today a huge potential for the redistribution of the population within metropolitan regions. This happens due to several interconnected reasons. First, external migration is still present and, although it is low at the moment, represents a significant portion of the growth in Brazil's urban peripheries. Additionally, intrametropolitan migration remains sizeable, and the vegetative growth of these areas can make a difference to the spatial redistribution of the population.

Hence, although the figures showing that our metropolitan regions, especially the SPMR, are growing at a slower rate are incontestable, the same cannot be said when we turn to the municipalities and, especially, the region's neighborhoods and districts, as Marques and Requena clearly show in Chapter 5 of this book.

As will be shown, even if the "core" municipalities showed very little or even negative growth, the pace of expansion of some peripheral municipalities remains impressive. Each decade they are located farther and farther from what was once considered the metropolitan center. Obviously the original idea of center and periphery no longer fits what is observed in these regions. Perhaps the notion of "polynucleated" metropolitan regions (Gottdiener 1988) is more appropriate, particularly in the SPMR, for this new spatial formation. However, the fact is that increasingly distant cities stand out due to their significant demographic rises in a region that is growing little. These municipalities, despite not being home just to the popular classes any longer, still comprises areas that receive a large proportion of migrants both from outside (Torres 2005) and from the region itself.

In this sense, knowing the impact of migration on these municipalities, as well as their nature in terms of the migrants' areas of origin, is of great importance for the understanding of the causes and the consequences of the demographic dynamic of Brazil's metropolitan regions.

In this chapter, therefore, the aim is to show that, despite the decline in population growth—which forms the rule in all regions of Brazil—and the fall in their net migratory gains, the metropolitan regions, particularly SPMR, remain the leading figures in the country's demographic and social dynamic as well as the areas where much of the Brazilian population lives and certainly where some of the biggest challenges are to be found in terms of finding solutions for their inhabitants' basic needs. Last, it is in the metropolitan region that spatial mobility, whether everyday or "residential," has become more intense, deserving special attention due to both its demographic and socioeconomic impact.

Metropolitan Brazil: The Main Trends and Regional Diversity

"Metropolitan Brazil" is not homogenous and much less regionally localized. It is diverse and dispersed across the national territory, and although certain patterns recur, especially in terms of the trends in territorial and demographic expansion, it shows spatial-temporal and regional divergences in terms of formation and specificities in terms of economic and political conditioning factors. According to Santos (2005, p. 58), "In the urban system, the categories considered homologous, the levels takes as parallels, are increasingly differentiated from each other. . . . Today each city is different from the other, irrespective of size, since there are differences between the metropolises too."

Although it can be identified as one of the main outcomes of the intense process of Brazilian urbanization, especially during the country's period of industrialization, this "metropolitan Brazil" is less significant in demographic terms. For example, while the nine federal metropolitan regions were responsible for more than 40 percent of national GDP in 2010,[2] in population terms they represented a little more than 26 percent. Even in the case of the SPMR, according to Santos (2005, p. 59) the "polar area of Brazil" or the "omnipresent metropolis in Brazilian territory," its 20 million inhabitants account for just 10.2 percent of the Brazilian population.

Whatever the case, it is important to mention that what in the view of various authors (Baeninger 2011, Santos 2005, Souza 2004) was the period of highest metropolitan deconcentration in the country (post-1980), the relative participation of the metropolitan regions maintained itself with little modification. In fact, the proportion of the Brazilian population in these areas changed from 29.8 percent in 1980 to 31.9 percent in 2010. In the case of the SPMR, this proportion was reduced from 10.4 to 10.3 percent. Indeed, in some cases like the Federal District[3] and Belo Horizonte, there was even a slight increase.

It is this information that provides the grounds for arguing that it would be too hasty to conclude that a process of metropolitan deconcentration, or even de-metropolitanization, has taken place in Brazil. As the authors cited earlier recognize, what has been observed is a degree of deconcentration, although arguably even this conception is somewhat wide of the mark.

Cities with millions of inhabitants, or agglomerations and conurbations with high population numbers, have increased significantly in Brazil since the 1970s (Santos 2005), "absorbing" an important proportion of the supposed deconcentration. In fact, the same can be said concerning the equally widely advertised growth in middle-sized cities since many of the latter are located in these agglomerations. The data presented by Baeninger (2011) reinforce this claim, demonstrating that, between 1991 and 2000, cities with between 100,000 and 500,000 inhabitants increased their share of the Brazilian population in both metropolitan and nonmetropolitan regions, although in the latter case the increase was larger.[4] In other words, if this reading of the data is taken to be correct, it would be somewhat inappropriate to talk about a process of interiorization or even de-metropolitanization: Instead we see an amplification of metropolitan-type urban agglomerations or even a dispersal of metropolitanization.

In this particular case, Reis Filho (2006) argues for the emergence of what he calls dispersed urbanization, which to some extent interferes in the organization of the every day, acquiring a regional dimension.

> The picture taking shape involves the reorganization of everyday life. The life of a significant portion of the population is becoming organized at a regional scale. Cities are ceasing to be the centers of everyday life and transforming instead into poles of a system articulated on a wider regional scale in which everyday life unfolds. For a narrower percentage

of the population, this everyday life also develops at an inter-regional level, as in the cases of some inhabitants from the Metropolitan Regions of São Paulo and Campinas, the Baixada Santista and the Vale do Paraíba, who commute daily between two of them.

(Reis Filho 2006, p. 91)

In the case of São Paulo, the recent discussion surrounding the "São Paulo Macrometropolis," proposed by Emplasa and predicted by Souza (1978, cited in Santos 2005) at the end of the 1970s, leaves little doubt about something that until very recently many authors rejected—namely, the complementarity between the SPMR and the urban agglomerations (three of them: Campinas, Baixada Santista and Vale do Paraíba, today officially metropolitan regions) that surround it (Emplasa 2011 and 2012). This complementarity is corroborated not only by economic and infrastructural relations but also by the social relations existing between these areas represented, for example, by commuter mobility (Cunha et al. 2013).

Hence, we can agree with Rodriguez and Busso (2009, p. 124), who referring to the situation of the metropolitan regions of São Paulo and Rio de Janeiro, suggest:

> What may be happening is that in both cities most emigrants are moving to nearby localities, suggesting that the 'decline in attraction' is somewhat fictional and that, in fact, what is unfolding is an expansion of their zone of influence or the constitution of an extended metropolitan area.

As well as demystifying the idea of metropolitan deconcentration, the aim here then is to show that in Brazil—even taking into account that only a third of the population was living in metropolitan urban agglomerations at the start of the 2010s[5]—these areas play key roles in the national demographic dynamic and in migration patterns in particular. Although it is indeed true that migration to these areas has declined, it is also undeniable that with the "closure" of the agricultural frontier and thus the dwindling of possibilities for interiorizing the Brazilian population, the metropolitan phenomenon—or, more generally, the large urban agglomerations—will remain the central issue to be considered when examining the spatial redistribution of the national population.

As we shall see later on, one example of this is the fact that the data from the 2010 census suggest that after a significant fall in net migration to these areas—the result not only of the reduction of interstate migration but also of the intensification of return migration—these areas, in particular the SPMR, show some degree of recuperation that, not coincidentally, is occurring in parallel with the economic recuperation of these areas after a long downturn in their respective labor markets.

As has already been pointed out by various other studies, like the Brazilian population as a whole, metropolitan Brazil has also seen a decline in demographic growth, undoubtedly sharper since in these cases migration (and not just the birth rate) has a decisive impact.

However, the expansion of the population residing in these areas was differentiated both regionally and temporarily. As can be seen in Table 4.1, while the metropolitan regions in the Southeast (São Paulo and Rio de Janeiro) were already growing at rates close to or below the national average in the 1980s, others like the Federal District and Salvador showed intense demographic growth almost twice as high as the rate recorded for Brazil as a whole. In the 2000s, it was perceived that many metropolitan regions, like Curitiba, Salvador, the Federal District, Fortaleza and Belém, were still growing more quickly than the overall Brazilian population, showing that the metropolitan phenomenon was still strong.

As well as the exaggerated perception that a demographic deconcentration is happening in the country,[6] perhaps what has most hampered recognition of the enormous contribution of the metropolitan regions to Brazil's demographic dynamic is the failure to consider the huge redistributive potential existing in these cities. Hence, as well as the importance of metropolitanization—or, to paraphrase Santos (2005), "macrourbanization"—due to their concentration not only of advantages, such as the increased availability of modern activities, but also disadvantages, like the effects of the crisis and above all poverty (Santos 2005, p. 87), we should also take into account that the power of spatial demographic transformation present in these areas is still very high.

We can also note in Table 4.1 that despite the fact that the central municipalities in metropolitan areas grew more slowly, most of the region called the "periphery"[7] still today shows an intense pace of demographic growth, which, as will be seen in the case of the SPMR, is to a significant extent explained by transferences within the population.[8] It can be observed that the largest growth occurred in the 1980s and 1990s, but significant levels of population growth were still recorded in the 2000s in some regions.

Considering that natural growth in Brazil has not been higher than 1.17 percent a year,[9] it is clear that the rates recorded not only in the "periphery" but also by many central municipalities can only be explained by the impact of migration. However, we also need to recognize the differences existing not only in terms of the periods studied but also between the metropolitan regions themselves.

The impact of migration on the demographic growth of the metropolitan regions can be captured in approximate form using census data on residency five years before the census.[10] The average demographic growth[11] and net migration rates for three distinct periods (1986–1991, 1991–2000 and 2005–2011) show not only the cooling down of the impact of migration on demographic growth (bearing in mind the falls in net migration rates) but also a significant reduction in the volume of net migration. In the case of the SPMR, the net migration rate, which was already very low in the 1980s (0.18 percent per year), became negative in the 2000s (−0.02 percent per year). The same kind of result was found in Rio de Janeiro and Recife,

Table 4.1 Average annual population growth rates by areas: Brazilian Metropolitan Districts and the Federal District—1991–2010.

Metropolitan Districts and the Federal District	Percentage		
	1980/91	1991/2000	2000/2010
São Paulo	1.88	1.64	0.97
Center	1.16	0.88	0.76
Periphery	3.21	2.81	1.25
Rio de Janeiro	1.03	1.17	0.83
Center	0.67	0.74	0.76
Periphery	1.49	1.73	0.91
Belo Horizonte	2.53	3.8	1.17
Center	1.15	1.15	0.59
Periphery	4.95	6.82	1.65
Curitiba	2.95	3.21	1.53
Center	2.29	2.11	0.99
Periphery	4.28	4.97	2.24
Porto Alegre	2.58	2.04	0.79
Center	1.06	0.83	0.35
Periphery	3.85	2.83	1.05
Distrito Federal	3.03	3.52	2.33
Center	2.84	2.79	2.28
Periphery	3.59	5.42	2.45
Belém	2.92	2.79	1.59
Center	2.65	0.32	0.85
Periphery	5.36	14.14	3.24
Fortaleza	3.5	2.81	1.94
Center	2.78	2.15	1.36
Periphery	6.27	4.72	3.27
Recife	1.85	1.5	1.01
Center	0.69	1.02	0.78
Periphery	2.91	1.86	1.18
Salvador	3.19	2.14	1.69
Center	2.98	1.83	0.91
Periphery	4.31	3.59	4.5
Brazil	1.77	1.61	1.18

Source: IBGE demographic censuses 1980, 1991, 2000 and 2010.

where the rates reached in the same decade were –0.14 and –0.08 percent per year, respectively. According to the 2010 census, however, other regions still presented demographic attractiveness, such as Curitiba (1.543 percent per year), the Federal District (2.33 percent per year) and Salvador (1.69 percent per year).

We can also highlight the fact that the declining impact of migration—including in some cases a negative migratory balance—has been more pronounced in the oldest metropolitan regions, consolidated with greater economic concentration and that, therefore, were the most affected by the economic crisis. In fact, this trend is consistent with the strong decline in the intensity and volume of interstate migration, emphasized in various studies, including those by Cunha and Baeninger (2005 and 2013). In regions that flourished in the 1980s and 1990s, benefitting from the economic deconcentration, it can be noted that migration, though also affected, behaved differently. One final aspect that deserves attention concerns the apparent recovery in migration levels in the 2000s in the SPMR. This question will be examined later.

To finalize this overview of "metropolitan Brazil" in terms of migration, it is important to investigate the internal composition of migration patterns considering interstate, intrastate and intrametropolitan flows for the same selected metropolitan regions.[12]

The censitary data suggest differences between the metropolitan regions in terms of the impact of migration originating from inside and outside their respective states. For example, in the case of the more consolidated metropolitan regions, like São Paulo and Rio de Janeiro, it is clear that the reduction in their migratory balances is related to the net losses to the interior of their states, though in the case of Rio de Janeiro, the negative balance recorded over the entire period considered was also due to interstate migratory exchanges. In the case of the Curitiba metropolitan region and the Federal District, on the other hand, we can note that the net migratory gains result from favorable exchanges in the two spatial scales. Finally, although the Recife and Salvador metropolitan regions increased their populations through their exchanges with the interior of their states, these are balanced by their net losses to other states.

In other words, the heterogenic behavior of the metropolitan regions involves not only the impact that migration has on their demographic growth but also the nature of this migration, with the process of "interiorization" promulgated by some authors clearly a phenomenon occurring in the Southeast, more specifically São Paulo and Rio de Janeiro. In the other metropolitan regions, we can note that their influence as an area of demographic attraction remains high.

The São Paulo Metropolitan Region: Demographic and Territorial Expansion and Spatial Mobility of the Population

The demographic dynamic of the SPMR has already provided the topic for various studies (Antico 2003, Baeninger 2011, Bogus & Pasternak 2009, Cunha 1994b, Torres 2005, Torres & Marques 2001), which though involving distinct approaches and questions, converge in terms of showing some aspects characteristic of the region. First, the SPMR's large demographic contingent of almost 20 million inhabitants, albeit representing just a little more than 10 percent of the Brazilian population in 2010, places the region among the largest urban agglomerations in the world.

Another element that should be highlighted concerning the region is its share of the population of the state of São Paulo, which despite a slight reduction over the last decades, remains very high, surpassing 47 percent. This level of demographic concentration was not reached by chance. It results from the region's leading economic role over much of the 20th century. During the period of large industrial growth and the strong Brazilian rural exodus, it was not the state of São Paulo but its main metropolitan region that attracted thousands and thousands of people from all parts of the country, especially the Northeast. In other words, from the demographic viewpoint, the process of concentration led by the SPMR is due to a large extent to the impact of external migration over various decades and internal migration (from within the state) until at least the 1970s.

Having grown over almost 40 years at average rates higher than 5 percent per year, the SPMR's rate of expansion began to decline in the 1980s, a tendency linked not only to the reduced intensity of migration but also the fall in birth rates.

This demographic growth led to its continual territorial expansion, involving municipalities ever more distant from the capital and thus from the metropolitan nucleus. As already pointed out in the previous section, the fact that its overall area is growing at a decreasing rate does not mean that the SPMR has lost its demographic dynamism, especially when we observe what is happening within its boundaries, in particular in some municipalities.

Migration played an important role in the demographic growth of the SPMR, especially its municipalities. However, over recent decades the SPMR has experienced significant changes in terms of migration (Baeninger 2012). In fact, much of what has been said about migratory behavior in the state of São Paulo is associated with what has been observed in the SPMR. The census data indeed show that among migrants recorded in the metropolitan municipalities, the biggest reduction occurred with respect to those from other states (Cunha 2013). In all events, it can be stated that the region historically was and remains the main entry point for these immigrants.

As another study has argued (Cunha 2013), it would not be reasonable to expect that the SPMR went back to showing the same migratory performance of the past—particularly in terms of migration levels—bearing in mind that, with the fall in birth rates, the demographic pressure on traditional areas of origin has reduced substantially. The data presented here suggest that the SPMR in fact never ceased to be an area of attraction and that all the indications to the contrary revealed processes related to its importance, whether returns—caused by the crisis—or losses to the "interior of the State," which seem to be processes related to a "concentrated deconcentration" (Rodriguez & Busso 2009) to nearby areas within large urban agglomerations (like Campinas and the Baixada Santista). Furthermore, according to studies cited earlier, these processes have led to the constitution of a more complex territorial entity, the Macrometropolis.

Despite the reduction in external migration, the region possesses a considerable internal demographic dynamism, which implies an important redistributive potential among its population, which in turn, contributes to the expansion of its territory. Following data provided by Nobre and Young (2012, p. 93), for example, between 2002 and 2007 the urban areas of the SPMR increased more than 232 km^2, even in a context of the low demographic increase of the region as a whole.

This redistributive potential is revealed in the intense residential mobility found in the region. Even though the data considered here show just a portion of this mobility,[13] the levels are impressive. While during the 1986-to-1991 period around 463,000 people moved between municipalities within the SPMR, between 1995 and 2000 this amount was 586,000 and, in the five-year period from 2005 to 2010, 470,000. Although clearly less intense over course of this period, the volume of people involved suggests the impact that these movements can have on the dynamic of the metropolitan municipalities, especially smaller ones. In the 2000s, the impact of internal migration is very high in the majority of municipalities outside the "metropolitan nucleus."

Just to give to the reader an idea of the weight of the intrametropolitan migration, it is estimated that in 31 out of the 39 municipalities of the region, these flows are responsible for more than 70 percent of the net estimated migration. This importance tends to be even more pronounced in large municipalities, with more than 200,000 inhabitants.

In sum, it can be concluded that although a decline in demographic growth and migratory gains can be identified within the SPMR as a whole, when we observe the demographic dynamic of its municipalities, a strong redistributive trend within the region clearly emerges, represented by intense intrametropolitan migration. As shown, this reached impressive figures of around 50,000 people per year moving to more peripheral regions. However, since previous decades, migratory movements of the upper and middle income population were also observable, explaining the growth of municipalities with high numbers of closed condominiums, as in the case of Santana de Parnaíba.

Figure 4.1 allows us to visualize the main internal redistributive trends within the SPMR, showing migratory flows involving more than 4,500 people. As can be noted, similarly to the behavior seen in the 1980s (Cunha 1994a, 1994b), the municipality of São Paulo remains the largest "supplier" of migrants to increasingly distant areas, the same occurring, obviously at a much lower magnitude, with the municipalities of Osasco, the ABC[14] and Guarulhos, the size, strength and diversity of latter effectively making them regional sub-poles.

In this internal redistributive process, the specificities in the profiles of migrants reveal the existence of a sociospatial diversification of these movements. Based on the data on the educational level of the intrametropolitan

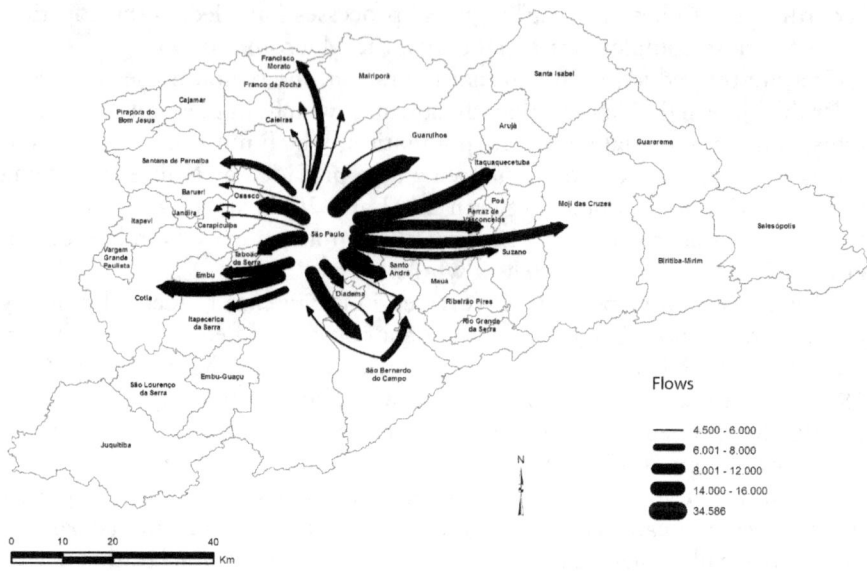

Figure 4.1 Intrametropolitan migratory flows over 4,500 people, SPMR—2005/2010.
Source: IBGE demographic censuses 2000 and 2010 (elaborated by Alberto Jakob, Nepo/Unicamp).

migrants, we can see the clear consolidation of a trend merely glimpsed a few decades ago (Cunha 1994b Matos 1994), namely that the "path to the periphery" is not predominantly a phenomenon observed among the low-income population. Examining Table 4.2, which presents data on the educational level of migrants for groups of municipalities in the SPMR,[15] it becomes very apparent that residential mobility has also increased in importance among people from higher socioeconomic strata.

The data presented here show, on one hand, that the profile of migrants heading to the "pole" municipalities (São Paulo), "sub-poles" and "elite peripheries" clearly have higher levels of education, presenting a percentage of more than 30 percent with completed higher education (first and third columns in the table); on the other hand, this figure is much lower for "traditional peripheries," especially the most distant (9.5 percent). It is worth noting that in the SPMR migrants with this level of schooling represent less than 23 percent of the total.

The same table shows too that these municipalities also receive the highest proportion of migrants with higher levels of education, the exception being the case of the "nearby traditional periphery," which receives more than 21 percent of these migrants.[16]

Even recognizing, therefore, that more than 45 percent of the intrametropolitan migrants are still composed of migrants with non-completed

Table 4.2 Intrametropolitan migrants by educational level and share of migrants and groups of municipalities.(*)

Destination groups of municipalities	Educational Level			
	No schooling and non-completed primary education		Higher education	
	Percentage of migrants	Percentage of migrants from total migration in the region	Percentage of migrants	Percentage of migrants from total migration in the region
Pole (São Paulo)	14.4	5.0	42.0	18.9
Sub-Pole	23.7	24.7	30.1	40.4
Elite Periphery	28.1	9.8	30.0	13.4
Nearby Traditional Periphery	32.5	43.0	12.9	21.9
Distant Traditional Periphery	39.9	17.6	9.5	5.4
Total	28.6	100.0	22.2	100.0

Source: IBGE demographic census 2010 (special tabulations—Nepo/Unicamp).

(*) see Note 15

secondary education[17] and thus involving an even more significant volume of people belonging to lower social groups, the differences between these flows do not just reflect the effects of the deconcentration of economic activity within the region (as in the case of the sub-poles) but also the consolidation of new kinds of settlements, particularly those that stimulate the high-income population to seek out new housing alternatives in the peripheries.

Final Remarks

All the indicators for the SPMR are impressive: In economic terms it accounted in 2010 for almost 56 percent of the state GDP and more than 18 percent of national GDP; in demographic terms, this picture is repeated since around 46 percent of São Paulo's inhabitants lived in the region in the same year. Even considering, then, that this area comprises part of a much more complex system of urban agglomerations within Brazil, which results, as emphasized earlier, in its low primacy within the country's urban system, there is no denying the "omnipresence" (Santos 2005) of the SPMR in the country.

It is very true that over the decades, the SPMR has seen a substantial reduction in its demographic growth, remaining below that observed in other metropolitan regions in the country, particularly those of the Northeast. It is also true that this shrinking in demographic dynamism was linked to some important changes in the national migratory process that historically gravitated around the region. Likewise, it can be said that, in economic terms, the SPMR also experienced a certain decline in importance.

Nonetheless, what this chapter has aimed to show is that despite these transformations, there are no motives for downplaying the importance that the SPMR still holds today, whatever dimension we look at. From a demographic viewpoint, the observed trends toward a (small) reduction in the relative weight of the SPMR in terms of the state and national populations and in its migratory gains are not sufficiently strong to support hypotheses of deconcentration or even a de-metropolitanization.

Even in the case of migration, which has undoubtedly fallen in volume and intensity, there is no denying that the importance of the SPMR remains imprinted in the figures revealed by the censuses: While in the 1980s the annual flow of migrants to the region was estimated at around 93,000 people, over the last decade this figure, despite declining, still amounted to around 60,000 people per year. In other words, the negative migratory balances presented by the area over recent decades seem insufficient to disregard the SPMR as the main entry point to the state of São Paulo. Hence this study argues that the net migratory losses recorded by the region are much more closely linked to an extension of the process of metropolitanization (or a concentrated deconcentration process) than a deconcentration in the strict sense of the term.

Another reason why the importance of the SPMR's demographic dynamic cannot be assessed solely through its global growth is related to its huge redistributive potential, still observed today. As shown, the intensity of intrametropolitan migration, which reached figures of more than 47,000 people per year in the 2000s, contributes substantially to the demographic dynamism of the municipalities, especially those further out from the metropolitan center, which as Torres (2005) demonstrated, have also been the destination for much of the migration from outside. It is indeed striking to note that the internal migratory dynamic recorded in the region in the 1970s (Cunha 1994a, 1994b), even with all the changes occurring in the 2000s—productive restructuring, the shift to the service economy, globalization and so on—can still be observed, with just one difference: The municipalities involved are increasingly distant from the main center. Obviously, as this study has shown, it is very clear that new forms of urban settlement have emerged in this process, the biggest novelty perhaps being the consolidation of the movement of the high-income population to the peripheries.

Without any doubt, the SPMR remains a place of opportunity, but unfortunately it has also never ceased to be an area with immense social problems and challenges. The "metropolitan citizen" still lacks progress in terms of public policies (housing and access to land, mobility, health care and so on) to combat or mitigate the effects that the redistribution of the population in space has on people's everyday lives.

Notes

1. Terms like "population turnaround" (Gottdiener 1988), "nonmetropolitan population turnaround" (Fuguitt 1985) and "counter-urbanization" (Champion 1998) were used to denominate this phenomenon.
2. Examining the division between the metropolitan centers and peripheries in terms of wealth generation, we can observe something interesting: While the former account for 26 percent of national GDP, the peripheries represent just 14.8 percent. Turning to the behavior of each of the metropolitan regions reveals even more pronounced differences: While the center of the SPMR was responsible for 18.67 percent of the national GDP in 2010 and the Rio de Janeiro MR for 7.3 percent, the peripheries of these regions represented no higher than 4 percent.
3. In fact the official name for the metropolitan region centralized by the Federal District is the "Integrated Development Region" (RIDE), reflecting the fact that it includes municipalities from three federal units (the Federal District itself and the states of Goiás and Minas Gerais). However the simplified notation will be used in this text.
4. According to data presented by Baeninger (2011), municipalities of this size in the "non-metropolitan" context increased from 10.2 to 17.3 percent and in the metropolitan context from 7.4 to 8.7 percent. In addition, it should be recognized that the metropolitan regions studied by the author (the nine federal metropolitan regions plus Campinas and Federal District) omit various other important agglomerations, such as Manaus, Florianópolis, Baixada Santista and Goiânia, just to mention some of them.
5. The low primacy alluded to in the introduction to this text is reflected when we compare Brazil with some other South American countries. In Argentina in 2010, for example, more than 55 percent of the population was living in the province of Buenos Aires or the country's federal capital; in Chile in 2002 around 40 percent of the inhabitants lived in the metropolitan region of Santiago; and in Uruguay in 2006 more than 40 percent of the population resided in the province containing the capital (Montevideo). Meanwhile in Mexico, in 2010, the behavior was similar to Brazil since its largest metropolitan region contains just 21.4 percent of the national population.
6. Another way used to explain this deconcentration is to observe the reduction in the relative weight of the "metropolitan" component in the urban population; however, this interpretation of the data may be considered somewhat fallacious. To give an example, the total population of the nine federal metropolitan regions and the Federal District increased in relative terms between 1980s and 2010 by two percentage points compared with the total national population (from 29 to 31 percent). However, when we consider the urban population alone, the situation inverts since the "metropolitan part" of the country loses around six percentage points (from 42 to 36 percent). However, this increase is unsurprising given that even in the areas most dependent on farming activities, such as the North and Center-West of the country, and more specifically the small Brazilian municipalities, the population has become urbanized very rapidly. This in turn has inevitably provoked the "deconcentration" suggested by the data. What we are faced with, therefore, is a "reclassification" effect rather than a demographic reality.
7. Without ignoring the existing debate on the significance and suitability of the "center/periphery" dichotomy today, the contrast is used in this text merely from a spatial perspective, looking to distinguish the metropolitan city core (center) from the rest (periphery).

8. It is important to emphasize that the impact of intrametropolitan migration is not the same for all regions. Studies elaborated for the Campinas metropolitan region, for example, show a much smaller impact of this type of migration on the growth of peripheral municipalities (Cunha 2011, Dota 2015).
9. Taking into account that the impact of international migration on Brazil's demographic growth in Brazil is very low, its rate of population increase (1.17 percent per year.) can be taken as a proxy for national natural growth, even though in states like São Paulo this rate is probably lower due to lower birth rates.
10. The information on residency five years earlier, available in the 1991, 2000 and 2010 censuses, allows us to estimate immigration and emigration volumes for the five-year period immediately prior to the census. However these estimates must be approached with some caution. First, they do not include the migration of children under the age of five (not yet born at the reference time of the information), and second, there is a declaration problems on the part of the interviewees. For more details on how to use the census information, see, for example, Rigotti (2011) or Cunha (2012).
11. It should be noticed that demographic growth rates refer to the inter-census period and the net migration rates in the five-year period immediately prior to the census. Hence, direct comparisons between the demographic growth and the net migration rates would consider that this latter rate is representative of the entire inter-census period, which may not be fully accurate.
12. Based on the data on residence five years previous to the census, we can classify as "interstate" immigrants those individuals whose previous declared municipality was outside the state of the municipal region in question. Intrastate immigrants are those who came from another municipality within the state concerned, with the exception of metropolitan municipalities. In these cases, the immigrants are classified as intrametropolitan.
13. The data used in this study presents a number of limitations in terms of ascertaining residential mobility. First, it refers only to movements between municipalities, which obviously excludes movements within municipalities, which in the case of some cities may be intense. Second the data refer only to the five-year period immediately prior to the census, thus omitting everything that occurred in the other five years, including the five-year period covered by the census. This information fails to identify the total migration that occurred within the SPMR since, by its very nature, it ignores the internal movements of those who had been living outside the region five years earlier. Finally the data fails to capture the migration of children under five, not born at the time of reference established in the census question.
14. The ABC region is composed of three highly industrialized municipalities, making them among the richest in the SPMR: Santo André, São Bernardo and São Caetano.
15. Here a simplified classification is used based on the educational profile of household heads and on the added value generated by the municipalities. The terms "poles" and "sub-poles" refer to the municipalities with large economic and demographic weight. The peripheries, meanwhile, have been classified as "elite" when a high percentage of people with high levels of education was observed, and "traditional" when the population is predominantly composed of people with low levels of schooling. The groups correspond to the following municipalities: pole: São Paulo; sub-pole: São Caetano do Sul, São Bernardo do Campo, Santo André, Guarulhos and Osasco; elite peripheries: Mogi das Cruzes, Santana do Parnaíba, Cotia; nearby traditional periphery: Poá, Ribeirão Pires, Barueri, Arujá, Caieiras, Suzano, Rio Grande da Serra, Mairiporã, Taboão da Serra, Mauá, Diadema, Carapicuíba, Ferraz de Vasconcelos, Franco da Rocha, Embu, Santa Izabel and Itaquaquecetuba; distant

traditional periphery: Jandira, Vargem Grande Paulista, São Lourenço da Serra, Salesópolis, Cajamar, Guararema, Embu-Guaçu, Itapecerica da Serra, Juquitiba, Itapevi, Pirapora do Bom Jesus, Biritiba-Mirim and Francisco Morato. Obviously this classification takes into account the "average characteristics" of the municipalities, ignoring the considerable internal heterogeneities found within them.
16. This result is explained by the heterogeneity existing in some of the region's municipalities, as in the cases of Barueri and Arujá, for example, whose areas contain urban settlements composed of high-income people, generally residing in closed condominiums.
17. The percentages of migrants for all levels of schooling were not presented to simplify the analyzed information. For the SPMR these figures are: "without schooling and non-completed primary education" = 28.6 percent; "completed primary and non-completed secondary" = 16.5 percent; "completed secondary and non-completed higher" = 32.8 percent; "completed higher" = 22.2 percent.

Bibliography

Antico, C. (2003). *Onde morar e onde trabalhar: espaço e deslocamentos pendulares na Região Metropolitana de São Paulo*. PhD thesis—Institute of Philosophy and Human Sciences, Campinas State University, Campinas.

Baeninger, R. (2012). *Fases e faces da migração em São Paulo*. Campinas: Nepo/Unicamp.

Baeninger, R. (2011). Nova Configuração Urbana no Brasil: desaceleração Metropolitana e Redistribuição da População. In: Randolph, R. and Candice, B. (eds.) *Expansão Metropolitana e Transformação das Interfaces entre Cidade, Campo e Região na América Latina*. Rio de Janeiro: Editora Max Limonad, pp. 41–68.

Bogus, L. and Pasternak, S. (eds.) (2009). *Como anda São Paulo. Rio de Janeiro, Letra Capital, Observatório das Metrópoles* (Conjuntura Urbana, 3).

Brito, F. (2009). *As migrações internas no Brasil: um ensaio sobre os desafios teóricos recentes*. Belo Horizonte: Cedeplar/UFMG (Texto para discussão, n. 366).

Castells, M. (2009). *The rise of the network society. The information age: Economy, society, and culture*. Volume I, 2nd Edition. Oxford: Wiley-Blackwell.

Champion, A. (1998). Population distribution in developed countries: Has counterurbanization stopped? In: United Nations (ed.) *Population distribution and migration*. New York, pp. 66–83.

Cunha, J. (2011). Movilidad espacial, vulnerabilidad y segregación socioespacial: Reflexiones a partir del estudio de la Región Metropolitana de Campinas, 2007. *Notas de Población, Santiago-Chile*, (38)93, pp. 169–209.

Cunha, J. (2005). Cenários da migração no Brasil nos anos 90. *Cadernos do CRH*, 18(43), pp. 87–101.

Cunha, J. (1995). Expansão metropolitana na transição migratória: o papel dos subcentros regionais. *São Paulo em Perspectiva*, 9(3), pp. 71–79.

Cunha, J. (1994a). Processo de metropolização e migração: uma análise comparativa entre a Região Metropolitana de São Paulo e Campinas. *São Paulo em Perspectiva*, 8(4), pp. 109–116.

Cunha, J. (1994b). *Mobilidade populacional e expansão urbana: o caso da Região Metropolitana de São Paulo*. IFCH/Unicamp: PhD thesis.

Cunha, J. (1987). As correntes migratórias na Grande São Paulo. *São Paulo em Perspectiva*, 1(2), pp. 6–15.

Cunha, J. M. P. (2012). Retratos da mobilidade espacial no Brasil: Os censos demográficos como fonte de dados. *Revista Interdisciplinar de Mobilidade Humana—EMHU*, Brasília, Ano XX, n. 39, pp. 29–50.

Cunha, J. and Baeninger, R. (2013). *Internal migration in Brazil: Trends at the beginning of the 21st Century*. Busan, Korea: XXVII IUSSP International Population Conference.

Cunha, J. M. P. and Baeninger, R. (2005). Cenários da Migração no Brasil nos anos 90. *Caderno CRH*. Salvador, Vol. 18, n. 43, Jan./April. pp. 87–1.

Cunha, J., Stoco, S., Dota, E. M., Negreiros, R., Miranda, Z. A. I. A. (2013). A mobilidade pendular na Macrometrópole Paulista: diferenciação e complementariedade socioespacial. *Cadernos Metrópole*, (15)30, pp. 433–459.

Davidovich, F. (2004). A 'volta da metrópole' no Brasil: referências para a gestão territorial. In: Ribeiro, L. (ed.) *Metrópoles entre a coesão e a fragmentação, a cooperação e o conflito*. São Paulo/Rio de Janeiro: Ed. Perseu Abramo/Fase, pp. 197–229.

Dota, E. (2015). *Mobilidade Residencial Intrametropolitana na RM de Campinas: uma abordagem a partir da distribuição espacial dos migrantes*. IFCH/Unicamp: PhD thesis.

Emplasa. (2012). *Macrometrópole paulista*. São Paulo: Empresa Metropolitana de Planejamento da Grande São Paulo. Available at: http://www.emplasa.sp.gov.br/emplasa/, Consulted 17 January 2013.

Emplasa. (2011). *Rede urbana e regionalização do estado de São Paulo*. São Paulo: Empresa Metropolitana de Planejamento da Grande São Paulo.

Faria, V. (1991). Cinqüenta anos de urbanização no Brasil: tendências e perspectivas. *Novos Estudos Cebrap*, 29, pp. 98–119.

Frey, W. (2006). Metropolitan America in the new century. *Urban Land*, 65(6), pp. 99–107.

Frey, W. (1988). Migration and metropolitan decline in developed countries: A comparative study. *Population and Development Review*, 14(4), pp. 595–628.

Fuguitt, G. (1985). The nonmetropolitan population turnaround. *Annual Review of Social*, 11, pp. 259–280.

Gottdiener, M. (1988). *The social production of urban space*. Austin, TX: University of Texas Press.

Harvey, D. (1991). *The condition of postmodernity: An enquiry into the origins of cultural change*. Oxford: Wiley-Blackwell.

Krätke, S. (2007). Metropolisation of the European economic territory as a consequence of increasing specialisation of urban agglomerations in the knowledge economy. *European Planning Studies*, 15(1), pp. 1–27.

Lattes, A. (1998). Population distribution in Latin America: Is there a trend towards population deconcentration? In: United Nations (ed.) *Population Distribution and Migration*. New York: United Nation Press, pp. 117–136.

Martine, G. (1987). Migração e metropolização. *São Paulo em Perspectiva*, 1(2), pp. 28–31.

Matos, R. (1994). *A desconcentração populacional em Minas Gerais e as mudanças na Região-Core*. Encontro Nacional De Estudos Populacionais, 9, Caxambu. Anais: Belo Horizonte: ABEP.

Nobre, C. and Young, A. (eds.) (2012). *Vulnerabilidades das megacidades brasileiras às mudanças climáticas: Região Metropolitana de São Paulo—relatório final*. São José dos Campos: Inpe/Unicamp.

Pasternak, S. (2009). Aspectos demográficos da Região Metropolitana de São Paulo. In: Bógus, L. and Pasternak, S. (eds.) *Como anda São Paulo*. Rio de Janeiro: Letra Capital, Observatório das Metrópoles (Conjuntura urbana; 3), pp. 11–38.

Reis Filho, N. (2006). *Notas sobre urbanização dispersa e novas formas de tecido urbano*. São Paulo: Via das Artes.

Rigotti, J. (2011). Dados censitários e técnicas de análise das migrações no Brasil: avanços e lacunas. In: Cunha (ed.) *Mobilidade espacial da população: desafios teóricos e metodológicos para o seu estudo*. Campinas: Núcleo de Estudos de População Unicamp, pp. 141–156.

Rodriguez, J. and Busso, G. (2009). *Migración interna y desarrollo en América Latina entre 1980 y 2005: un estudio comparativo con perspectiva regional basado en siete países*. Santiago do Chile: Cepal.

Santos, M. (2005). *A urbanização brasileira*. São Paulo: Hucitec.

Sassen, S. (2006). *Cities in a world economy*. Thousand Oaks, CA: Pine Forge Press.

Souza, M. (2004). Alguns aspectos da dinâmica recente da urbanização brasileira. In: Fernandes, E. and Valença, M. (eds.) *Brasil urbano*. Rio de Janeiro: MaijaoEditora, pp. 57–74.

Torres, H. (2005). Fronteira paulistana. In: Marques, E. and Torres, H. (eds.) *São Paulo, segregação, pobreza e desigualdades sociais*. São Paulo: Editora Senac, pp. 101–119.

Torres, H. and Marques, E. (2001). Reflexões sobre a hiperferiferia: novas e velhas faces da pobreza no entorno metropolitano. *Revista Brasileira de Estudos Urbanos e Regionais*, 4, pp. 49–70.

United Nations. (1998). *Population distribution and migration: Proceedings of the United Nations expert group meeting on population distribution and migration*. New York: United Nations.

5 Diverse Demographic Trajectories and Heterogeneity

Eduardo Cesar Leão Marques and Carolina Requena

In this chapter, we discuss intraurban demographic growth in the SPMR. The topic is of considerable academic interest given that many of the urban problems typical of Brazil's large cities, experienced primarily by their resident low-income populations, have been blamed on a pattern of urbanization that typically involves the expansion of peripheries and favelas combined with high demographic growth. The topic is also of great interest for public policies since the pressure on public policies and services caused by high rates of population growth in the 1960s and 1970s contributed to the creation of large inequalities in terms of access, especially for the poorest. This is emphatically the case of Brazil's metropolises with their trajectory of increasingly extensive urban fabrics and serious negative impacts on access to services, urban mobility and day-to-day sociability, especially among low-income groups.

The São Paulo metropolis recorded very modest demographic growth in the 2000s—around 1 percent per year, following a trend established in the region since the 1980s and the general dynamic of Brazilian metropolitan regions more recently. At least in São Paulo's case, though, these average figures concealed substantially uneven paces of intraurban growth. Studies such as those by Jannuzzi and Jannuzzi (2002) and Torres (2005) showed that since the 1980s, the low rates of average growth had contributed to hide the demographic decline of the more central regions and the continuation of very high growth rates in peripheral areas. This growth followed a clear radial and concentric pattern with a central population decline and intense growth in the more outlying belts of the metropolis (Torres 2005), reinforcing the perception of a city organized in rings (Taschner & Bógus 1998), a pattern that became even clearer when the census districts and municipalities—fairly highly aggregated units—were taken as the units of analysis or when the data were collated into larger scales of analysis. More recently, following release of the first batch of information from the 2010 census, the idea spread that the main trend for the decade would be that "the center has started growing again" (PMSP 2011). The aim of this chapter, then, is to discuss this trend, showing that the recent dynamic is much more complex than a mere resumption of growth in the central region. As we shall see, when the information is disaggregated and the processes analyzed in more detail, it becomes clear that this observation is at once true—some areas of the expanded center have indeed returned to growth—and fairly incomplete since not only did a portion of the central area continue to decline demographically in the 2000s, but areas of the peripheries also began to fall in population terms, while others continue to grow at a strong rate, albeit at a lower level than before. We believe that these findings provide additional evidence of the São Paulo metropolis's complexity, as already highlighted in works like Marques and Torres (2005), which have indicated the existence of an intense heterogeneity behind the more general patterns.

It is important to stress that these dynamics bear little or no relation to what was observed in large cities of the Global North from the postwar period to the 1970s. In the United States case, for example, the central areas of the country's large cities lost their high-income population, which relocated to suburban districts or regions on the outer ring of the metropolis. This population was replaced by low-income groups as the central regions entered into an increasing state of abandonment and urban degradation (Fischer & Styles 2006), configuring what would subsequently appear as "inner city problems" (Wilson 1987). In the case of São Paulo, a similar process occurred solely in the historic center of the metropolis, which experienced a demographic decline for decades and then slowly became populated by low-income residents. However, the population reduction over the much larger central region—referred to as the expanded center —was not accompanied by a relative increase in the presence of lower-income groups. In this case, the phenomenon was associated with a change to a construction style associated with elite occupation and the dissemination of lower-density housing solutions in the expanded center itself. As we shall see in Chapter 6, though, this extensive region has become even more exclusively occupied by sectors of the elite over the last decade.

In the next section, we discuss the general tendencies as seen through the extant literature. We then present the intraurban patterns of the demographic dynamic in the 2000s, drawing on data from the 2000 and 2010 censuses. The final section explores the main growth trends present in the observed patterns, using census information on income, age structure, migration and precarious housing as well as data on private-sector housing developments originating from another source of data.

The Demographic Dynamics in São Paulo

The SPMR registered increasingly higher growth rates in the first half of the 20th century, peaking in the 1950s, when they reached 5.9 percent per year, and the metropolis absorbed 2.1 million new residents over the decade, a figure that would still continue to grow steadily over the following decades. Table 5.1 shows the region's population and overall growth rates, indicating just the overall demographic trend, already known through works like

Table 5.1 Population and demographic growth, SPMR—1920 to 2010.

Year	Population	Growth Rate (% p.a.)
1920 (*)	579,033	–
1940	1,568,045	5.11
1950	2,688,901	5.44
1960	4,791,245	5.93
1970	8,178,241	5.56
1980	12,549,856	4.38
1991	15,369,305	1.86
2000	17,852,637	1.68
2010	19,683,975	0.98

Source: IBGE census 2010, Baeninger (2012) and http://www.ibge.gov.br/home/presidencia/noticias/notasaopaulo.shtm.

(*) Population of São Paulo municipality only

Baeninger (2012). In absolute demographic figures, peak growth was in the 1970s when the metropolis absorbed 4.4 million new inhabitants in 10 years. However, from the 1960s a slow and monotonic decline in the growth rates was already observable. This trend grew more pronounced in the 1980s when the largest relative fall in rates took place. Although the figures for the São Paulo municipality as a whole reversed over the decade (Perillo & Perdigão 1998), the trend toward peripheralization seen in the previous decade was repeated (Taschner & Bógus 2001), similar to the experience of other Brazilian metropolises (Cunha 2003). The decline in growth rates continued in the 2000s.

However, when growth rates for the interior of the metropolis are disaggregated, a change in this scenario can already be observed in the 1980s. Works like Jannuzzi and Jannuzzi (2002) and Torres (2005) showed that slowing population growth rates were accompanied over this decade by the continuation of intense growth in peripheral areas as well as an absolute decline in population numbers at the more internal regions of the metropolis. Jannuzzi and Jannuzzi (2002) showed how disaggregating growth at the level of census districts reveals an absolute population reduction in various regions of the expanded center during the 1980s. The data by district show the same dynamic continuing in the 1990s, spreading to regions in the first belt surrounding the expanded center—from the North of the Tietê River to regional centers and the West. At the same time, peripheral areas showed very high positive growth rates. Since the 1980s, therefore, the São Paulo metropolis has registered a pattern of absolute decline in its central areas, which tended to spread through a wider region in the following decade but was accompanied by the maintenance of high rates in the peripheries.

This analysis was complemented by Torres (2005), who explored the intrametropolitan dynamic in more detail. The author worked with data from 1991 and 2000, disaggregated by the census weighting areas. His findings generally reinforced the data from Jannuzzi and Jannuzzi (2002) for the central areas reported, though the work focused mainly on the peripheral areas. The growth rates observed in the more outlying regions of the metropolis proved to be much higher than anticipated by the debates on the topic, demonstrating that the outskirts continued to grow at rates typical of the 1970s. The author eloquently showed the correlation between demographic growth and average household income, nuanced by cross-referencing with the localization of each of the areas. While the consolidated city, to use Torres's expression, had medium or high income and declined in population terms, the so-called urban frontier presented very high growth and low income levels. Moreover the production of social indicators for these areas suggested that this growth was associated with the strong presence of recent low-income migrants with less access to urban infrastructure, a clear continuation of the pattern of peripheralization seen in the 1970s.

Publication of the 2010 census by the São Paulo Municipality (PMSP 2011), exploring the growth of the São Paulo municipality over the past decade, caused an impact by reporting a return to growth for the city's central region. The report analyzed the recent IBGE data at the level of the municipal districts and demonstrated demographic growth in the region known as the expanded center as well as continuing decline in some areas of the North Zone and part of the first ring around the center in addition to moderate growth in peripheral areas. These data were once again analyzed in PMSP (2012a) with a similar diagnosis.

Observation of this growth at a spatial level, however, reveals much more complexity than the depiction obtained by analyzing the census districts. The next section analyzes the same data but at a more detailed level—the weighting areas—indicating distinct scenarios of moderate growth, decline and rapid growth in various regions. Furthermore, the patterns that emerge from the study of this more disaggregated information cannot be correlated with income or recent migration as straightforwardly as in the previous decade, suggesting greater heterogeneity and differentiation of the São Paulo metropolitan fabric than imagined up to now.

The Spatial Distribution of Growth

The best available scales of comparison for the geographical data from the Brazilian censuses are the weighting areas, given the intense changes to the boundaries of the census sectors between each census.[1]

The maps in Figures 5.1 and 5.2 display the distribution of growth for each of the two periods. As Figure 5.1 shows, growth in the 1990s tended to follow a concentration distribution strongly associated with income, as

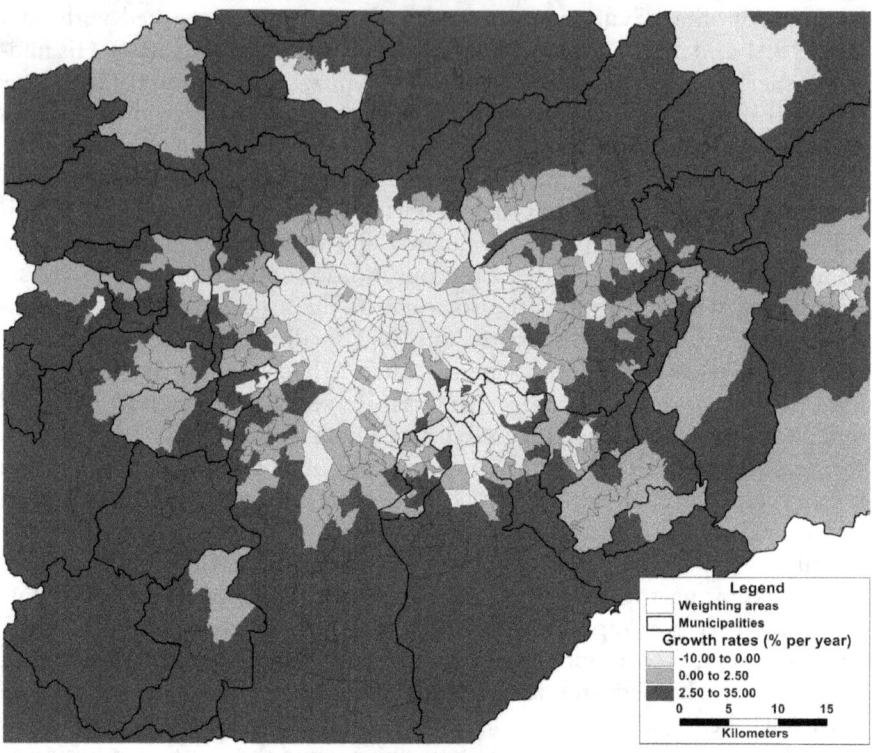

Figure 5.1 Demographic growth, weighting areas, SPMR, 1991–2000.
Source: IBGE demographic censuses and base maps produced by the CEM.

Torres (2005) adroitly explored.[2] The regions with the highest growth were those with the lowest income, located in the most peripheral regions of the metropolis, where growth rates typical until the 1970s could be found, a phenomenon the author calls the "urban frontier." At the same time, a significant proportion of the expanded center displayed negative growth, also analyzed by Torres (2005), continuing a process that began in the 1980s and was analyzed by Jannuzzi and Jannuzzi (2002).

The spatial distribution of growth changes significantly in the following decade, as we can observe in Figure 5.2.

Various trends are evident, but we can summarize them as follows:

- As well as a substantial part of the periphery showing growth cooling to lower rates, some areas presented negative growth, as in the case of areas to the south. These regions include the nucleus of one peripheral municipality to the east, which had already displayed negative growth and once again recorded a declining population. A population

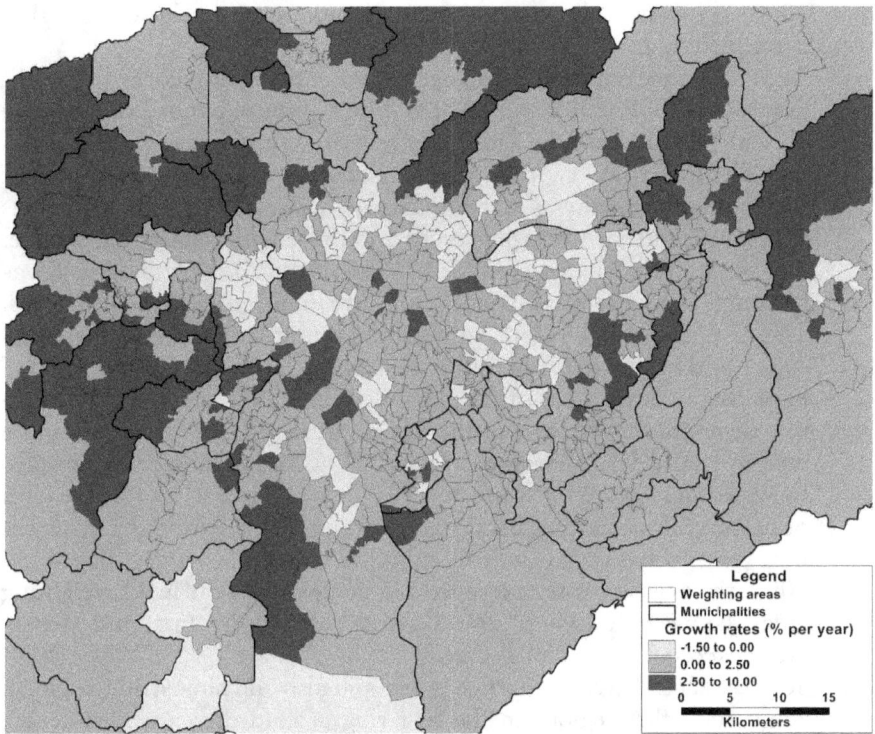

Figure 5.2 Demographic growth by weighting area, SPMR, 2000–2010.
Source: IBGE demographic censuses and base maps produced by the CEM.

reduction was similarly recorded to the west. Parts of this region had already presented this behavior in the previous decade, but now the patch with negative growth was larger, reaching municipalities within the region that had grown at very high rates during the previous decade.

- Other areas of the metropolis's peripheries continued to show high growth rates, however, albeit much lower than those seen during the previous decade. These included areas that had already grown intensely in the previous decade, such as areas in the far south of São Paulo municipality. These provide clear examples of the general downward trend of growth rates for the metropolis in the 2000s, in which just a few areas (from 633, the total number of areas) showed rates above 5 percent per year between 2000 and 2010, while 142 areas equaled or exceeded this rate in the 1990s. Additionally, the highest rates of weighting areas in the 1990s had been 32 and 20 percent per year, while in the 2000s these had fallen to 10 and 8 percent per year. Hence

the region that had been exhibiting urban frontier behavior (Torres 2005) grew much less over the last decade, even in those areas that continued to grow.
- The central area of population decline was no longer recorded, as highlighted in PMSP (2011 and 2012a). Most of the expanded center grew at relatively modest rates, generally reversing the trend toward population decline. However, it would be inaccurate to describe the center of São Paulo generically as starting to grow again since the central areas contain localities with high growth and those with continuing decline.
- For some areas of the expanded Center, a reversal of the trend was recorded with the establishment of very high growth in the 2000s. These are areas with recent, intense real estate activity in the historical center and in the first ring to the west of the latter.
- However, in other areas of the expanded center, the trend toward negative demographic growth of the last decades did not cease, as can be seen in Figure 5.2. The list of spaces still in decline includes a substantial portion of the West Zone as well as a patch to the south. The level of negative growth rates decline, however, and many of these areas are now close to stable. It is worth observing that while between 1991 and 2000, the negative rates exceeded 2.5 percent per year in 22 weighting areas, between 2000 and 2010 no area reached this rate, and just six areas exceeded 1 percent negative.
- To these central areas in decline we should also add almost all the North Zone and other regions in the first ring around the expanded center, which had already experienced the process of negative growth in the previous decade and continued to lose occupants. In the 2000s, though, this decline reached a substantial part of the outer portion of the municipality's East Zone. These include various localities that showed intense growth until the previous decade. In this case the process of negative growth that during the previous decade had expanded as far as the central portion of the East Zone continued to expand toward the peripheries.

It should be stressed that only more detailed analyses, including study of the weighting areas, enable these nuances to become observable. The use of districts conceals relative de-occupation and the accompanying growth of adjacent areas to the southeast of the map (Figure 5.1). In studies based on districts, these regions are shown generically as low growth, but they displayed behavior of peripheralization and negative growth in the 1990s and 2000s, respectively.

Which processes can be associated with these trends? Did the return to growth in the central localities involve a substitution of population? Did those regions that continued to increase demographically repeat the pattern of peripheral growth associated with the migration and poverty classically found in the metropolis? The next section turns to other data from the census to provide some preliminary responses to these questions.

Exploring the Processes and Causes Behind Growth Patterns

The first general point to emphasize concerns the lower levels of growth in the last decade compared to the previous, both the positive and negative rates.

Torres (2005) showed that growth rates in the 1990s were associated with the average income of the weighting areas[3] as well as their geographic localization. As we saw in Figure 5.1, these tended to be radial and concentric. Between 2000 and 2010, the association between demographic behavior and income changed significantly. In statistical terms, the association between growth rates over the decade and the average incomes of the household head in the weighting areas in 2010 vanished.[4] Although most of these areas present low income and low growth, various low-income bands are found in regions with low and high growth, except for some divergent areas with low income and very high growth rates. The same is found in areas that contain individuals from high-income bands.

Although growth rates have generally cooled down, therefore, areas inhabited by wealthy social groups and those inhabited by the poor both displayed high and low growth rates over the last decade. But was this, for example, because of the deeper change in demographic growth patterns associated with a fall in birth rates and the shrinking in average household density or the social transformation of locations driven by urban processes like real estate development and gentrification? A region that grew little (or decreased in population size) may have begun to be occupied by lower-income populations over the decade and presented higher growth rates in the 1990s. Conversely, areas once inhabited by the poor (with high growth rates) may have become occupied instead by higher-income groups (growing at lower rates).

We can begin our analysis by comparing the incomes of residents from each weighting area in each census and ascertain whether places that underwent intense change experienced a significant substitution in their population. For the region as a whole, the average income across all weighting areas was R$1,049 in nominal terms (with a standard deviation of R$943) in 2000 and rose to R$1,678 (with a standard deviation of R$1,460) in 2010. As we are interested only in the variations relating to places, we can divide the income of each area by the average income of the metropolitan region each year.[5] Comparing these indicators reveals the relative positions of the areas in each census, neutralizing the effects of the decade's dynamic. This data suggests that the social makeup of the weighting areas, as measured by income, was substantially maintained throughout the metropolis as a whole:[6] In 2010, the vast majority of the weighting areas were occupied by inhabitants relatively similar, at least in terms of income, to those living in the areas 10 years earlier. This stability also suggests the persistence of the high patterns of segregation present in the city, though the analysis of this dynamic demands specific investigation. For the metropolis overall, therefore, the great majority of places remained with relatively similar social makeups.

Even if there were no significant changes in relative incomes, or it proves impossible to associate the growth of income bands directly, as was possible in the 1990s, can we delimit the types of transformations happening over the decade? What were the typical growth trajectories delineated by the demographic changes of the 2000s? Analysis of the data suggests that three key trajectories exist: (1) areas that decreased in population size until 2000 and grew significantly over the last decade; (2) areas that decreased over both decades; and (3) areas that grew intensely over the two decades.

In the next section, we explore these trajectories by comparing the average social composition of the residents of each of these areas in 2010 with those of the other areas of the metropolis. To do so we make use of variables from the census that allow us to characterize the population according to income, age structure, skin color, residential type (house, apartment and villa or condominium) and access to infrastructure as well as indicators for recent migration, housing development production, the presence of individuals born between the censuses and favelization. Before examining the findings, however, a few explanations are needed apropos the indicators employed to measure these last four processes.

In the case of migration, first we used the information from the sample of the 2010 census relating to migrants who had arrived in the municipality over the nine years prior to the census. The data serves as an indicator but does not enable a precise measurement of the phenomenon that we need to control since it fails to differentiate intraurban migration. Nonetheless, it is the best information available concerning the process. Thus, the proportion of the population in each area that migrated to the municipality during the last nine years is the variable used to test the importance of the recent migration in the demographic trend. Recent migration continues to be a central dimension in the explanation of demographic growth—the correlation between the growth rates between 2000 and 2010 and the proportions of inhabitants from the areas who are recent migrants is high.[7] As we shall see, though, in areas with distinct trajectories, migration can perform entirely different roles.

Second is private-sector housing production. We used the number of new residential units built by the formal private sector, recorded in the Empresa Brasileira de Estudos de Patrimônio (EMBRAESP) database and analyzed by the CEM, locating these new developments by their addresses first in isolation and subsequently in the weighting areas.[8] The limitation of this variable is that it fails to capture the movements of self-built housing, small-scale commissioned production and the informal market. The data, however, systemizes new property developments built by the formal housing sector.[9] We used the total number of new housing units built in each weighting area between 2000 and 2009.

A third indicator is the proportion of the population from the weighting area born between the 2000 and 2010 censuses. This indicator tests the demographic effect of births on the growth of the areas. However this is merely an indication for two reasons: First, the correct variable would be the birth rate in each area, information we lack; second, we do not know whether the parents of children age 10 and under living in any given area in 2010 were already living there in 2000 or whether they themselves are migrants. However, even with these limitations, the variable tells us about the association between the growth process and the presence of young people born after 2000.

Finally, there are the favelas. In this case, we have used the information on the proportion of the population living in *subnormal* sectors in the 2000 and 2010 censuses in each weighting area. This information presents known limitations (Marques 2008, Saraiva & Marques 2005), but it is the only data available for comparison across the entire region. Since the classification of the subnormal sectors is a product of a specific methodology employed by IBGE and since the latter introduced an important update to its database between the censuses, we decided to follow a procedure similar to that adopted for incomes by dividing the proportions of inhabitants in subnormal sectors for each weighting area by the average for the metropolitan region in each census. In addition, the indicators for migration and housing developments described relate to flows, while the proportions of subnormal sectors relate to housing stock, meaning that to measure the importance of variations in the presence of favelas in each weighting area, we calculated the differences between the proportions for each year. There were three trajectories in growth patterns.

Population Decline in the 1990s and Growth in the 2000s

This trajectory includes the areas that shrank in demographic terms between 1991 and 2000 (any negative growth) and returned to substantial growth (more than 2.5 percent) between 2000 and 2010. This process obviously led to an increase in the average demographic densities over the last decade.

In 2000 these areas already had fairly high average income (R$2,300 compared to R$1,000 in the other areas). In 2010, the positive indicators tended to repeat themselves, with higher income (R$4,100, compared to R$1,100 in the other areas), proportionally more people living in apartments (60 percent compared to 18 percent in the other areas), higher proportions of people over the age of 65 (10 percent compared to 7 percent) and fewer teenagers (15 percent compared to 21 percent) as well as a lower proportion of black and brown people (24 percent compared to 38 percent).[10] A much higher percentage of domestic workers is also found among the residents (0.9 percent compared to 0.1 percent in the other areas).[11] On average at least, therefore, these are areas with a higher-earning and socially better positioned population.

Comparing indicators in these areas in 2000 and 2010 is also revealing. The proportion of households in apartments was 54 percent in 2000 and rose six percentage points in 2010, suggesting that at least some of the observed growth was associated with recent vertical housing developments. In addition, when we analyzed the changes in income between the two censuses (having already discounted the change in averages), significant and substantial positive results emerged: Relative income in 2010 is 22 percent higher than relative income in 2000. In other words, in those localities where the demographic decline was reversed, growing intensely in the 2000s, the average income grew much more than the average in the other weighting areas in the metropolis. At the same time, the data on the proportion of individuals born in these areas between the two censuses are below the average of the other areas (11.8 percent compared to 15.3 percent).[12]

This data seem to confirm the importance of formal housing production in reversing the downward trend in these areas. Moreover, the presence of housing developments in the 2000s is shown to be strongly concentrated in the areas with this growth trajectory. In these areas, an average of 2,100 new residential units was built, compared to an average of 500 units in the other metropolitan areas. Conversely, these areas revealed no significant variation in terms of their favela population or their proportion of recent migrants.

Since many of these variables are intercorrelated, we decided to conduct a final statistical test, investigating the combined effect on the trajectories of demographic change caused by housing developments, the difference in the proportion of subnormal areas, recent migration and the presence of people born between the two census dates. In the case of areas that fell demographically until 2000 and then grew until 2010, only housing developments and recent migration to the municipality proved significant and positive in a multivariate analysis.[13] This implies that the areas showing this trend received more migrants and new housing than the rest of the metropolis.

Six of the 10 areas in this situation are located in the expanded center and two in areas with rising average incomes. Another two areas comprised the center of a peripheral municipality (Taboão da Serra) and an area in the southern periphery adjacent to it, the latter with a much lower average income. In these two areas a much lower number of new formal housing developments was seen—just 150 on average. The peripheral area was the only one showing a relatively high and increasing number of favela residents.

These areas include some with a recent surge in housing production. The pattern of housing developments in these regions—in large part a result of zoning policy—has led to the substitution of commercial or industrial use by residential use with a subsequent increase in population density. The inversion of the demographic trend results, therefore, from a particular pattern of housing production shaped by state regulation.[14]

Although the type of data analyzed here does not allow us to verify that a substitution of the population occurred, as in the gentrification processes described by the international literature (Hamnett 1991), the areas with this trajectory ended up with an even better off population, in terms of income, living increasingly in apartments. These areas were also subject to a mass investment in housing production by the formal market, suggesting that the return to growth was associated with a boom in housing production for high-income residents and a consequent rise in demographic densities.

Continuous Population Decline Over the Two Decades

The second trajectory comprises areas that declined in demographic terms in the 1990s and continued to fall over the 2000s (negative growth in both periods). In this case, income is slightly higher than the other areas, both in 2000 and in 2010 (R$2,300 and R$1,990 in the two years compared to R$1,000 and R$1,650 in the other areas), but substantially lower than in the areas analyzed. However, relative incomes indicate that the areas with a trajectory of population decline also lost income in relative terms. In the case of this trajectory, therefore, in 2010 we find a population with a lower income in relative terms than the level seen in 2000.

Other indicators suggest a social makeup close to the metropolitan average but slightly higher. Already in 2000 there were lower proportions of children and adolescents (7 and 22 percent compared to 9 and 26 percent in the other areas), a higher number of senior citizens (9 percent compared to 5 percent in the other areas) and higher literacy rates (63 percent). The proportion of apartments was also slightly higher (23 percent compared to 20 percent in the other areas) and basic infrastructure more extensive (100 percent connected to the water supply, 95 percent of bathrooms linked to the sewage system and 99 percent covered by waste collection). The difference between the indicators in these areas and those of the other areas tended to be repeated in 2010.

In these areas there was no specific concentration of formal housing production. But while there were relatively fewer inhabitants in favelas in 2000–3 percent compared to 8 percent in the other areas—this proportion fell even further in relative terms in 2010. In fact, the proportion remained stable, but the proportion in all other areas rose to 10 percent in 2010. As the classification of the subnormal sectors was widened and ended up including more areas in 2010, it is reasonable to suppose that the areas with this trajectory tended to lose favela residents in relative terms over the last decade. Additionally, these areas have fewer individuals born between the two censuses than the average for other areas (12.2 percent compared to 15.5 percent). Finally, the areas with this trajectory absorbed fewer recent migrants than the others—8 percent compared to 13 percent for the rest of the metropolis.[15]

Once again, since many of these variables are intercorrelated, we performed a multivariate statistical test similar to the one conducted for the previous trajectory. In this case, the variables for recent migration for the municipality, formal housing production and the population born between the censuses proved to be significant and negative.[16] This indicates that the population decline in these areas is related to low migration, a low number of births between the census dates and low housing production.

This growth situation involves 61 weighting areas located mainly in the first ring surrounding the expanded center in areas of the North Zone, in large part in Osasco municipality and in the centers of older municipalities like Santo André, São Caetano and Mogi das Cruzes. The same situation is also found in some areas of the expanded center with high incomes.

Although recent housing production by the formal private sector was also observable in some of these areas, the kind of construction involved has not generated denser population levels, unlike the previous situation: In this case the horizontal or two-story residential urban fabric has been replaced by verticalized developments that have nonetheless prioritized open spaces and leisure areas, resulting in a reduction of density per block.

However, it should be reemphasized that in the set of areas that show continuing population decline, the rates seen in the 2000s were not particularly high and mostly remained between 0 and −1 percent per year. Indeed the average rate of the areas showing this downward trajectory between 1991 and 2000 was −1.1 percent per year, while the rate between 2000 and 2010 was −0.4 percent per year. Although the decline has been continuous, then, it was less intense over the last 10 years than in the 1990s.

In fact, even between 1991 and 2000, the negative growth rates were fairly slight compared to the positive growth rates elsewhere. Even in that decade, only 22 areas presented negative rates more than 2.5 percent, while 268 areas presented positive rates more than 2.5 percent. Curiously, until Torres (2005) had shown the intense growth of the so-called urban frontier, the local debate was primarily concentrated on the less intense pole of the processes underway—the population decline of the central areas. Even in the 1990s, therefore, the downward trend was already less accentuated than the upward trend, a tendency that remained observable in the 2000s, albeit at a less intense level.

Intense and Continuous Growth Over the Two Decades

To explore this trajectory we analyzed the areas that grew strongly in the 1990s (more than 3 percent per year) and continued to grow in the 2000s (more than 2.5 percent per year). As we saw previously, the positive growth rates tended to decline overall in the metropolis and, while reaching a striking average rate of 8.4 percent per year in the 1990s, slowed down to a still very substantial 4.0 percent per year between 2000 and 2010.

In this case, the indicators suggest a social situation opposite to the previous ones. The income in 2000 was low (R$640 compared to R$1,100) and remained significantly low (R$1,150 compared to R$1,750 in the other areas) in 2010. In 2000, the proportion of children and adolescents was higher (12 percent compared to 9 percent and 31 percent compared to 25 percent, respectively) and the proportion of elderly people lower (3 percent compared to 6 percent in the other areas). The vast majority of households were houses (91 percent) and access to infrastructure was more precarious—just 88 percent of households were connected to the water supply, compared to 96 percent in other areas, and just 54 percent had a bathroom connected to the sewage system, compared to 81 percent in other areas.

In 2010, this social makeup remained present in relative terms. Young people between 5 and 18 continued to be overrepresented (6 and 26 percent compared to 5 and 21 percent, respectively), and the proportion of children born between the two censuses were above the average the other areas (18.5 percent compared to 15.2 percent). Similarly, elderly people were underrepresented (4 percent compared to 8 percent), as well as people declaring themselves to be black and brown (7 and 41 percent, respectively, compared to 6 and 31 percent in the other areas). Although improved over the decade, basic infrastructure remained less present: water supply at 90 percent compared to 96 percent and bathrooms linked to the sewage system at 66 percent, compared to 85 percent for households elsewhere.

Once again, given that most of these variables are intercorrelated, we conducted a multivariate statistical test similar to those carried out for the previous trajectories. In this case just recent migration to the municipality and the population born between the censuses proved significant and positive,[17] indicating that areas with this trajectory systematically received more migrants, and had a population age of up to 10, than the remainder of the metropolis.

Overall, the data suggest that these involve areas similar to those that Torres (2005) calls the urban frontier, confirmed by their pattern of localization. In total, 72 weighting areas are found in this situation. The vast majority is located on the metropolitan periphery and shows low income levels. However, this situation also extends to three areas with very high income and strong growth—part of Morumbi and two areas in a peripheral municipality (Santana do Parnaíba) almost certainly are all associated with occupation by high income groups in closed luxury condominiums. For these areas, the relative increase in income was 27 percent between the averages of the two censuses, an opposite trend to the other areas sharing this trajectory of demographic growth.

Comparison of the relative incomes indicates stability or a small fall relative to the income in the weighting areas in this situation compared to the other areas: The average income of these areas in 2010 was 1 percent lower than the average income of the these same areas in 2000. Recent migration seems to be closely associated with this trajectory. The proportion of recent migrants is 18 percent in these areas, compared to 12 percent in the rest of the metropolis.

In this case, the information on houses and apartments remained relatively stable. The formal housing production proved negative and significantly associated with the areas with this growth trajectory.[18] However, the lower number of formal private-sector housing developments is not counterbalanced by a growth in favelas. In fact, in none of the two censuses did these areas have larger populations in favelas relative to the others. This does not mean that this trajectory, which is spatially associated with areas that can still be considered part of the urban frontier in Torres's sense (2005), is not linked to precarious housing. We have no information available on clandestine or irregular settlements, which are in fact much more characteristic of São Paulo's peripheries than the favelas.

Hence the large majority of areas that grew continuously over the last two decades are poor, possess less infrastructure, continue to receive recent migrants and are located in peripheral areas, as described by Torres (2005) under the term of urban frontier. As we saw in Figure 5.2, however, areas with this trajectory represent just a portion of the peripheral areas in 2010, and their growth levels tend to be lower than those observed in the previous decade. It can be concluded that although the production of the peripheries as a process continues to unfold in a form similar to the pattern classically described in the literature, it no longer occupies all or even the majority of the peripheries, which are becoming more and more diverse.

Summarizing Patterns

The most general aspect to emphasize concerns the slowing down of both positive and negative growth rates in SPMR. As in earlier decades, the average figures conceal locally higher rates, but their levels in the 2000s were substantially more subdued than in the 1990s.

We also observed a considerable heterogeneity in growth patterns at a spatial level. In contrast to the emphasis given in the local debate, the idea that the center returned to growth conceals trends involving moderate growth, intense growth and continuing decline, all of which are present in the expanded center. Similarly, some peripheral areas continue to be marked by the processes classically attributed to urban outskirts, but in other regions we can observe reduced growth or even a depopulating of the area. The structuring of the growth processes does not show a clearly concentric behavior in the 2000s.

These patterns allow us to delimit at least three major growth trajectories over the last two decades, explained by distinct processes. In some of the central areas, de-occupation was replaced by intense growth, associated with recent private-sector housing developments, an increase in relative income and the intensification of territorial occupation. In these areas the metropolis became more compact and its residents better off financially compared to metropolitan averages. In another trajectory, other central areas, as well as regions close to them, continued to decline demographically. These are areas with a relatively high income that have not been targeted by the housing production market or subject to favelization or recent migration. Some high-income areas of the expanded center follow this pattern, contradicting the idea that the center generically has returned to growth. A third and final trajectory includes mostly peripheral areas with low income and a lower presence of services (though coverage is improving), which continued to expand in the 2000s at high rates, albeit lower than previously in average terms. These areas represent just part of the peripheral regions, reinforcing earlier narratives on the growing heterogeneity of these spaces.

Notes

1. The census sectors are more detailed spatial disaggregation units for which the IBGE provides information from the census universe, while the weighting areas comprise the units with the highest detail from the census sample, composed by the IBGE through sector aggregations. Given the intense changes to the boundaries of the census sectors between censuses and the subsequent alterations made to the census sector limits, the decision was taken to work to make the weighting areas compatible by aggregating the 812 areas from 2000 with the 633 from 2010. It should be added that these databases are made freely available by CEM at http://www.fflch.usp.br/centrodametropole/en/.
2. The map is not identical to the one presented by Torres (2005) due to the choice of a band of 2.5 percent growth per annum rather than 3 percent per annum, as selected by the author.
3. A statistical correlation indeed exists between the 1991-to-2000 growth and the average household head income in 2000—0.426, significant to a 99 percent confidence level.
4. The correlation coefficient between the two variables in this case is low and statistically insignificant.
5. The information on income from the two censuses is not entirely comparable due to changes introduced to the census questionnaires, as well as the effects of inflation, the rise in the minimum wage and the increase in the coverage of income transfer programs, all impacting on the absolute figures. Dividing by the average for each census eliminates these effects.
6. The correlation coefficient between incomes normalized by the averages indicates an almost complete association—0.987, significant to 99 percent reliability.
7. Correlation coefficient of 0.449, significant to 99 percent.
8. This database is made freely available by CEM at http://www.fflch.usp.br/centrodametropole/en/.
9. For a detailed analysis of the development industry since the 1980s, see Chapter 10 by Telma Hoyler.
10. About the methodology on data on race in Brazil, see Chapter 7 by Danilo França.
11. Note that these involve domestic workers (maids) who sleep at their workplace and were therefore recorded in the census as living in the area, not residents employed elsewhere as domestic workers. The figure may seem small but in fact means that almost one in 100 residents in these areas is a domestic worker residing at his or her place of work.
12. Differences significant to 99 percent.

13. A logistic regression analysis was conducted with the four cited variables as well as the dependent variable for the trajectory in question. The two variables indicated presented a significance of 99 percent.
14. This interpretation was suggested by Raquel Rolnik during one of the preparatory seminars of this book, whom we thank.
15. All the differences are significant to 99 percent.
16. A logistic regression was carried out with four variables (the three cited plus the variable difference in the proportion of subnormal areas) as well as a dependent variable of the trajectory in question. The indicated variables presented a significance of 99 percent.
17. A logistic regression was conducted with the four cited variables as well as a dependent variable of the trajectory in question. The two variables indicated presented a significance of 99 percent. Interestingly, the multivariate model assesses the occurrence of a joint effect on the trajectory. As migration and the presence of young people are usually associated, the expectation would be for one of them to cease being expressive when introduced jointly in the test. The fact that the two remained present indicates a very strong and independent effect from each of them.
18. In average terms, the areas with high and continuous growth received just 190 new units, compared to 570 in other areas, on average, a significant difference of 95 percent reliability.

Bibliography

Baeninger, R. (2011). Crescimento da população na região metropolitana de São Paulo: desconstruindo mitos do século XX. In: Kowarick, L. and Marques, E. (eds.) *São Paulo: novos percursos e atores: sociedade, cultura e política*. São Paulo: Ed. 34/CEM, pp. 53–78.

Bógus, L. and Taschner, S. (2001). São Paulo, o caledoscópio urbano. *São Paulo em Perspectiva*, 15(1), pp. 31–44.

Cunha, J. M (2003). Redistribuição espacial da população: tendências e trajetória. *São Paulo em Perspectiva*, 17(3–4), pp. 218–233.

Fischer, C. and Styles, J. (2006). Where Americans lived: The redrawing of America's social geography. In: Fischer, C. and Hout, M. (eds.) *Century of difference: How America changed in the last one hundred years*. New York: Russell Sage Foundation, pp. 162–185.

Hamnett, C. (1991). The blind men and the elephant: The explanation of gentrification. *Transactions of the Institute of British Geographers*, 16(2), pp. 173–189.

Jannuzzi, P. (2007). Cenários futuros e projeções para pequenas áreas: método e resultados para os distritos paulistanos 2000–2010. *Revista Brasileira de Estudos da População*, 24, pp. 109–137.

Jannuzzi, P. and Jannuzzi, N. (2002). Crescimento urbano, saldos migratórios e atratividade residencial dos distritos da cidade de São Paulo: 1980–2000. *Revista Brasileira de Estudos Urbanos e Regionais*, 4(1–2), pp. 107–127.

Marques, E. (2008). *Assentamentos precários no Brasil urbano*. Brasília: Ministério das Cidades/CEM.

Marques, E. and Torres, H. (2005). *São Paulo: segregação, pobreza e desigualdades sociais*. São Paulo: Ed. SENAC.

Perillo, S. and Perdigão, M. (1998). *Cenários migratórios recentes em São Paulo*. Paper presented at the XI Encontro Nacional da Associação Brasileira de Estudos

Populacionais-Abep, Caxambu, Brazil. http://www.abep.org.br/?q=publicacoes/anais/anais-1998-migra%C3%A7%C3%A3oPMSP. (2012a). *Plano Diretor Estratégico a Cidade de São Paulo, 10 anos*. São Paulo: Prefeitura Municipal de São Paulo.

PMSP. (2012b). *São Paulo 2040: A cidade que queremos*. São Paulo: Prefeitura Municipal de São Paulo.

PMSP. (2011). *Informes Urbanos*. São Paulo: Prefeitura Municipal de São Paulo.

Saraiva, C. and Marques, E. (2005). As condições de vida nas favelas paulistanas. In: Marques, E. and Torres, H. (eds.) *São Paulo: segregação, pobreza e desigualdades sociais*. São Paulo: Ed. Senac, pp. 148–168.

Taschner, S. and Bógus, L. (1998). Continuidades e descontinuidades na cidade dos anéis. In: Migração, N. Patarra (ed.) *Condições de vida e Dinâmica Urbana 1980–93*. Campinas: Ed. Unicamp/Fapesp, pp. 135–157.

Torres, H. (2005). Fronteira urbana. In: Marques, E. and Torres, H. (eds.) *São Paulo: segregação, pobreza e desigualdades sociais*. São Paulo: Ed. Senac, pp. 101–120.

Wilson, W. (1987). *The truly disadvagntaged*. Chicago: University of Chicago Press.

6 The Social Spaces of the Metropolis in the 2000s

Eduardo Cesar Leão Marques

The SPMR shows intense residential segregation. This pattern is visible when we observe the population distribution by income bands or education and when we consider occupational classifications such as EGP classes. This pattern has been widely explored by the literature since the 1970s in a narrative, qualitative or monographic form by classic studies like Camargo (1976), Kowarick (1979) and Bonduki and Rolnik (1982) and, more recently, using data from the 2000 census to construct segregation indices applicable to income and schooling (Torres 2005) or to diverse occupational classification models (Marques et al. 2012, Preteceille & Cardoso 2008). This chapter analyzes residential segregation in the metropolis in the 2000s.[1]

The chapter is divided into four sections. In the first, we discuss the main conceptual elements involved in the analysis through a review of the existing literature, while in the second we analyze the general pattern of residential segregation in 2000 and 2010, considering income and social class. In the following section we develop a typology of spaces based on the distribution of these classes at the two census points to capture a snapshot of the changes occurring in these spaces. The fourth and final section compares the two classifications and investigates the distribution of space types within the metropolitan area.

Residential Segregation Under Debate

As is well-known, São Paulo is intensely segregated in the same way as many other Brazilian and Latin America cities (Carvalho et al. 2004, Centeno 2009, Dureau & Vanegas 2009, Píres 2009, Villaça 2000). Classic studies of the city have already highlighted this segregation pattern as one of its most important and constitutive characteristics (Camargo 1976, Kowarick 1979). Since the 1970s, the overall structure of residential segregation was also typically described as radial and concentric (Bonduki & Rolnik 1982). In this structure, amenities, services and wealthier social groups were located in the center of the metropolis. Moving outward, space was organized in gradients of declining social conditions and precarity toward the peripheries (Bonduki & Rolnik 1982), a place of sociability at once specific and similar to the rest of the city (Durham 1988).

More recently, some analyses have emphasized the persistence of this structure over time (Bogus & Taschner 2000, Maricato 2003, Villaça 2000), while others have stressed the growing heterogeneity of the metropolitan territory, especially on the peripheries (CEM 2004, Marques & Torres 2005) but also in the favelas (Saraiva & Marques 2005), matching studies of Rio de Janeiro (Valladares & Preteceille 2000). Evidence provided by ethnographic studies has reinforced these analyses by highlighting the significant levels of heterogeneity found in peripheral spaces (Feltran 2011). Interestingly, this heterogeneity had already been emphasized in classic works (Bonduki 1991, Vetter et al. 1979), although the mainstream reading until recently had stressed the homogeneity of these urban peripheries.

In the debates on São Paulo in the 1990s, this heterogeneity was explained as the outcome of a combination of diverse processes. On one hand, it was supposedly produced by a shift in state policy since the return to democracy in the late 1980s, impelled by the campaigns of urban social movements and by reformist technical bureaucracies in an environment of competition between political parties, increasingly shaped by electoral politics (Faria 1992, Marques & Bichir 2003). This change in turn led to an increased supply of policies and services, even to the poorest of the poor (Figueiredo et al. 2006). At the same time, authors argued that the social composition of these peripheral spaces was also being altered through intense demographic changes (Baeninger 2012), poverty (Marques et al. 2016) and wider social structures that were also slowly but steadily transforming. Finally, these patterns of heterogeneity were seen to have reinforced by the dissemination of new housing developments linked to closed condominiums located in peripheral spaces, aimed in particular at wealthy social groups (Caldeira 2000).

These transformations are somewhat at odds with the international debates on the major urban trends of the last decades. We can group the international studies on the topic into two sets, already partially covered in Chapter 2. The first set centers on discussing the restructuring of production from the 1970s onward and its consequences for cities, based on early contributions like Sassen (1991) and Leborgne and Lipietz (1990) to cite just two of the most influential (and distinct) traditions. The second set of studies more clearly belongs to the traditional line of analyses of residential segregation in space, a canonical theme in urban studies since the pioneering works of the Chicago School (Park et al. 1925) and the first attempts to measure the phenomenon (Duncan & Duncan 1955). A quick review of the recent arguments is important since these tell us about the main hypotheses available for explaining the transformations occurring over recent decades and observed empirically in the remainder of the chapter.

As described earlier, Sassen (1991) argued that the transformations of capitalism introduced since the 1970s had concentrated business command in the large cities, leading to a decline in secondary activities more clearly connected to Fordist production. The social structures of these metropolises thus underwent transformative processes that led to social and occupational polarization. This hypothesis was originally formulated with respect to New York, London and Tokyo but later became applied to many other societies (Knox & Taylor 1995).

Setting out from very different theoretical premises associated with regulation theory, authors like Leborgne and Lipietz (1990) arrived at a similar diagnosis. The authors argued that the crisis in Fordism of the 1970s and 1980s in the central economies of the capitalist world generated diverse responses from economic and government actors, most of them involving various forms of flexibilization. These included altering relations among firms, labor contracts and factory processes per se, with innumerable consequences for capital, labor, legal and ideological frameworks. What most interests us here, though, is once again the diagnosis of urban polarization, both in terms of social structure and geographically with the territorial concentration of activities and wealth in already privileged places.

In both cases, therefore, social and spatial polarization are foreseen as a response to tertiary activities linked to business command, with spatial polarization identified as a consequence of the new dynamics involved in the production of spaces and urban renewal projects. As we saw already in Chapter 2, this polarization of the social structure was not found in São Paulo.

These hypotheses have since been subject to critique, especially in recent debates on residential segregation in large metropolises, which prompts me to briefly review the latter debate. First, it needs to be pointed out that some aspects of the hypotheses described passed the test of time better than others. On one hand, the emergence of a social group of superrich and a market for property speculation oriented toward business command seems to be a consensus. This process has had important spatial consequences on land markets, housing and urban policies, leading to numerous urban renewal projects (Fainstein 2008) as well as important gentrification processes (Butler 1997) in cities around the world.

The hypothesis of social polarization, by contrast, has been heavily criticized since the local effects of global processes seem to vary substantially. According to some authors, different welfare regimes buffer the influence of global processes (Hamnett 1996a, Lehto 2000, Vaattovaara & Kortteinen 2003). Consequently, labor markets can be subject to processes of depreciation, improvement or stability in jobs as well as polarization, properly speaking, as we saw earlier. For many commentators, the recent dynamics have mostly involved a substantial growth in professional jobs, along with the development of a series of new, intermediary positions in the occupational structure of cities like London (Hamnett 1994 and 1996b), Paris (Preteceille 1995), Tokyo (Fujita & Hill 2012) or Oslo (Baum 1999).

In terms of social structure, therefore, our hypothesis is to test not only the occurrence of polarization in São Paulo but also the professionalization of its occupational structure.

There also appears to be a consensus that the spatial impact of these transformations in production on the urban fabric is mediated by a variety of dynamics and structures in contrast to the original hypothesis advanced by Sassen (1991). In cities like Athens (Maloutas 2007), Budapest (Kovacs 2012) and Paris (Preteceille 1995), the urban histories and structures were of primordial importance in constructing the current situation, while in Madrid the local land and housing markets played fundamental roles (Dominguez et al. 2012). Local political processes and public policies seemed to have been crucial in diverse places like London (Hamnett 1994 and 1996b), Paris (Preteceille 2006), Copenhagen (Andersen 2012) and Helsinki (Wessel 2000) as well as in various cities studied by the Urbex project (Musterd & Murie 2002). Testing the existence of spatial polarization in São Paulo, therefore, comprises a second important analytic task.

How, then, can the international debate on segregation provide an insight into the processes taking place in Brazil's metropolises? An excellent comparison of 11 cities can be found in Maloutas (2012). The author lists some of the major trends observed, which reverberate with the results that we present in the following sections. First, as already emphasized earlier, global trends are not necessarily found locally, given that local processes heavily influence the observed results. In most cases, the main axis of segregation is socioeconomic, and although ethnic-racial dimensions make themselves present, they overlap with the former dimension. In this respect, the rich are generally more segregated than the poor, despite the fact that debates usually highlight segregation of the latter. Segregation levels depend heavily on state policies but not necessarily in the way originally predicted by formulators. Furthermore, Maloutas (2012) argues that in most cities one can observe an increase in the social differentiation of places with a growing spatial approximation of diverse social groups, with closed condominiums and gentrification being just part of this process. Finally, reductions in segregation do not necessarily signify inequality or greater contact among social groups.

We can turn now to explore how these processes have unfolded in São Paulo, maintaining a dialogue with the hypotheses cited.

Residential Segregation in São Paulo

The panorama of residential segregation provided by the 2010 census confirms a strong continuation of the urban form, both in terms of the simple observation of thematic income maps, for example, and in the analysis of spatial statistics indicators. An initial measurement of segregation can be achieved by analyzing the spatial distribution of income using the Moran Index, which measures spatial autocorrelation for a defined variable. Mathematically, the index varies between -1 and 1 and expresses the correlation between the values of the variable concerned in each area and the averages of this same variable for the neighboring areas so that the closer to 1, the stronger the relation (Anselin 1995). The Moran Index for the household head income variable for the weighting areas was 0.704 in 2000 and 0.699 in 2010. Hence, though slightly lower, the index was practically the same.

However, the income provides us with an overly simple measure of segregation by social group. Another more detailed approach involves analyzing segregation by social class, measured by the Moran Indexes for the EGP classifications already used from Chapter 2 and constructed according to the procedures set out in Barbosa and Marschner (2013). To provide a clearer picture, the rural categories—now fairly residual—were excluded from the analysis, leaving eight classes in total.

We use two indexes, the Moran Index and the Dissimilarity Index, since each has its advantages and disadvantages. The Moran Index is less sensitive to group size but is less intuitive to interpret, while the Dissimilarity Index is influenced by the relative sizes of the groups. The manual classes, for example, present much lower Dissimilarity Indexes compared to their Moran Indexes since they represent large groups, predominant over a wide geographic area, though concentrated in segregated areas (the peripheries).

Examining the Moran Index first, values more than 0.6 are usually taken to indicate high segregation. In the case of São Paulo, the data suggests medium-high to high levels of segregation, especially for higher occupational categories. The index for high-level professionals, for example, was 0.80 in 2000 and dropped to 0.75 in 2010.[2] The other classes presented lower indexes, between 0.6 and 0.65. This indicates a certain reduction in the concentration of these classes, though the result may also express a proportional expansion of these classes over the decade, as we have already seen. We can also observe a rise in segregation for skilled and unskilled workers (isolated cases of rising Moran Indexes).

The middle occupational classes present the lowest indexes. In these classes we can also observe more pronounced changes, especially among both high- and low-level, routine, nonmanual workers. Although these were not the most segregated classes in 2000, they became the least segregated in 2010, with indexes of 0.46 and 0.58, respectively. We shall see that the falling concentration of these middle categories forms part of a recent trend toward expansion, precisely of mixed spaces. Employers, along with technicians and supervisors, also showed substantial reductions, though this result may simply express sample variations due to the size of these classes.

Turning next to the Dissimilarity Index, this varies between 0 and 1 and totalizes the differences between the distributions of attributes of interest, taking one particular distribution as a reference point. This may seem somewhat obscure, but in fact its interpretation is fairly intuitive, indicating a proportion of the population with an attribute of interest (e.g., a particular migratory origin) that would have to be spatially relocated to match the distribution of the population as a whole or another attribute (e.g., the population with a different origin). As an example, in 2000 37 percent (or 0.37) of the population of high-level professionals would have to be moved for the distribution of this class to match that of the general population in the weighting areas. The information for the whole metropolis suggests indexes from moderate to low (between 0.1 and 0.23) except in the case of high-level professionals (0.37 and 0.35 in 2000 and 2010, respectively) and owners (0.39 and 0.43).[3] Not by chance, the higher occupational classes already presented very high Moran Indexes.

From the viewpoint of both indexes, therefore, the higher classes are the most segregated,[4] while the other classes show segregation levels ranging from median to high. Over the decade, the classes that most grew in proportional terms tended to become deconcentrated, while those whose populations fell increased in terms of their segregation.

However, these results still relate to the metropolis as a whole. We can also calculate the Dissimilarity Index between occupational classes, investigating how social groups become segregated from each other. Table 6.1 presents information for 2010. As an example of how these indicators can be interpreted, Table 6.1 shows that the Dissimilarity Index between high-level professionals and skilled manual workers, for example, was 0.49. This means that 49 percent of high-level professionals would have to be relocated in 2010 to match the same distribution of skilled workers. This proportion fell slightly since 2000, when it reached 0.42. The highest index in 2010 was between owners and low-level manual workers, 0.57, a fairly high figure. The highest indexes, therefore, related to elite groups, taking the lower occupational classes as a reference point. On the other hand, the Dissimilarity Index levels between middle and lower groups ranged between median and low.

Examining the table reveals another important dimension. As we can see, the indices are perfectly ordered between the classes. When we move along rows or up and down the columns, the indicators increase for the higher classes and reduce for the lower classes. For the middle classes, they reduce and then rise, albeit at a lower magnitude. The data fairly clearly suggests, therefore, that the greater the social distance between classes, the greater the segregation. Social segregation in São Paulo is, thus, strongly hierarchical in social terms with a clear sense of social avoidance. Between elite occupational classes, or between lower classes, therefore, the Dissimilarity Indexes are very low, while they increase substantially between elite and lower occupational groups. The spatial distributions of the middle classes are much closer to those of lower groups than those of the elites, reinforcing the impression that the metropolitan fabric tends to be relatively heterogeneous, except for the localization of those classes at the top of the social structure.

The comparison between 2000 with 2010 indicates stability, but the indices tend to increase slightly between low-level professionals and all the middle and lower occupational categories as well as between owners and the same categories. The indices reduce between high- and low-level professionals.

Table 6.1 Dissimilarity Indexes between classes, SPMR, 2010.

	Owners and employers	Professionals, high level	Professionals, low level	Routine nonmanual, high level	Technicians and supervisors	Routine nonmanual, low level	Skilled manual workers	Unskilled manual workers
Owners and employers	–	0.18	0.27	0.41	0.48	0.51	0.56	0.57
Professionals, high level	0.18	–	0.16	0.32	0.39	0.43	0.49	0.50
Professionals, low level	0.27	0.16	–	0.19	0.28	0.30	0.38	0.39
Routine, nonmanual, high level	0.41	0.32	0.19	–	0.15	0.16	0.22	0.25
Technicians and supervisors	0.48	0.39	0.28	0.15	–	0.16	0.17	0.21
Routine, nonmanual, low level	0.51	0.43	0.30	0.16	0.16	–	0.13	0.15
Skilled manual workers	0.56	0.49	0.38	0.22	0.17	0.13	–	0.10
Unskilled manual workers	0.57	0.50	0.39	0.25	0.21	0.15	0.10	–

Source: CEM and author's calculations based on IBGE data.

The São Paulo metropolis emerges as segregated, therefore, especially in relation to the higher occupational classes. The overall structure of segregation is strongly hierarchical, and the middle and lower classes tend to mix more, but in spaces uninhabited by the elites. Segregation generally remained stable over the decade, though perhaps with an increased segregation of the higher classes and a reduced segregation of the lower classes, which became more mixed with the middle classes. We can now examine how this process unfolds spatially.

Types of Spaces

To explore social structure in the São Paulo space in 2010, as well as the transformations observed over the course of the decade, spaces were classified on the basis of occupational classes. First, a factor analysis was conducted, departing from the distribution of the classes in areas with data from the two censuses contained in the databases: This resulted in 1,266 "cases" or "areas" (633 from each census with each duplicated area). The analysis suggested a large concentration of the phenomenon in two factors with an Eigen-value higher than unity, which explain 78.9 percent of the variance. The first factor was associated strongly (and positively) with the presence of owners and professionals and negatively with manual workers. The second factor was associated mainly with technicians and supervisors and high- and low-level, routine, nonmanual workers.

Next, a cluster analysis was applied to the areas based on these two factors, which generated five groups. The distribution of the classes for 2010 can be observed below. The results are similar to the ones obtained for 2000, although the mixed middle class and the manual spaces present larger differences, what is consistent with the higher growth rates observed in some peripheries, as we saw in the previous chapter. Measures of dispersion indicate that the internal variability of the groups is fairly low. As can be seen in Table 6.2, as we shift from 1 to 5, the groups show a declining proportion of higher classes—owners and professionals—and a growing proportion of manual workers. The intermediary classes tend to appear more strongly in the intermediary groups, characterized by mixed social composition, but with a low relative presence of higher groups.

These groupings precisely delimit spaces inhabited by specific class compositions. This can be confirmed by the averages of indicators not used in the analysis, showing a clear descending order to the space types in terms of their social and urban conditions. For example, the indicator ISEI, which as we saw earlier summarizes class positions by taking into account classes, education level and income, declines continuously as we move down the list. While the spaces predominantly occupied by the higher classes reached an index of 59 and 51 in 2010, the figure was 34 and 37 for the spaces occupied by manual workers and by the mixed lower-middle classes, respectively. Interestingly, the spaces of higher classes are further away from the average

Table 6.2 Proportional distribution of classes and groups, SPMR, 2010 (%).

	Number of WAs	Population 2010	% of the population	Owners and employers	Professionals, high level	Professionals, low level	Nonmanual, routine workers, high level	Nonmanual, routine workers, low level	Technicians and supervisors	Skilled manual workers	Unskilled manual workers
Elite spaces	47	1,346,324	6.9	8.7	38.5	20.8	10.0	7.0	2.3	5.2	7.5
Upper middle-class spaces	53	1,711,317	8.7	6.2	24.4	17.5	13.7	13.5	3.2	12.9	8.6
Mixed middle-class spaces	136	4,325,736	22.1	2.4	13.3	13.4	15.4	17.3	4.8	21.3	12.1
Lower, middle-class, mixed spaces	214	7,029,647	35.9	1.2	6.3	7.7	11.8	19.2	4.1	29.5	20.2
Manual worker spaces	183	5,188,244	26.5	0.5	3.4	4.8	9.0	18.5	3.9	35.4	24.5
Total	633	19,601,268	100.0	2.2	10.9	9.9	11.8	17.2	4.0	25.4	17.8

Source: CEM and author's calculations based on data from IBGE.

than those occupied by manual workers, an outcome of the inequalities present in the metropolis's social structure (and its residential segregation).

Similarly, incomes tend to fall substantially between the groups, just as when we compare quotients to the metropolitan average in 2010, from 3.5 in elite spaces to 1.0 in mixed, middle-class spaces and 0.5 in manual workers' spaces. Again the spaces of higher occupational class are much more distant from the average than the lower occupational spaces. The social composition indicates a wealthier, older, less black and brown, and more highly schooled population in higher occupational spaces with a gradual inversion of this makeup as we drop down social structure.

Taken as a whole, the indicators suggest the following configuration of characteristics for this set of spaces in 2010:

1—Elite Spaces

These were characterized by the high presence of owners and professional workers (68.0 percent), with a very high income (four times the metropolitan average), high ISEI (about 50 percent higher than average) and high levels of schooling. The presence of children was low, so too people self-classified as black or brown, who represented a quarter of the metropolitan average. Manual workers tended to be residual (12.5 percent). These spaces included mostly apartments (69.5 percent), a low household density, and almost complete access to infrastructure (over 96 percent coverage in relation to all urban services). These spaces clearly represent the areas occupied by higher social groups. They declined in population in the 1990s with negative average growth rates of –1.1 percent per year. However the rates reversed in the 2000s and grew by 1.1 percent per year.

2—Upper Middle-Class Spaces

Owners and professionals were also predominant, though not forming a majority: 48.1 percent. In addition, these spaces also contained above-average proportions of high-level, routine, nonmanual workers, 13.7 percent, totaling 61.8 percent of these classes in their population. The income and ISEI were medium high but much lower than those of the elite spaces (the average income was a little more than half that of the previous spaces). These spaces were also predominately made up of apartments (43.9 percent) and condominiums (2.8 percent, the highest figure among the different groups) and complete infrastructure (practically equal to the previous group). These areas also showed a fall in the 1990s—negative rates of –0.7 percent per year on average—and also returned to growth in the 2000s—1.2 percent per year.

3—Mixed Middle-Class Spaces

These spaces had characteristics near to average for the metropolis in relation to almost all indicators, though with slightly higher than average proportions of professionals, high level, routine, nonmanual workers and technicians and supervisors. The proportion of the latter class is the highest across the metropolis. These undoubtedly represented mixed areas but with a predominance of middle occupational classes and also the presence of higher occupational groups. The individuals self-declaring black and brown represented 29 percent of the population. Generally speaking, their characteristics were slightly higher than average in terms of social composition. Apartments comprised a minority in terms of residence—inhabited by just 22 percent of the population—but urban conditions remained fairly high and infrastructure close to universal. These spaces almost showed demographic stability in the 1990s—a negative rate of 0.1 percent per year—and a low growth rate in the 2000s—an average rate of 0.5 percent per year.

4—Lower Middle-Class Mixed Spaces

These were areas with a predominance of manual workers (skilled and unskilled) but also low-level, nonmanual, routine workers and technicians. These four classes totaled 71.6 percent of the population. These spaces presented the highest presence of low-level, routine, nonmanual workers: 18.5 percent. The relative income and ISEI were between medium and low. These were areas with mixed social characteristics between middle classes and low social groups and with a high presence of black and brown individuals: 44 percent. The predominant type of residence was houses (with just 9 percent living in apartments), and the *subnormal* sectors were more frequently present than the metropolitan average. These spaces displayed high growth in the 1990s—2.8 percent per year—and continued to grow in the 2000s at an average of 1.1 percent per year. The infrastructural conditions were close to the metropolitan average or even better than average for the majority of indicators.

5—Manual Worker Spaces

The final group presented a high and clear predominance of skilled and unskilled manual workers: 58.9 percent. The only other occupational class with a proportion higher than the metropolitan average was low-level, routine, nonmanual workers, with 18.5 percent. Income and ISEI levels were very low. Almost all the population lived in houses (91.7 percent), and residents from subnormal sectors were widely present (a 50 percent higher proportion than the preceding type of space). Self-declared black or brown individuals were predominant: 51.7 percent (the only type of space with this prevalence in the metropolis), and young people were abundant. These areas experienced a demographic explosion in the 1990s—6 percent per year—and continued to grow at high rates in the 2000s—1.9 percent. The infrastructural conditions were highly precarious in relation to almost all indicators: Just 72 percent of households had bathrooms for their own exclusive use, 72 percent had garbage collected by a collection service, and 73 percent of the households had access to metered electricity. Notably, the five types of spaces discussed in this section showed little variation in terms of infrastructural conditions with high rates of coverage close to the metropolitan averages. The only spaces that diverged from this pattern were precisely those occupied by manual workers where all the indicators showed lower-than-average coverage (sometimes substantially so), and the indicators relating to the precarity of the surrounding area indicated very precarious conditions. This information will be explored in more detail in the chapter relating to urban conditions.

Comparing Spaces in the 2000s

Did the areas already have these characteristics in 2000, though? What types of transformations took place in terms of the social makeup of these spaces? To analyze this dimension, we compared the two classifications constructed previously. These are not strictly comparable since the average levels and the distribution of conditions changed between censuses. We, therefore, undertook a two-stage analysis. First we controlled the changes between the different types of spaces before subsequently investigating the changes in classification for each space in particular.

To control the changes in the social makeup of the space types in each census, we began by analyzing the differences of the classes in the groups, which can tell us about alterations in the social compositions of the spaces delimited previously (see Table 6.3). If we subtract the relative proportions of the classes in the areas in the two censuses, we obtain the following result (differences lower than 1 or –1 percent have been omitted to improve clarity).

As we can see, substantial differences exist only among the high- and low-level professional classes (positive) and among manual workers (negative). It should be noted that the presence of the professional classes increased across all groups, even where they were in a significant minority. At the same time, the presence of manual workers declined across all types of spaces, reinforcing the emergence of a process of professionalization, as explored in the second chapter.

The most striking change, however, was the increased presence of high- and low-level professionals in the spaces where these classes were already concentrated—the spaces of elites and the upper-middle classes. Furthermore, it is also important to stress that it was precisely in these higher occupational spaces where unskilled manual workers most declined in presence. These spaces therefore became more exclusive over the decade. Skilled manual workers, by contrast, became relatively less present in the lower occupational spaces where they were predominant. These spaces also observed the highest relative growths in high-level, routine, nonmanual workers as

Table 6.3 Differences between proportions in the areas: 2000/2010, SPMR (%).

2010–2000	Owners and employers	Professionals, high level	Professionals, low level	Technicians and supervisors	Nonmanual routine workers, high level	Nonmanual routine workers, low level	Skilled manual workers	Unskilled manual workers
Elite spaces	-1.9	9.5	2.6	-1.8	-2.8	-1.0	-1.7	-3.1
Upper middle-class spaces	-1.3	7.0	3.5		-2.1	-1.2	-2.2	-3.4
Mixed middle-class spaces	-1.2	3.8	2.8			-1.2	-2.4	-2.0
Lower middle-class mixed spaces		1.7	1.2		1.4		-3.6	
Manual worker spaces		1.1			2.5		-4.0	
Total		3.2	1.7				-2.7	-1.4

Source: CEM and author's calculations based on data from IBGE.

Note: Differences lower than 1 or –1 percent omitted.

The Social Spaces of the Metropolis in the 2000s 151

well as substantial increases in professionals. It is worth adding that, as we saw in Chapter 2, low-level, routine, nonmanual workers showed a higher income and occupational status (measured by ISEI) than manual workers, which reinforced the improvement in the average configuration of lower occupational spaces.

From the viewpoint of the types of spaces, therefore, the presence of high- and low-level professionals generally increased while that of manual workers (both skilled and unskilled) declined. The higher classes also became more predominant in higher occupational spaces, while the lower occupational spaces became less dominated by factory and manual workers and more linked to routine, nonmanual workers as well as to higher classes. The lower occupational spaces which, as we shall see, tend to be more peripheral, are thus becoming more heterogenic.

But what about the geography of these transformations? To analyze this question, we begin by comparing how each area was classified in 2000 and in 2010. As the exercise set out from the classification combining both years, methodologically closely comparable groups were created. Despite the similarities in the general pattern, the areas did not present an identical classification, suggesting patterns of change. The majority of areas—93.8 percent—was classified in the same groups in both censuses, but the investigation of the remaining 6.2 percent can tell us a lot about the changes in the metropolis over the decade when we compare the distribution of the types of spaces in each census.

The spatial distribution of social groups changed little during the decade. Figure 6.1 displays the distribution of groups in 2010. As would be expected, the space of the elites is strongly concentrated in the Southeast of the expanded center. Here, the spaces of the elite can be seen spreading out toward the centers of the wealthiest municipalities of São Paulo's ABC region: São Caetano, Santo André and, to a lesser degree, São Bernardo do Campo. Surrounding this elite area, middle-class regions function as a transition zone to the peripheral areas, showing a significant level of heterogeneity.

In the spread of this region in the Southeast, we can clearly identify the Paraisópolis favela as an enclave of manual workers within the continuous territory of the elite (marked as "d"). Located between the two continuous darker patches in the Southeast of the expanded center and close to the boundary with the municipality of São Caetano is another manual and mixed, lower middle-class space, in this case the Heliópolis/São João Clímaco complex of favelas. These are the only cases of micro-segregation in the entire central region, not by chance the only two large-scale favelas in São Paulo's expanded center.

Standing out to the east and the north of the largest patch of elite are the regions of Tatuapé and Santana, both also elite spaces, though small in size. To the northeast and east, the center of Guarulhos and Mogi das Cruzes appear as upper middle-class spaces. To the west, the region of closed

152 *Eduardo Cesar Leão Marques*

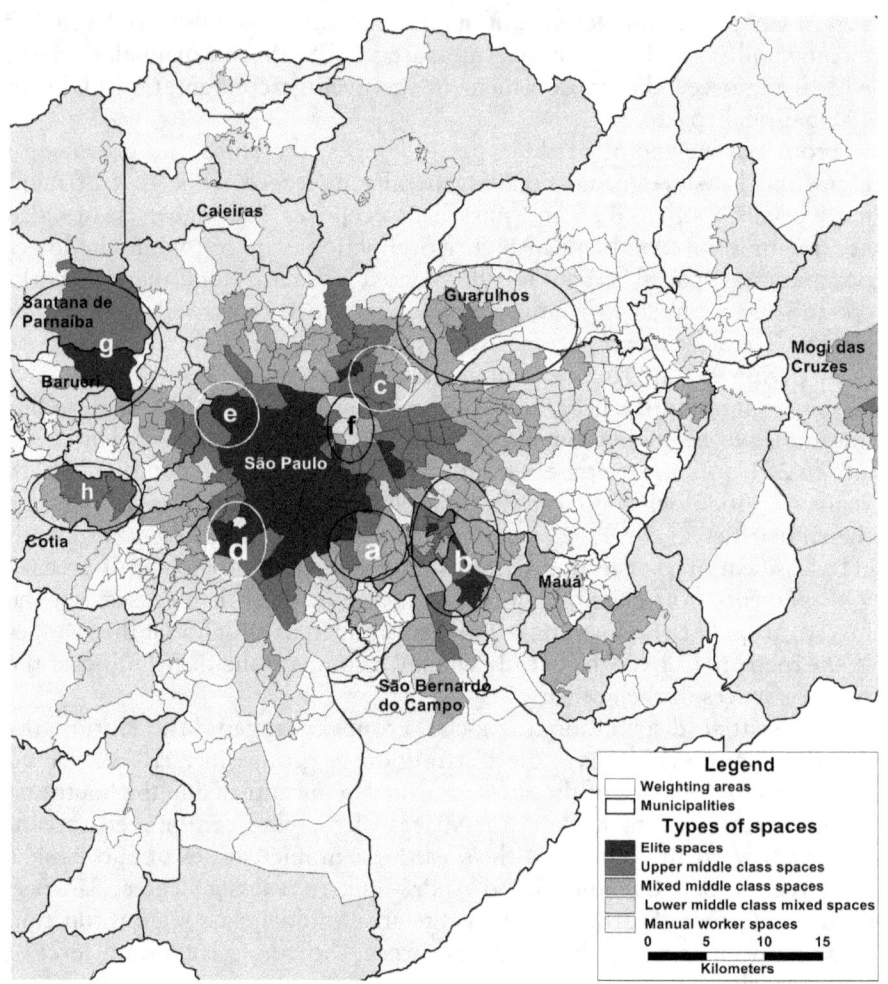

Figure 6.1 Distribution of groups, SPMR, 2010.
Source: CEM and author's calculations based on data from IBGE.

condominiums stands out, classified as upper-middle class in Santana do Parnaíba and elite spaces in Barueri as well as an area forming part of the municipality of Cotia.

The historical center appears as a predominantly mixed lower-middle class and manual worker space. Also as expected, the more peripheral regions correspond primarily to mixed lower-middle class and manual worker spaces, albeit with spatial discontinuities and a high presence of mixed middle-class spaces, especially toward the East Zone of São Paulo municipality.

The main trends of changes can be summarized as follows (and are marked in Figure 6.1):

a. Expansion of the Elite Patch of the Expanded Center

The elite central patch next to the center spread toward the southeast over areas formerly classified as upper-middle class (area marked "a") in the direction of the São Paulo ABC region. The same was found toward the west and southwest (region marked "d") and to the north and northwest of the elite patch (area marked "e" in Vila Leopoldina).

b. Popularization of the Historical Center

In the historical center, a larger quantity of areas presented mixed middle-class characteristics and now has a mixed, lower middle-class configuration, making it more popular than before (area marked as "f").

c. Closed Condominiums Accompanied by Continuing Peripheralization

In the west of the region, an area in Barueri shifted to an elite space, while others in this same municipality, as well as in Cotia and Santana do Parnaíba, became upper-middle class.

Other areas in the same region transformed in the opposite direction as they went from mixed upper-middle class to mixed middle class. In the far southwest of São Paulo municipality, various areas previously classified as mixed lower-middle class became manual, while others took the opposite path. In Guarulhos, various spaces became more popular, not very far from the increasingly elite areas already highlighted.

It is worth adding that closed condominiums are usually treated as a synonym of elite housing by the academic literature, when in fact, they present a fair degree of internal heterogeneity.[5] Exploring more closely, the two patches to the west indicated in Figure 6.1 as "g" and "h" include two different configurations of closed condominiums. The grouping further north represents a pioneering region of condominiums and generally shows more elite socioeconomic characteristics. The grouping to the south mainly includes condominiums whose original building style was based on a larger inclusion of green areas and lower levels of infrastructure and equipment.

However, each of these regions is also highly heterogeneous, including condominiums with distinct occupation and housing patterns. Figure 6.2 illustrates this point. In each sequence, as we move from left to right, we shift from housing developments with wide institutional spaces and large-scale plots with customized houses commissioned by the owners, built in the center of the plot (on the left), to clusters of semi-detached houses built in a standardized form by the developer.

Figure 6.2 Types of residences in the Western region.
Source: CEM, produced by Carolina Requena, taken from satellite images.

Summarizing, therefore, we can state that the decade was marked by the coexistence of processes of expansion of the wealthiest region of the city, impoverishment of its central areas, and elitization and peripheralization of peripheral areas, making the structure of the metropolis even more complex, despite the persistence of segregation.

Access to Services and Policies

Finally, here are a few remarks on how urban services have advanced in the São Paulo metropolis. On average for the metropolis as a whole, the recent dynamic has involved an expansion in access, at least in quantitative terms. As emphasized previously, the expansion in services and policies for poorer sections of the population over the last decades in Brazil has reintroduced inequalities in access and introduced diverse social inequities in terms of quality. However, the lack of systematic data on these dimensions limits our capacity to detect this phenomenon.

In quantitative terms, the water supply and waste collection services were already practically universal in 2000, with 95 percent of households covered in both areas, a figure that rose to 95 percent and 96 percent, respectively, in 2010. The urban service with the lowest access rates continued to be sewage treatment, although average coverage rose from around 77 percent in 2000 to 85 percent in 2010 but with considerable heterogeneity. It is worth stressing that these rates include not only connection to the sewage system but also (many) connections to the water drainage system with harmful effects on health and the environment. The lowest levels of coverage were concentrated in the areas inhabited by the poorest population: In the 47 areas with the worst indicators, for example, just 36 percent of households were covered on average.

However, while we compare types of spaces, coverages tend to decline as we move from the elite spaces to those of manual workers—from 99.8 to 90.1 percent in water, 98.7 to 90.6 percent for garbage and 98.9 to 85.7 percent in electrical supply, all for 2000. Generally, coverage has tended to improve over the course of the decade, especially in the spaces with a lower presence of services in 2000, though these still remained some distance from becoming universal. The lowest coverage was and remained sewage services and continues to present the largest levels of inequality between classes—varying from 98.5 to 60.5 percent in 2000 and between 98.8 and 74.8 percent in 2010. Qualitative studies, furthermore, suggest the presence of very important variation in the quality of the services for elite areas and peripheries. Unfortunately, the only indicator we have about quality is indirect and associated with households linked to the electricity grid, along with the use of mains meters. While coverage of the service varied little in 2010 (98.9 to 95.7 percent), the presence of metering clearly distinguished the different spaces (94.4 to 73.1 percent), showing the persistence of significant differences in service quality despite the overall expansion of services.

Summarizing Trends

It is fairly difficult to provide a single assessment of all these trends. Overall, São Paulo can be described as a fairly segregated city, especially in relation to the higher classes. The middle and lower classes are much less segregated and tend to coinhabit the same spaces more frequently. The overall structure of segregation, however, indicates a clear hierarchy between groups, pointing to a pattern that we can call social avoidance on the part of the higher classes. This structure changed little over the decade, both in terms of segregation indicators and in the spatial distribution of income and social classes.

This stability is reinforced by the overall analysis of the types of social spaces. However, a detailed analysis of the composition of these types, as well as their spatial distribution, points to important transformations. The types of spaces of the metropolis indicate more exclusive higher occupational class spaces in 2010, at the same time that manual and popular spaces became less associated with industrial workers and more mixed by the end of the decade. The higher-class spaces, therefore, became even more homogenous, while the other spaces of the metropolis, including the peripheries, remained more heterogenic.

Spatialization of the information confirms this analysis and shows how diverse trends coexisted in territorial terms over the decade. While the data showed an expansion of the wealthiest region of the expanded center (which tended to become even more elite in profile), areas of the old center became more popular. In the sprawling peripheries of the metropolis, we were able to observe both processes of elitization (linked to condominiums, increasingly heterogeneous, but not only to them) and the continuity of classic trends toward peripheralization, making the structure of the metropolis more heterogenic over the decade, with more diversified peripheries, albeit with a more exclusive elite core and larger territorial dimensions.

Finally, in terms of access to basic urban services, an improvement was observed in average indicators, with the exception of sewage services, which remained much scarcer. On the other hand, there are strong signs of persisting inequalities, especially in terms of quality.

Notes

1. Since there is no geographical identification available for the sample data from the 1991 census, generating the same information for that year is impossible.
2. It should be added that the Moran Indexes and Dissimilarity Indexes reported here referring to 2000 are slightly different from those presented in Marques et al. (2012) due to the geographical scale used to analyze the segregation. In the case of this earlier study, the indicators were produced on the basis of weighting areas for the year 2000, compatibilized with 1991, covering 814 areas in total. In the case of this chapter, we used the year 2000 as a basis, compatibilized with 2010. On the methodological effect of the scale of areas on segregation measures, see Sabatini (2004).
3. To provide a scale of comparison for the Dissimilarity Index, it is worth noting that the highest Dissimilarity Index between different linguistic groups in Paris in 1999 was observed between native French speakers and Turkish immigrants: 0.47. The vast majority of other indexes between ethnic groups did not exceed 0.4 (Preteceille 2006). In Hong Kong in 2006, the Dissimilarity Index between the richest and poorest deciles was 0.57 (YIP 2012). In Athens in 2001, the Dissimilarity Index between high-level professionals and routine manual jobs was 0.40 (Maloutas 2007).
4. These results confirm the findings for various cities reported by Maloutas (2012) as well as the comparative analysis of Rio de Janeiro and Paris produced by Preteceille and Cardoso (2008). Despite segregation being higher in Rio de Janeiro than in Paris for all categories, it is higher for the higher occupational classes in both cities. The same kind of result was found in relation to Santiago in Chile by Sabatine et al. (2008). This argument had already been advanced vis-à-vis Brazilian cities by Villaça (2000), analyzing spatial patterns in thematic maps up to 1991.
5. For more details, see Marques, Requena and Hoyler (2016).

Bibliography

Andersen, H. (2012). The solidity of urban socio-spatial structures in Copenhagen. In: Maloutas, T. and Fugita, K. (eds.) *Residential segregation in comparative perspective*. London: Ashgate, pp. 177–196.
Anselin, L. (1995). Local Indicator of Spatial Association—LISA. *Geographical Analysis*, 27(2), pp. 93–115.
Baeninger, R. (2012). Crescimento da população na região metropolitana de São Paulo: desconstruindo mitos do século XX. In: Kowarick, L. and Marques, E. (eds.) *São Paulo: novos percursos e atores: sociedade, cultura e política*. São Paulo: Ed. 34/CEM, pp. 53–78.
Barbosa, R. and Marschner, M. (2013). *Uma proposta de padronização de classificações em pesquisas do IBGE Censos 1960–2010 e PNADs 1981–2011: educação, setores de atividade econômica e ocupação ISCO-88, EGP11 e ISEI*. Working paper. São Paulo: CEM, Mimeo.
Baum, S. (1999). Social transformations in the global city: Singapore. *Urban Studies*, 36(7), pp. 1095–1117.
Bonduki, N. (1991). Depoimento. *Espaço e Debates*, 42, pp. 1–12.
Bonduki, N. and Rolnik, R. (1982). Periferia da Grande São Paulo: reprodução do espaço como expediente de reprodução da força de trabalho. In: Maricato, E. (ed.) *A Produção Capitalista da Casa e da cidade do Brasil*. São Paulo: Alfaômega, pp. 117–154.
Butler, T. (1997). *Gentrification and the middle-classes*. London: Ashgate.
Caldeira, T. (2000). *Cidade dos muros*. São Paulo: Editora 34.
Camargo, C. (1976). *São Paulo, 1975—Crescimento e pobreza*. São Paulo: Ed. Loyola.
Carvalho, I., Souza, Â. and Pereira, G. (2004). Polarização e Segregação Socioespacial em uma Metrópole Periférica. *Cadernos CRH*, 17(41), pp. 281–297.
CEM. (2004). *Mapa da Vulnerabilidade Social da População da Cidade de São Paulo*. São Paulo: CEM/Cebrap, SAS/PMSP.
Centeno, P. (2009). *Lima, diversidade y fragmentación de uma metrópoles emergente*. Quito: Olacchi.
Dominguez, M., Leal, J. and Goyter, E. (2012). The limits of segregation as an expression of socioeconomic inequality: The Madrid case. In: Maloutas, T. and Fugita, K. (eds.) *Residential segregation in comparative perspective*. London: Ashgate, pp. 217–236.
Duncan, O. and Duncan, B. (1955). A methodological analysis of segregation indexes. *American Sociological Review*, 20(2), pp. 210–217.
Dureau, F. and Vanegas, A. (2009). Las diferentes expresiones del proceso de segregacion en Bogotá. In: Jaramillo, S. (ed.) *Bogotá em el cambio de siglo: promesas y realidades*. Quito: Olacchi, pp. 195–220.
Durham, E. (1988). A sociedade vista da periferia In: Kowarick, L. (ed.) *As Lutas Sociais e a Cidade*. Rio de Janeiro: Paz e Terra, pp. 169–192.
Fainstein, S. (2008). Mega-projects in New York, London and Amsterdam. *International Journal of Urban and Regional Research*, 32(4), pp. 768–785.
Faria, V. (1992). A conjuntura social brasileira: Dilemas e perspectivas. *Novos Estudos Cebrap*, 33, pp. 103–114.
Feltran, G. (2011). *Fronteiras de tensão*. São Paulo: Ed. Unesp/CEM.
Figueiredo, A., Torres, H. and Bichir, R. (2006). A conjuntura social brasileira revistada. *Novos Estudos Cebrap*, 75, pp. 173–184.

Fujita, K. and Hill, R. (2012). Residential income inequality in Tokyo and why it does not translate in class-based inequality. In: Maloutas, T. and Fugita, K. (eds.) *Residential segregation in comparative perspective*. London: Ashgate, pp. 37–68.

Hamnett, C. (1996a). Why Sassen is wrong: A response to Burgers. *Urban Studies*, 33(1), pp. 107–110.

Hamnett, C. (1996b). Social polarization, economic restructuring and welfare state regimes. *Urban Studies*, 338, pp. 1407–1430.

Hamnett, C. (1994). Social polarization in global cities: Theory and evidence. *Urban Studies*, 31(3), pp. 401–424.

Knox, P. and Taylor, P. (1995). *World cities in a world-system*. Cambridge: Cambridge University Press.

Kovacs, Z. (2012). Residential segregation in Budapest before and after transition. In: Maloutas, T and Fugita, K. (eds.) *Residential segregation in comparative perspective*. London: Ashgate, pp. 197–216.

Kowarick, L. (1979). *A Espoliação Urbana*. Rio de Janeiro: Paz e Terra.

Leborgne, D. and Lipietz, A. (1990). Flexibilização defensiva ou flexibilização ofensiva. In: Valladares, L. and Preteceille, E. (eds.) *Reestruturação urbana: tendências e desafios*. Rio de Janeiro: Nobel/Iuperj, pp. 17–43.

Lehto, J. (2000). Different cities in different welfare states. In: Bagnasco, A. and Le Galés, P. (eds.) *Cities in contemporary Europe*. Cambridge: Cambridge University Press, pp. 112–130.

Maloutas, T. (2012). Introduction: Residential segregation in context. In: Maloutas, T. and Fugita, K. (eds.) *Residential segregation in comparative perspective*. London: Ashgate, pp. 1–36.

Maloutas, T. (2007). Segregation, social polarization and immigration in Athens during the 1990's: Theoretical expectations and contextual difference. *International Journal of Urban and Regional Research*, 31(4), pp. 733–758.

Maricato, E. (2003). Metrópole, legislação e desigualdade. *Estudos Avançados*, 17(48), pp. 151–167.

Marques, E. and Bichir, R. (2003). Public policies, political cleavages and urban space: State infrastructure policies in São Paulo, Brazil—1975–2000. *International Journal of Urban and Regional Research*, 27(4), pp. 811–827.

Marques, E. and Torres, H. (2005). *São Paulo: segregação, pobreza e desigualdades sociais*. São Paulo: Editora SENAC.

Marques, E., Bichir, R. and Scalon, C. (2012). Residential segregation and social structure in São Paulo: Continuity and change since the 1990s. In: Maloutas, T. and Fujita, K. (eds.) *Residential segregation around the world: Why context matters*. London: Ashgate, pp. 135–152.

Marques, E., Requena, C. and Hoyler, T. (2016). Estrutura social, segregação e espaços em São Paulo. In: Kowarick, L. and Frugoli, H. (eds.) *Pluralidade urbana em São Paulo*. São Paulo: Ed. 34, pp. 215–247.

Musterd, S. and Murie, A. (2002). *The spatial dimensions of urban social exclusion and integration*. Amsterdam. Available at: www.frw.uva.nl/ame/urbex

Park, R., Burgess, E. and Mackenzie, R. (1925). *The city*. Chicago: Chicago University Press.

Píres, P. (2009). *Buenos Aires, la formación del presente*. Quito: Olachi.

Preteceille, E. (2006). La ségrégation sociale a-t-elle augmenté? La métropole parisienne entre polarization et mixité. *Societé Contemporaines*, 62(2), pp. 69–93.

Preteceille, E. (1995). Division sociale de l'espace et globalization. *Societé Contemporaines*, 22–23, pp. 33–67.

Preteceille, E. and Cardoso, A. (2008). Rio de Janeiro y São Paulo: ciudades duales? Comparación con Paris. *Ciudad y Território: Estudios Territoriales*, XL(158), pp. 617–640.

Ribeiro, L. and Preteceille, E. (1999). Tendências da Segregação Social em Metrópoles Globais e Desiguais: Paris e Rio de Janeiro nos Anos 80. *Revista Brasileira de Ciências Sociais*, 14(40), pp. 143–162.

Sabatine, F., Wormald, G., Sierralta, C. and Peters, P. (2008). La segregación residencial en Santiago: Tendencias 1992–2002 y efectos vinculado con su escala geografica. In: Sabatini, F., Salcedo, R., Wormald, G. and Gáceres, G. (eds.) *Tendências de la segregación en las principales ciudades chilenas*. Santiago: INE, pp. 19–41.

Sabatini, F. (2004). Medición de la segregación residencial: reflexiones metodológicas desde la ciudad latino-americana. In: Cáceres, G. and Sabatini, F. (eds.) *Barrios cerrados em Santiago de Chile: entre la exclusión y la integración residencial*. Santiago: PUC/Lincoln Institute, pp. 278–307.

Santos, C. and Bronstein, O. (1978). Meta-urbanização—o caso do Rio de Janeiro. *Revista de Administração Municipal*, 25, pp. 6–34.

Sassen, S. (1991). *The global city: New York, London and Tokyo*. Princeton: Princeton University Press.

Taschner, S. and Bógus, L. (2000). A cidade dos anéis: São Paulo. In: Queiroz, L. C. (ed.) *O futuro das metrópoles: desigualdades e governabilidade*. Rio de Janeiro: Revan/Fase, pp. 87–99.

Taschner, S. and Bógus, L. (1998). Continuidades e descontinuidades na cidade dos anéis. In: Patarra, N. (ed.) *Migração, Condições de vida e Dinâmica Urbana 1980–93*. Campinas: Ed. Unicamp/Fapesp, pp. 148–168.

Torres, H. (2005). Medindo a segregação. In: Marques, E. and Torres, H. (eds.) *São Paulo: segregação, pobreza e desigualdades sociais*. São Paulo: Ed. SENAC, pp. 81–100.

Vaattovaara, M. and Kortteinen, M. (2003). Beyond polarization versus professionalization? A case study of the development of the Hensinki region, Finland. *Urban Studies*, 40(11), pp. 2127–2145.

Valladares, L. and Preteceille, E. (2000). Favela, favelas: unidade ou diversidade da favela carioca. In: Queiroz, L. (ed.) *O futuro das metrópoles: desigualdades e governabilidade*. Rio de Janeiro: Observatório/Ed. Revan, pp. 375–406.

Vetter, D., Massena, R. and Rodrigues, E. (1979). Espaço, valor da terra e equidade dos investimentos em infra-estrutura no Município do Rio de Janeiro. *Revista Brasileira de Geografia*, 41(1–2), pp. 79–92.

Villaça, F. (2000). *Espaço intra-urbano no Brasil*. São Paulo: Ed. Nobel.

Wessel, T. (2000). Social polarization and socioeconomic segregation in a welfare state: The case of Oslo. *Urban Studies*, 37(11), pp. 1947–1967.

Yip, N. (2012). Residential segregation in an unequal city: Why are there no urban ghettos in Hong Kong? In: Maloutas, T. and Fujita, K. (eds.) *Residential segregation around the world: Why context matters*. London: Ashgate, pp. 179–194.

7 Inequalities and Residential Segregation by Race and Class

Danilo França

Introduction

In this chapter I present a general outline of racial inequalities and residential segregation by race and class in the SPMR between 2000 and 2010. On the latter topic, I highlight the differentials found in the residential patterns of black and white populations belonging to similar social classes, giving greater emphasis to the middle and upper classes. Its objectives are to present the interconnections between race and social class as an important dimension in the study of residential segregation in Brazil and to ascertain how segregation patterns are related to the profile of racial inequalities.

Traditionally, the study of residential segregation in Brazilian cities has been guided by the debate on the polarization between a wealthy center and a poor periphery. Urban studies placed greater emphasis on the processes of segregating poor people and migrants on the peripheries, metropolitan areas far from the center and lacking infrastructure, and the consequences of this segregation for the reproduction of social inequalities in the city. More recently, the increased availability of data and the use of new measuring and analytic techniques led to a fresh discussion of the center-periphery model, highlighting the social heterogeneity of urban space. The presence of upper classes was identified in "fortified enclaves" located far from the center, while favelas and pockets of poverty were found in wealthy areas. In peripheral areas, once thought to be homogenously poor, considerable social diversification was identified as well as improvements in the urban infrastructure and greater access to the services offered by the state in many localities (see Caldeira 2000, Bichir 2006, Marques & Torres 2005).

However, even with the substantial methodological advances that have allowed previously underexplored dimensions of residential segregation to be revealed, it is usually proclaimed that housing patterns in Brazilian metropolises are basically—if not entirely—organized through inequalities in social class.

The academic literature exploring the connections between race and urban space in Brazil is fairly sparse. A group of qualitative studies has focused on symbolic aspects and identity issues, researching favelas and peripheral districts and making use of notions such as "black territories" or "racialized spaces." Appeal is made to these ideas as part of the argument that areas with a high concentration of black people are less problematic in terms of sociability for the population concerned. Moreover, the stigmas attributed to this population are also associated with the representations of particular spaces of the city, which can acquire new meanings in the form of identity discourses (e.g. Carril 2003, Oliveira 1996, Rolnik 1989, Silva 2004, Vargas 2005).

The other set of research comprises quantitative studies that examine the question of segregation based on skin color through the analysis of census data. This type of analysis is already present in some of the classic works on the sociology of race relations in Brazil, such as Donald Pierson's (1971 [1942]) analysis of Salvador, Fernando Henrique Cardoso and Octávio Ianni's (1960) investigations of Florianópolis, and the study by Costa Pinto (1998 [1953]) on the black population of Rio de Janeiro. However, these authors suggested that race was not an important factor in segregation, which they considered to be conditioned strongly by social class instead. Since then segregation has been a question little explored in this field of studies.

The research on segregation along racial lines only acquired some degree of attention decades later with the work of US sociologist Edward Telles (1993, 1995, 1996 and 2012 [2004]), who introduced this discussion into the broader framework of Brazilian race relations and presented evidence that racial segregation was more strongly expressed in the higher social classes.

In Telles's studies, this theme was explored more systematically by census data from 1980 to develop synthetic indicators, looking to measure the phenomenon in 35 Brazilian metropolitan regions. The author applied the kinds of segregation indices (indices of dissimilarity, exposure and isolation) widely used in US studies but that had never been employed in Brazil. These revealed moderate levels of segregation—when compared to the US—that became more acute in the higher income bands.

After publication of Telles's research, quantitative analyses were carried out using segregation indices and other forms of measurement on residential segregation by race, based on data from the 2000 census, in more specific contexts like the cities of Salvador (Carvalho & Barreto 2007, Garcia 2006), Belo Horizonte (Costa & Ribeiro 2004, Rios Neto 2005), Rio de Janeiro (Garcia 2006, Préteceille & Cardoso 2008, Ribeiro 2007) and São Paulo (Préteceille & Cardoso 2008, Torres 2005).

In earlier research on race, class and residential segregation in São Paulo municipality (França 2010), I used the database from the 2000 census sample and applied a variety of segregation measurement techniques. Among the results, we can highlight the finding that the degree of racial segregation—initially very low among the low-income groups—tends to increase when we examine the residential patterns of the black and white populations in higher social classes. To this we can add that for the higher household income bands, the concentration of black people in peripheral areas is much higher than of white people, while the proportion of higher-income white people in elite areas is much higher than for blacks. Finally, I also showed that the white population, even among the lower classes, is more strongly represented, comparatively speaking, in wealthier areas of the city than the black population.

However, in the period from 2000 to today, Brazil has experienced important socioeconomic transformations, including a reduction in inequality and the growth of the middle classes. In city areas, there has also been a strong warming of the real estate market and the construction sector. These circumstances may generate a variety of impacts on social classes and racial groups as well as on the residential segregation patterns of such groups. In this context, the availability of more recent census data, collected in 2010, offers an important opportunity for us to empirically assess the actual amplitude of these transformations in the SPMR.

Working toward this aim, I shall be guided by the following questions: How have the social transformations experienced by the country over the last decade impacted on the inequalities between black and white people in the SPMR? To what extent are these inequalities reflected in patterns of residential segregation by race and class? Were there alterations to these patterns in the period under consideration? These questions serve as a starting point for demonstrating the relevance of an approach that incorporates the race variable in the analysis of residential segregation in Brazilian cities.

In the next section I describe racial inequalities in education, income and occupation based on data from the 2000 and 2010 censuses. Next I measure residential segregation between black and white people ranked in sociooccupational groups.

Racial Inequalities in the São Paulo Metropolitan Region

One key factor for describing race relations in a given social context is the population's racial composition. Historically, Brazilian censuses have shown diverse changes in the population's racial composition through the use of the "race/color" variable. More recently, a decline has been observed in the proportion of people declaring themselves white (*branco*), with a growth in black (*negro*) and brown (*pardo*).

The population of the SPMR has risen from 17.9 to 19.7 million inhabitants, or around 10 percent, from 2000 to the present. Over this period there has been both an absolute and relative decline in the white population (from 65.5 to 58.7 percent) and a substantial increase in the black (from 4.9 to 6.3 percent) and brown (from 27 to 33 percent) populations. Hence, the white population continues to be a majority, though their number fell by 1.4 percent, while the brown population grew 34 percent and black 42 percent in relative terms.

These transformations largely stem from miscegenation and demographic trends such as migration, fertility and mortality rates. Nonetheless, racial reclassification—individuals changing their race/color declaration over the course of their lifetime—has become increasingly relevant in the contemporary context due to the intense mobilization of identities and the implementation of public policies with a racial dimension.

In terms of the educational advances of the Brazilian population, we can note substantial evolutions at the beginning of the 21st century: Primary education (almost) became universalized, while there was significant growth in secondary education and a notable improvement in overall access to higher education. These educational advances have been clearly observable in the SPMR population too.

In relation to the education level of individuals over the age of 25 (an age when most individuals have already completed their educational cycles and have joined the labor market, making use of their qualifications), important increases were observed over the period in terms of the population's educational levels, including substantial growth in the groups of people completing secondary and higher education. However, almost half of the black and brown population still has educational levels below complete primary level. For these groups, the main advance in terms of education over the period was the increase in the proportion of individuals with a secondary school certificate: from around 15 percent in 2000 to 25 to 30 percent in 2010. Possession of university diplomas increased among all groups, though the white population still monopolized access to these opportunities: Almost 86 percent of individuals with higher education are white. In sum, despite the general improvement in education, racial inequalities remain strong in this area: 52.6 percent of whites have at least secondary education, while 79.9 percent of blacks were unable to complete primary education. These education inequalities should be reflected in income inequalities. Table 7.1 allows us to evaluate how far this in fact occurs.

Table 7.1 displays the averages for the monthly income earned from the primary work of the employed white, brown and black populations over the age of 25. In 2000, the value of the income for the black and brown populations was very close and represented a little less than half the amount earned by the white population. This situation altered little in 2010. Furthermore, we can observe that income inequalities are lower in the two categories, with less schooling and stronger in those categories with more schooling. In other words, in concordance with the recent literature on racial inequalities (e.g., see Ribeiro 2006), we can note that these become more pronounced at the top of the social hierarchy, contradicting earlier expectations that access to education would lead to more equality between the black[1] and white populations.

Hence, despite advances in education in the decade 2000 to 2010, income inequality between blacks and whites remains practically identical. The only educational level where a small decline in racial inequality could be observed was among those completing secondary education, a group that saw a large

Table 7.1 Racial inequalities in income[1] by educational level, SPMR, 2000 and 2010.

Educational Level	Race / Color	2000		2010	
		Average Income	Difference[2]	Average Income	Difference[2]
No schooling and incomplete primary level	White	1,087		1,149	
	Brown	865	−20.4%	863	−24.9%
	Black	830	−23.7%	872	−24.2%
	Total	982		999	
Complete primary and incomplete secondary level	White	1,557		1,434	
	Brown	1,121	−28.0%	1,014	−29.2%
	Black	1,098	−29.5%	1,084	−24.4%
	Total	1,405		1,251	
Complete secondary and incomplete higher level	White	2,591		1,873	
	Brown	1,551	−40.1%	1,207	−35.6%
	Black	1,521	−41.3%	1,233	−34.2%
	Total	2,349		1,623	
Complete higher level	White	5,678		4,852	
	Brown	3,251	−42.7%	2,700	−44.4%
	Black	3,093	−45.5%	2,560	−47.2%
	Total	5,485		4,529	
Total	White	2,564		2,525	
	Brown	1,135	−55.7%	1,142	−54.8%
	Black	1,174	−54.2%	1,207	−52.2%
	Total	2,113		1,997	

1 Monthly income from main work, in Reais (R$), 2010.
2 Percentage difference in relation to white population.
Source: IBGE 2000 and 2010 censuses.

increase among black and brown residents. However, the income value of educational qualifications fell substantially during the period, losing 31 percent (average income dropped from R$2,349 to R$1,623). In other words, while the black and brown populations became better qualified, obtaining more secondary school certificates, and these qualifications lessened their income gap in relation to whites, the devalorization of the diploma meant that the financial gains for this section of the black population were slight.

As Comin and Barbosa (2011) have already shown, the average income of those completing university has also been falling. In the case of the SPMR, the higher education diploma fell 17.4 percent in value in the decade under analysis. Moreover, as we have seen, the white population still monopolizes most higher education diplomas, while racial inequalities in income for university-trained workers worsened slightly.

However, the connection between educational qualifications and a return in revenue is mediated through employment positions in the labor market. Next, therefore, I evaluate the changes in the distribution of the population by EGP occupational categories, a classification system internationally used in comparative studies (Barbosa & Marschner 2013, Erikson et al. 1979).

Comparing the distributions of the black and white populations by occupational category, we can observe some clear differences. The black population shows a higher concentration in lower categories, principally among manual workers (60.7 percent in 2000 and 55.9 percent in 2010), while the white population is better distributed across the different categories of the socio-occupational hierarchy. In 2010, the employed white population was almost equally divided into three parts: employers and professionals (32.8 percent), technicians and nonmanual workers (34.1 percent) and manual workers (33.1 percent).

Over the decade, the proportion of manual workers decreased, and the proportion of high-level professionals increased for both the white and black groups. An increase was also observed in the proportion of black people in all categories, matching their increased participation in the employed population. Though still concentrated more in manual worker categories, the black population showed growth in middle categories—such as high-level, routine, nonmanual workers (a 35 percent increase)—and high categories like high-level professionals (a 60.5 percent increase).

In sum, the evidence presented here shows us that recent improvements in educational coverage have enabled advances for the black and brown populations, principally in terms of their completion of secondary schooling. It is very likely that this increase in the proportion of black people with completed primary education is related to their increased representation in middle-level occupations such as technicians, supervisors and high-level, routine, nonmanual work. The growth trend in high-level professional occupations also clearly benefitted the black population. However, these evolutions were still insufficient to reverse the predominance of black people in manual occupations or reduce the income inequality between blacks and whites, which—in the context of "wage losses," especially for those with secondary and higher education diplomas—remains the same.

Residential Segregation Between Black and White Populations in the São Paulo Metropolitan Region

According to Maloutas (2012), inequalities and discrimination (based on the labor market, wealth accumulation and ethnic-racial hierarchies) are an important causal factor in the process of housing allocation, which in turn, results in residential segregation. Given the pattern of inequalities described in the previous section, I evaluate the transformations in residential segregation by race between 2000 and 2010.[2] In this section I present the measurement of segregation through two techniques: the Dissimilarity Index and LISA (Local Indicator of Spatial Autocorrelation) Maps.

The Dissimilarity Index is a traditional measure of residential segregation that captures the degree to which two social groups are unevenly distributed within a city's space. Evenness is defined, therefore, by the proportion of each group in the composition of the city's total population and the extent to which the distribution of these groups in the different areas of the city replicates this composition. In other words, the indicator shows the relation between the composition of the population in each spatial unit and the composition of the population of the city as a whole.[3] The Dissimilarity Index ranges from 0 to 1, where 1 signifies complete segregation and 0 complete uniformity in terms of the distribution of the groups.

The Dissimilarity Index between the black and white populations was 0.27 in 2000 and increased to 0.29 in 2010, showing the persistence of racial segregation in the SPMR. This Dissimilarity Index is usually interpreted as an indication of the proportion of the population of a particular group within the city that would have to move to another area to obtain an even residential pattern from the viewpoint of the proportion of each group in the city's overall demographic composition. Hence, in 2000, 27 percent of the population would have had to move from one weighting area to another for the distribution of racial groups to be evened out, while in 2010 this proportion rose to 29 percent.[4] Since they are below 0.30, these indices can be considered moderate compared to US patterns—the country with the biggest tradition in applying these measures.

Very often, this indicator of segregation between black and white populations is interpreted as an effect of residential segregation by social class (very well described by Eduardo Marques in Chapter 6 of this volume) since most of the black population is poor and the upper socioeconomic classes are predominantly white. However, here I shall try to highlight the racial component of segregation. As a first step in the analysis, therefore, the SPMR population is classified, as proposed by Marques, Barbosa and Prates (in Chapter 2), into social strata based on EGP occupational class categories.[5] In the upper stratum are the owners, employers and high-level professionals; the middle stratum is composed of low-level professionals, technicians and manual work supervisors, and high-level, routine, nonmanual workers; the lower stratum includes low-level, routine, nonmanual workers, skilled manual workers and semi-skilled or unskilled manual workers. Combining these three strata with black and white racial groups results in six groupings, the segregation indices for which are shown in Table 7.2.

In Table 7.2 we can observe that the groups most segregated from the rest of the metropolitan population are higher occupational level whites with indices well above the next-highest groups, lower-level blacks and middle-level whites. The other groups—low-level whites, and middle- and upper-level blacks—are more evenly distributed across the metropolitan region's spaces.

Table 7.2 Dissimilarity Index between racial group and socio-occupational strata in the SPMR, 2000 and 2010.

	2000					
Groups	White Upper	Black Upper	White Middle	Black Middle	White Lower	Black Lower
Rest of the population	0.44	0.15	0.22	0.17	0.11	0.28
White upper	–	0.39	0.26	0.52	0.45	0.58
Black upper	0.39	–	0.20	0.19	0.19	0.27
White middle	0.26	0.20	–	0.30	0.23	0.38
Black middle	0.52	0.19	0.30	–	0.14	0.13
White lower	0.45	0.19	0.23	0.14	–	0.18
Black lower	0.58	0.27	0.38	0.13	0.18	–
	2010					
Groups	White Upper	Black Upper	White Middle	Black Middle	White Lower	Black Lower
Rest of the population	0.47	0.15	0.25	0.15	0.12	0.30
White upper	–	0.40	0.26	0.53	0.48	0.61
Black upper	0.40	–	0.20	0.19	0.19	0.29
White middle	0.26	0.20	–	0.31	0.26	0.41
Black middle	0.53	0.19	0.31	–	0.13	0.15
White lower	0.48	0.19	0.26	0.13	–	0.18
Black lower	0.61	0.29	0.41	0.15	0.18	–

Source: IBGE 2000 and 2010 censuses, author's elaboration.

The wealthiest whites present the highest level of isolation in the metropolis, separating themselves spatially from all the other groups. The group closest to them consists of middle-class whites (0.23 in 2000 and 0.26 in 2010). The next-closest group, already displaying a relatively high Dissimilarity Index (0.37 in 2000 and 0.39 in 2010), are higher-level blacks. On the other hand, if we evaluate the segregation indices of the higher-level black population (the second column of Table 7.2), the group that shares the same areas least with them are the higher-level whites. This data thus demonstrates the degree of isolation of the white elite in the São Paulo metropolis.

At the other end of the occupation hierarchy, the most segregated group is the poorest blacks. Comparison with the poorest whites reveals that the latter are more evenly distributed across the city's areas and closer to the middle and upper layers, while the lower-level black population tends to be more heavily concentrated in specific areas.

In the decade being analyzed, a tendency toward increased segregation can be noted among higher- and middle-level whites in relation to the rest of São Paulo's population (from 0.44 to 0.47 and 0.22 to 0.25, respectively) but mainly in relation to lower-level blacks and whites. The Dissimilarity Index between higher-level whites and lower-level blacks rose to 0.61 in 2010 (a value common in hyper-segregated US metropolises). Meanwhile, the higher-level black population became increasingly separated both from higher-level whites (from 0.39 to 0.40) and lower-level blacks (from 0.27 to 0.29).

These Dissimilarity Index results demonstrate that, beside the well-documented segregation between social classes in urban space, there is also an observable racial component to segregation. This becomes clearer when we compare the indicators for black and white workers from the same social level. The Dissimilarity Index revealed a greater racial proximity in the lower occupational classes compared to the middle and upper classes, especially in terms of the striking isolation of the upper-level white population.

Synthetic indicators like the Dissimilarity Index give us some idea of the total amount of segregation yet reveal little about where each of the groups is concentrated. To fill this gap, I present a segregation analysis based on the Moran Index (Anselin 1995) just for 2010, focusing on the occupational categories of professionals (high and low levels). The Moran Index is a measure of spatial autocorrelation; that is, as well as the distribution of groups by area, the measure takes into account the contiguity of the areas in which the different groups are located.[6] In other words, it shows the extent to which the groups under consideration are concentrated in sets of mutually adjacent areas.

This can be seen in detail via the use of LISA Maps (see Figure 7.1). These maps represent the spatial autocorrelation of the groups under analysis here. The darker areas denote a high concentration of the variable in question in neighboring areas. The light grey areas express the contiguity of areas with a low concentration of this variable. Areas in white have no statistically significant result.

A large agglomeration of areas with a concentration of white professionals is found in São Paulo's expanded center. Many areas from this large central cluster of white professionals are characterized by the low concentration of black professionals. The latter, meanwhile, show a greater diversification in the sets of spaces where they are concentrated and a stronger presence in various areas considered "consolidated peripheries" and in some parts of the old center of São Paulo city. In other words, black professionals are more highly dispersed across the space of the metropolis and little present in the expanded center. Indeed, a high concentration of both black and white professionals is found in just 11 of the 633 weighting areas from the SPMR.

In relation to the socioeconomic characteristics of the areas where the groups being analyzed are concentrated, the classification of the SPMR spaces developed by Eduardo Marques (Chapter 6 of this book) provides us with additional important information. Analyzing the distribution of the groups within these five types of spaces—(1) elite spaces, (2) upper middle-class spaces, (3) mixed middle-class spaces, (4) lower, mixed middle-class spaces and (5) manual worker spaces—a greater concentration of whites in upper areas and blacks in lower areas becomes evident, irrespective of social class.

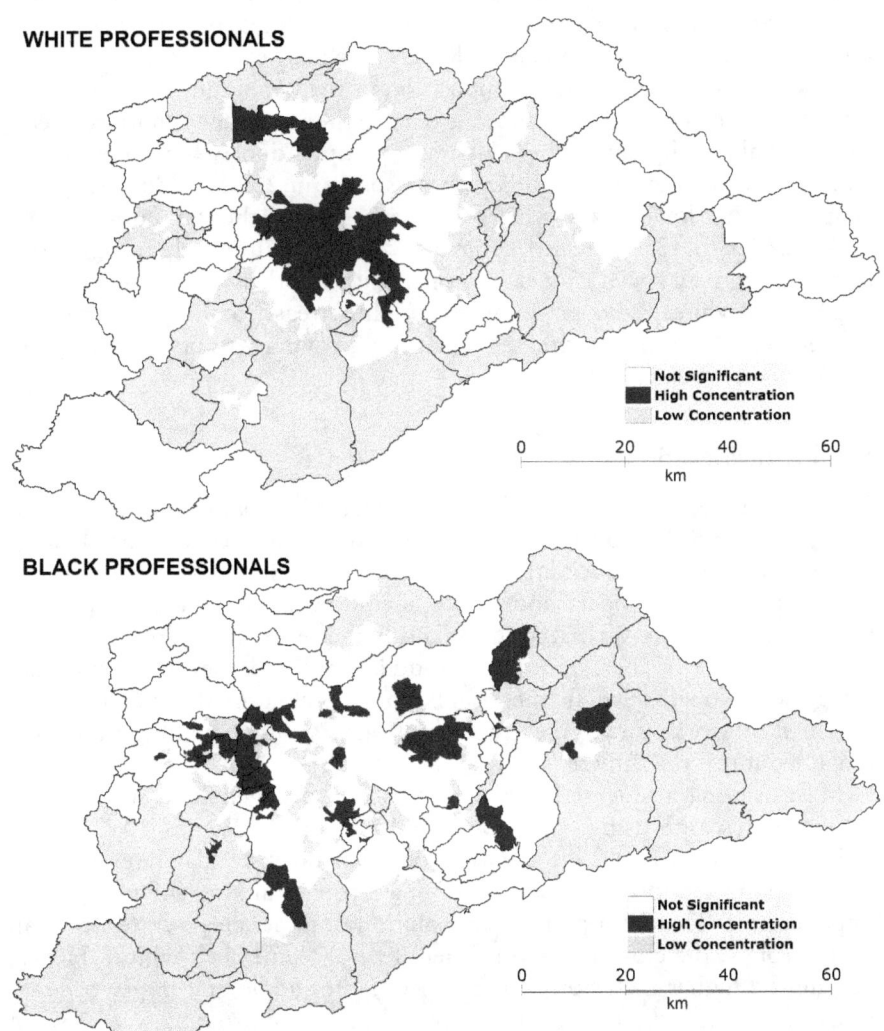

Figure 7.1 LISA Maps of the concentration of social groups, 2010.
Source: Calculations by the author from IBGE data.

Whites from the upper stratum continue to have a higher concentration in elite or upper middle-class spaces (around 53 percent in 2000 and 2010). More than half of upper-class blacks (about 54 percent for both years) resided in Type 4 spaces (mixed, middle lower-class spaces) and Type 5 (manual worker spaces).

Assessing just the lower classes during this period, we can note a growth of black and white groups in manual worker spaces. These types of spaces, along with the middle lower-class mixed spaces, are occupied by the absolute majority of lower classes but especially the black population in the lower occupational class: 65.6 percent of lower class whites live in Type 4 or 5 areas, compared to 79.1 percent of lower-class blacks.

Specifically in terms of the composition of the population of elite spaces (Type 1), we can note that during the decade they became even more exclusively inhabited by the higher-class white population, which represented 45.5 percent of the population of these spaces in 2010. Additionally, the proportion of lower-class whites in these spaces, though falling (from 17.7 percent to 13.7 percent), is greater than the sum of the proportions of blacks from all social classes (10.4 percent). In other words, middle- and upper-class whites, who predominate in elite areas (totaling 72.3 percent of their population), have greater residential proximity to poor whites than blacks of any social class.

Final Considerations

This chapter has shown some of the racial features in patterns of residential segregation in SPMR during the first 10 years of the 21st century. During this period, significant social transformations took place in relation to racial inequalities between blacks and whites, including an increase in the proportion of black people with secondary and higher education diplomas and a larger inclusion of these groups in middle- and higher-level occupational categories. Nonetheless, in the context of a decline in the income levels obtained by workers with these qualifications, racial inequalities in income remained much the same.

In this setting, residential segregation by race changed little. As observed by earlier research using data from the 2000 census (França 2010, Préteceille & Cardoso 2008), segregation between blacks and whites remains slight among the lower classes, becoming stronger among the middle and upper classes. There is a permanent isolation of upper-class whites from all other groups, the closest group to them being middle-class whites. Hence, despite the higher inclusion of black people in middle and upper occupational categories, there is no increased residential approximation between these groups and white people from the same social levels nor any increase in their residence in spaces associated with higher socioeconomic groups.

Given the stability of the residential segregation observed in the data described in this chapter, the most salient aspect is the large separation of middle- and upper-class whites from all other groups, which remain closer to each other. These are the main elements of the singular pattern of segregation by race and class observable in the São Paulo metropolis. If there were none of the racial specificities described here, and segregation were purely by social class, there would be a high proximity between blacks and whites from each class, not just among the poorest sectors. Nonetheless, what we observe here is not similar to a model—typical to US cities—in which race stands out as the main residential separator.[7]

The pattern of residential segregation by race and class in the SPMR seems to be strongly correlated with the structure of social stratification in Brazil. Pursuing this line of argument, we can cite the interpretation proposed by Edward Telles (2012 [2004]), who suggests that Brazilian society can be conceived according to a separation between a white middle and upper class and a multiracial poor class. This separation is conceived not only as socioeconomic hierarchies and inequalities (called "vertical relations" by the author) but also as "social distance," in the sense of the possibility of different groups inhabiting the same spaces ("horizontal relations").[8]

For Telles, "invisible barriers" exist that hinder the entry of black people into the middle classes, while a racist culture perpetuates the idea that they should occupy subaltern positions.[9] These limits to the inclusion and consolidation of the position of the black population in higher socioeconomic strata are, he argues, reflected in the greater residential distance between them and white people of similar social class. The "invisible barriers" and racist culture can be identified, then, in the distance between racial groups cultivated in the horizontal relations (of proximity and integration, including relations of sociability, neighborliness, intermarriage, etc.) of the middle and upper strata, which maintain the populations separate.[10]

These are proposals for interpreting the residential segregation by race demonstrated in the data presented here. However, this phenomenon still requires the development of specific analytic models as well as new empirical research aimed at a better description of its specificities in the Brazilian context while replying to a series of questions raised in the process.

Here the chapter has revealed the segregation between blacks and whites from similar occupational categories. We still do not know, however, to what extent the observed distances are associated with other factors like social networks, family ties, wages, wealth in terms of assets and properties and so on. Another factor that needs to be considered is that the higher socioeconomic standing of many black people is only recent. Studies are also needed on how race operates in the mechanisms generating these residential patterns. Along these lines, research into residential preferences and discrimination in the housing market could provide important material in terms of revealing such mechanisms.

Furthermore, having described the racial outlines of residential segregation, we need to ask to what extent these residential patterns impact differently on the experiences of the black and white populations, especially in terms of sociability, access to the city and urban public policies.

Notes

1. Here we use the category "black" to refer to the set of black and brown populations, given the similarity in the socioeconomic indicators of the two groups.
2. Residential segregation is defined here as the degree to which social groups are separate from each other, considering the localization of their residences in urban

space (Marques 2005, Massey & Denton 1988). This is the degree of concentration in space of one social category in relation to another. Hence, "segregation is primarily a relational phenomenon: segregation of a group only exists when another group segregates itself or is segregated" (Torres 2005, p. 42).
3. The spatial reference unit for measuring segregation in this chapter are the weighting areas delimited by the 2010 census.
4. According to Cortese et al. (1976), the Dissimilarity Index tends to inflate when membership of minorities is very small compared to the number of spatial units used in its calculation. Conversely, the higher the proportion of the minority, the lower the value of the index will be, though not necessarily lower segregation. In the case of the SPMR, there was an increase in the proportion of black and brown people, but there was also an increase in the Dissimilarity Index. This evidence dispels the possibility that the growth in the value of the indicator is a methodological effect. In other words, according to the conception of segregation informing the construction of the Dissimilarity Index, there was indeed an increase in racial segregation in São Paulo.
5. The expressions class, stratum or social level used here involves an operational definition of stratification based on the EGP occupational categories.
6. The Moran Index was calculated on the basis of the location quotient (LQ) of the black and white professionals in the 633 weighting areas of the SPMR. The LQ is a measure of concentration consisting of the ratio between the proportion of the population of a group living in a determined area and the proportion of the population of the same group in the city as a whole. Like the Dissimilarity Index, therefore, the LQ also weighs the extent to which the proportion of a given group in an area replicates the proportion of this group across the entire metropolitan region. However, while the Dissimilarity Index results in a single value for the groups under consideration, the LQ provides specific values for the concentration of each group in each area. In those areas where a given group is underrepresented, the LQ assumes values between 0 and 1; where the group is overrepresented, the values are above 1. In other words, the higher the LQ, the higher the concentration of the group in the area concerned.
7. Historically, black people from higher classes in the US are just as segregated from whites as the poorer sections of the population (Massey & Denton 1993). However, some research (e.g., Iceland & Wilkes 2006) has shown that more recently there has been a reduction in the segregation indices between middle- and upper-class blacks—who have seen improvements in education, income and jobs—and whites. Alba et al. (2010) show that middle- and upper-class blacks are closer to whites; however, their white neighbors are poorer than them, and the districts in which they reside have worse socioeconomic indicators than the districts typical to white people from the same social groupings.
8. From this viewpoint, residential segregation expresses these horizontal relations insofar as it reveals the degree of "social distance" between groups. In other words, based on the physical distance between the residences of different social groups in urban space, the study of segregation aims to apprehend the potential for exposure and contact between one group and another.
9. One striking outcome of these mechanisms is the fact that black people with higher income are not recognized as "middle class" and, as a result, are subject to constant distrust and discrimination (Figueiredo 2003 and 2004).
10. These proposals can be extended further if we turn to the theories of Pierre Bourdieu (1997), who argued that the inhabited physical space is a symbolization of social space, manifesting social hierarchies and distances: The hierarchizations of spaces correspond to and naturalize social hierarchies. We could say, therefore, that the possession of capital (economic, cultural, social, etc.) on the basis of which social space is organized shapes the physical space, which likewise acts, in turn, on the reproduction of the structures of social space.

Bibliography

Alba, R., Logan, J. and Stults, B. (2000). How segregated are middle-class African Americans? *Social Problems*, 47(4), pp. 543–558.
Anselin, L. (1995). Local indicator of spatial association—LISA. *Geografical Analysis*, 27, pp. 91–115.
Barbosa, R. and Marschner, M. (2013). *Uma proposta de padronização de classificações em pesquisas do IBGE (Censos 1960-2010) e PNADs (1981-2011): educação, setores de atividade econômica e ocupação (ISCO-88, EGP11 e ISEI)*. Working paper. Mimeo.
Bichir, R. (2006). *Segregação e Acesso a Políticas Públicas no Município de São Paulo*. FFLCH/USP: DCP, Unpublished master dissertation.
Bourdieu, P. (1997). Efeitos de Lugar. In: Bourdieu, P. (ed.) *A Miséria do Mundo*. Petrópolis: Vozes, pp. 159–166.
Caldeira, T. (2000). *Cidade de muros: Crime, segregação e cidadania em São Paulo*. São Paulo, Edusp/Ed. 34.
Cardoso, F. and Ianni, O. (1960). *Cor e Mobilidade Social em Florianópolis: Aspectos das Relações entre Negros e Brancos numa Comunidade do Brasil Meridional*. São Paulo: Companhia Editora Nacional (Coleção *Brasiliana*, vol. 307).
Carril, L. (2003). *Quilombo, favela e periferia: a longa busca da cidadania*. Tese de Doutorado em Geografia Humana. São Paulo: FFLCH-USP.
Carvalho, I. and Barreto, V. (2007). Segregação residencial, condição social e raça em Salvador. *Cadernos Metrópole*, 18(2), pp. 251–273.
Comin, A. and Barbosa, R. (2011). Trabalhar para estudar: sobre a pertinência da noção de transição escola-trabalho no Brasil. *Novos Estudos—CEBRAP*, 91, pp. 75–95.
Cortese, C., Falk, R. and Cohen, J. (1976). Further considerations on the methodological analysis of segregation indices. *American Sociological Review*, 41, pp. 630–637.
Costa, C. and Ribeiro, L. (2004). *Cor, Status e Segregação Residencial em Belo Horizonte: Notas Exploratórias*. XI Seminário sobra a Economia Mineira. Diamantina: CEDEPLAR/UFMG.
Erikson, R., Goldthorpe, J. and Portocarrero, L. (1979). Intergenerational class mobility in three Western European societies. *British Journal of Sociology*, 30, pp. 415–441.
Figueiredo, A. (2004). Fora do jogo: A experiência dos negros na classe média brasileira. *Cadernos Pagu*, 23, pp. 199–228.
Figueiredo, A. (2003). *A classe média negra não vai ao paraíso: trajetórias, perfis e negritude entre os empresários negros*. IUPERJ: Unpublished PhD thesis.
França, D. (2010). *Raça, Classe e Segregação Residencial no Município de São Paulo*. FFLCH/USP: DS, Unpublished master dissertation.
Garcia, A. (2006). *Desigualdades Raciais e Segregação Urbana em Antigas Capitais: Salvador, Cidade d'Oxum e Rio de Janeiro*. IPPUR/UFRJ: Unpublished PhD thesis.
Iceland, J. and Wilkes, R. (2006). Does socioeconomic status matter? Race, class, and residential segregation. *Social Problems*, 53(2), pp. 248–273.
Maloutas, T. (2012). *Residential segregation around the world: Why context matters*. London: Ashgate.
Marques, E. (2005). Elementos conceituais da segregação, da pobreza urbana e da ação do Estado. In: Marques, E. and Torres, H. (eds.) *São Paulo: segregação, pobreza e desigualdades*. São Paulo: Editora Senac, pp. 19–56.

Marques, E. and Torres, H. (eds.) (2005). *São Paulo: segregação, pobreza e desigualdade*s. São Paulo: Editora Senac.
Massey, D. and Denton, N. (1993). *American apartheid: Segregation and the making of the underclass*. Cambridge, MA: Harvard University Press.
Massey, D. and Denton, N. (1988). The dimensions of residential segregation. *Social Forces*, 67, pp. 281–315.
Oliveira, N. (1996). Favelas and ghettos: Race and class in Rio de Janeiro and New York City. *Latin American Perspectives*, 23(4), pp. 71–89.
Pierson, D. (1971 [1942]). *Brancos e pretos na Bahia*. São Paulo: Editora Nacional (Brasiliana; vol. 241).
Pinto, L. (1998 [1953]). *O Negro no rio de Janeiro: relações de raça numa sociedade em mudança*. Rio de Janeiro, Editora da UFRJ.
Préteceille, E. (2004). A construção social da segregação urbana: convergências e divergências. *Espaço e Debates*, 45, pp. 11–23.
Préteceille, E. and Cardoso, A. (2008). Río de Janeiro y São Paulo:11 ciudades duales? Comparación con Paris. *Ciudad y Territorio, Estudios Territoriales*, XL, pp. 617–640.
Ribeiro, L. (2007). *Status, Cor e Desigualdades Sócio-Espaciais na Metrópole do Rio de Janeiro*. XII Encontro da ANPUR. Belém: XII Encontro da ANPUR.
Ribeiro, C. A. C. (2006). Classe, raça e mobilidade social no Brasil. *Dados*, 49(4), 833–873.
Rios Neto, E. (2005). *Desigualdade Raciais nas Condições Habitacionais da População Urbana*. CEDEPLAR/UFMG. Mimeo.
Rolnik, R. (1989). Território Negros nas Cidades Brasileiras (Etnicidade e Cidade em São Paulo e no Rio de Janeiro). *Estudos Afro-Asiáticos*, 19, pp. 29–41.
Silva, M. (2004). *Nem para todos é a cidade: segregação urbana e racial em São Paulo*. Doutorado em Ciências Sociais. PUC-SP.
Telles, E. (2012 [2004]). *O Significado da Raça na Sociedade Brasileira*. Available at: http://www.princeton.edu/sociology/faculty/telles/
Telles, E. (1996). Identidade racial, Contexto Urbano e Mobilização Política *Afro-Ásia*, 17, pp. 121–138.
Telles, E. (1995). Race, class and space in Brazilian cities. *International Journal of Urban and Regional Research*, 19. pp. 295–406.
Telles, E. (1993). Cor da Pele e Segregação Residencial no Brasil. *Estudos Afro-Asiáticos*, 24, pp. 5–22.
Torres, H. (2005). Medindo a segregação. In: Marques, E. C. and Torres, H. G. (eds.) *São Paulo: segregação, pobreza e desigualdade*s. São Paulo: Editora Senac, pp. 81–100.
Torres, H. (2004). Debate: A pesquisa sobre segregação: conceitos, métodos e medições. *Espaço e Debates*, 45, pp. 87–109.
Vargas, J. (2005). Apartheid brasileiro: raça e segregação residencial no Rio de Janeiro. *Revista de Antropologia*, 48(1), pp. 75–131.

Part III
Processes of Space Production

8 The Dynamics of São Paulo's Favelas
Socioeconomic Conditions and Territorial Patterns

Camila Pereira Saraiva

Introduction

The so-called favelas in Brazil (similar to *tugurios, barrios de invasión, villas miseria*, slums or informal settlements in other countries) are the result of situations of extreme urban poverty associated with ineffective state housing policies. Since the favelas are characterized by illegal access to land and disorderly occupation, they usually lack basic urban infrastructure and public facilities. The increasing numbers of people living in such conditions, especially during the second half of the 20th century, brought favelas to the center of urban studies.

Since then, the measurement and description of these settlements and their populations have become essential to the development of policies for better living conditions. Nevertheless, the lack of any agreed definition of what constitutes a favela (or other similar settlements) in most countries makes its measurement a difficult task.

According to the UN "Habitat Global Report on Human Settlements," published in 2003, slums in many countries have not been incorporated into existing monitoring instruments, such as national population censuses or demographic surveys. Instead, proxies or related variables like " 'proportion of unauthorized housing" or "proportion of squatters" are provided in some surveys (UN-Habitat 2003).

Since 1991, Brazil's national population census[1] has used the concept of the *aglomerado subnormal*, or substandard tracts, defined as a set of at least 51 households that occupy (or have recently occupied) public or private land owned by third parties, usually characterized by disordered layout, high density and a lack of essential public services.

Over the 1990s and 2000s, there was a steady improvement in the definitions and techniques used by municipal administrations to gather and process primary data on favelas, including a growing investment in geographic information systems. These efforts and the increased exchange of information between municipal councils and the IBGE enabled the 2010 demographic census to make significant advances in terms of mapping substandard tracts.

Drawing on the most recent national census, conducted in 2010, and the favela mapping produced by the municipality of São Paulo, this chapter presents a methodology for measuring and characterizing the metropolitan area's favelas. An initial study along these lines can be found in Saraiva and Marques (2005), which used the 2000 national census. In the present chapter, therefore, I explore the dynamics of São Paulo's favelas over the two last decades.

In the first section, I consider the relevance of measuring and characterizing favelas in a context where their urbanization has become perceived as a housing solution. Next, I present data on the socioeconomic composition, infrastructure and provision of services in São Paulo's favelas in 2010, as well as their surrounding areas, with the aim of identifying elements for assessing the impact of favelas on the territories in which they are embedded. In the third section, I compare the characterization of the favelas situated in the capital with those found in the other municipalities of the SPMR and proceed toward the construction of a typology of favelas for 2010.

Following the general trend verified in the metropolis, the findings indicate an overall improvement in the infrastructure and socioeconomic conditions of favelas. However, the gap between living conditions in the favelas and those in the formal city persists, highlighting the need for public responses to address the issue.

The Relevance of Favela Estimates

Although Latin American cities were already marked by poor neighborhoods during the first decades of the 20th century, studies of urban poverty in these cities only came to the fore after the 1950s, when the slums became a significant phenomenon in the majority of the continent's urban conglomerations.

In these first studies, urban poverty was seen to result from the inadequate adaptation of rural migrants to city life. The poor were thus seen as socially and economically marginalized in the urban environment. While the Economic Commission for Latin America (ECLAC) responded to this situation through economic policies, the Center for Latin American Economic and Social Development (DESAL) argued for grassroots policies promoting the social and cultural integration of the marginalized migrants (Vekemans & Giusti 1969).

However, the supposed incapacity of the poor to integrate was challenged by other studies from the 1960s onward, which focused on the strategies developed by these populations to overcome poverty. These works brought to light the everyday life and sociability of squatter settlements (Leeds 1969, Pearlman 1976).

Elsewhere, studies carried out by John Turner and William Mangin in different Latin American countries pointed to slums as a housing solution rather than simply a problem. These authors questioned the modernist solution based on high-rise residential blocks and advocated the development of alternative housing programs involving community construction and slum upgrading (Mangin 1967, Turner 1968).

Influenced by John Turner's proposals, UN-Habitat adopted the ideas of progressive development and local patterns in housing policies during the 1970s. This approach was implemented in pioneering fashion in the Peruvian Barriadas in the 1950s and involved experimental, low-cost techniques. Improving the physical conditions in slums thus became a viable alternative to their demolition.

In Brazil, the first of such initiatives can be traced back to the late 1960s when Community Development Company (CODESCO) was created in Rio de Janeiro. Nevertheless, the mainstream housing policy up until the mid-1980s was based on slum evictions as a prelude to building new residential developments. It was only in the late 1980s and especially during the 1990s that slum-upgrading projects became part of official housing policies. Initially, these policies were a municipal initiative, a reflection of the growing resistance of the local population to forced evictions, the absence of an efficient national housing policy and the decentralization mechanisms of Brazil's new national constitution, promulgated in 1988 as part of the redemocratization process. When the Ministry of Cities was created in 2003, a massive program of favela upgrading was launched at the national level. In this context, the measurement and characterization of favela conditions are crucial tasks.

In São Paulo, the favelas began to become a prominent feature of the urban landscape only around the end of the 1970s. Before this period, irregular housing developments and slum tenements (*cortiços*) predominated as an alternative for the low-income population unable to afford any other form of housing.[2] In 1973, just 1 percent of the city's population lived in favelas (Pasternak 2000). During the same decade, the favela population in Rio de Janeiro reached 13 percent (Valladares 1981), while the *barriadas* accounted for 25 percent of the population in Lima, Peru.

A survey conducted by the São Paulo municipality in 1987, however, indicated that the percentage of the municipality's population living in favelas had risen to 8.8 percent, totaling 812,764 inhabitants.

The 1991 demographic census registered 647,400 people living in substandard tracts in São Paulo municipality, equivalent to 6.7 percent of the total population. However, a research study by the Foundation Institute of Economic Research (Fipe/FEA-USP), undertaken in 1993 at the request of the municipal council, indicated that around 19.4 percent of São Paulo's population lived in favelas.

The substantial difference between the estimates based on census data and the figures resulting from local censuses is largely predictable and related to the difference between sociological definitions of the favela and IBGE's own methodology for surveying those sectors it terms substandard. In São Paulo, for example, where very small favelas are frequent, their number is generally underestimated.[3]

The explosive growth of favelas in the 1980s converged with the analyses of worsening social inequality and increasing unemployment, poverty, precariousness and urban violence during the 1980s and 1990s in diverse Brazilian cities (Maricato 1996, Pasternak & Bógus 2001).

Studies produced between 2002 and 2003 by the CEM, in partnership with the São Paulo municipality, confirmed a rise in the population living in favelas, although showing just moderate growth. The estimated favela population was around 891,673 people, or 9.2 percent of the total population, in 1991 and 1,160,597, or 11.2 percent of the total population, in 2000 (Marques et al. 2003, Torres & Marques 2002).

Analysis of the favelas in the 1990s had already shown a tendency for relative improvement in the indicators for infrastructure and the socioeconomic conditions of their residents as well as a greater degree of heterogeneity than usually considered.

São Paulo's Favelas in the First Decade of the 21st Century

Responding to the debate on estimating the favela population, the CEM created a method based on geoprocessing techniques. This involves inputting information from the cartographic database on the census tracts (produced by IBGE) to the favela mapping developed by the municipal administrations (Marques et al. 2003). As well as being replicable, this method takes advantage of both the municipal administrative data, especially its definition of a favela, and the collection of field data by IBGE in its demographic censuses.

In São Paulo municipality, for example, the municipal information on the favelas was seldom computerized and remained difficult to access until the start of the 2000s. Today, however, a continually updated digital map of favelas is made available to the public by the municipality. This allows us to observe that the mapping of the substandard tracts made by IBGE in this municipality, for the 2000 census is fairly proximate to the favela map used by the municipality.

In the other municipalities of the metropolitan region, meanwhile, although comparison with the maps produced by the municipal councils has proved impossible, it seems that their mapping of the substandard tracts has also improved, albeit to a lesser degree.[4]

Due to this change in the methodology for defining substandard sectors, the figures from the previous censuses are not directly comparable to the 2010 census. The number of census sectors in the SPMR in the 2010 demographic census, for example, is higher than in the 2000 census by around 1.4 times. At the same time, the number of sectors of substandard tracts is 1.6 times higher: 3,305 substandard sectors in 2010 compared to 2,053 sectors in 2000. At first sight, this would seem to indicate both the emergence of new favelas and an increase due to improvements in the mapping made by IBGE.

However, a comparison of the cartographic databases showed that more than 70 percent of the sectors mapped in 2010 already existed in 2000, albeit with geometric corrections.[5] The areas with a concentration of new polygons are all located on the periphery's outskirts. Although we cannot be sure whether these occurrences are due to corrections to the mapping methodology or the expansion in precarious housing areas, these areas deserve attention.

Observation at a reduced scale, supported by the use of aerial images, allows these areas to be divided into two groups: those that still include considerable portions of unoccupied land and those already densely occupied. The latter may indicate the formation of complexes—a group of very proximate or contiguous favelas—as occurs in Rio de Janeiro. However, only a specific examination of these territories can confirm this trend.

In the municipality of São Paulo, where we know that the information on favelas improved substantially over the last decade, the increase in the number of substandard sectors was 1.9 times. However, the number of favelas considered by the municipal council altered little.[6] The most recent information available from the municipal council was used, while the maps of favelas and urbanized nucleuses were obtained from the Habisp Web site on February 20, 2013, corresponding to a universe of 1,628 favelas and 354 urbanized nucleuses (totaling 1,982 settlements).

Having made the necessary provisos concerning the changes to how the cartographic databases were produced, I describe next the methodology used to characterize the favelas in São Paulo municipality. In relation to the techniques for the imputation of data between bases, the use of overlay and tag techniques was once again tested, with the latter proving more consistent with the household data continually updated on the municipality's cartographic database.[7]

The characterization of the 2010 favela population was made, therefore, through the imputation to the favela database of the densities of variables selected from the substandard tracts.[8] At first sight, the data suggests an increase in the favela population (including the urbanized nucleuses) at an average annual geometric growth rate lower than the São Paulo municipality as a whole: 0.41 compared to 0.84.

When we applied the same exercise to the census sectors to compare the results with the favela maps—that is, a spatial selection of the polygons from the 2010 database that touch on or contain polygons from the 2000 database, the result of which is used as the basis for selecting continuous polygons—328 of the total 1,628 favelas were discovered to be "new," while all the urbanized nucleuses existed previously. However, when the year of implantation of the favela was checked using information provided by the municipality, just 50 were observed to have sprung up after 2000.

On the other hand, the area corresponding to favelas in 2010—28,097,898 m²—is slightly lower than the area computed on the basis of 2000—28,350,469,00 m²—indicating that, despite identifying new polygons, the revision of the geometry of the favelas also led to a reduction in the area occupied by favelas within the municipality. In response to these changes, I suggest that the total population of favelas in 2000 may have been slightly overestimated. Consequently, the comparison between the absolute data presented in this chapter should be treated with caution.

In the 1990s, when the average geometric annual growth rate of the São Paulo municipal population reached 0.88, the same rate in the favelas was more than three times as high, namely 2.97 per year. In the last decade, however, the growth rate of the municipal population was 0.76 per year, slightly lower than the previous decade, while in the favelas—including the urbanized nucleuses—the population growth rate fell significantly to 0.41 per year.[9]

Although the favela population in 2010 is higher than the total registered in 2000—1.21 million versus 1.16 million—it is important to observe that in percentage terms, this population represents a smaller portion of the total population: 10.7 percent rather than the previous 11.1 percent. These results tell us that the total population in 2000 may have been overestimated due to imprecisions in the favela mapping, as previously mentioned.

Even so, without ignoring the corrections made to the cartographic databases, we can suggest a certain stability in the municipality's favela population in relative terms. Some stability can also be observed in the population density of the favelas over the last decade. This rose slightly from 409 to 431 inhabitants per hectare. However, as already emphasized, this rise may be due to cartographic corrections to the favela perimeters, which resulted in a shrinkage of the total area, aimed at higher precision in the delimitation of the favelas.

On the other hand, household density showed a tendency to fall at a higher pace in favelas compared to the municipality as a whole. Between 1991 and 2010 the household density of favelas was 4.6 (1991), 4.0 (2000) and 3.6 (2010) compared to 3.8, 3.5 and 3.1 in the municipality. Unfortunately the limited data available makes it impossible to offer any analysis of building density within the favelas. Even so, it seems plausible to work with the hypothesis that the consolidation of many of these settlements tends to be accompanied by an increase in building density, which may partly explain the population increase combined with a fall in household density.

In Table 8.1 I present the characterization of the favelas in 1991, 2000 and 2010. Generally speaking, the observation of location quotients—which allow us to separate the effect of an improvement in favela indicators from the effect of improvements at municipal level—suggested that conditions in the favelas altered relatively little in social terms but did improve in relation to infrastructure.

Table 8.1 Socioeconomic indicators in São Paulo and in favelas, 1991, 2000 and 2010.

Indicator	Relative Numbers (in %)						Location Quotients		
	1991		2000		2010		1991	2000	2010
	Favelas	SPM	Favelas	SPM	Favelas	SPM			
Children up to the age of 14	41.2	28.6	35.5	24.8	29.6	20.8	1.44	1.43	1.42
People age 65 or over	1.2	5.2	1.7	6.4	2.6	8.1	0.23	0.27	0.32
Literate population age five years old and over	61.3	80.0	84.0	91.9	89.6	95.2	0.77	0.91	0.94
Household head without income and up to three min. wages	77.9	42.7	73.2	40.1	95.6	68.6	1.82	1.83	1.39
Households connected to water supply network	89.7	98.3	96.0	97.6	97.3	99.1	0.91	0.98	0.98
Households connected to sewage system	25.1	81.2	49.2	87.2	68.2	91.9	0.31	0.56	0.74
Households covered by waste collection service	63.3	95.2	82.0	96.5	79.4	95.1	0.66	0.85	0.83

Source: Author's elaboration based on favela maps by PMSP and IBGE demographic censuses.

The observation of the indicators relatives to the age structure indicates a drop in the percentage of the population between 0 and 14 years old, accompanying the trend towards demographic transformation across the municipality. Similarly, there was a rise in the elderly population over the age of 65; in this case, however, the increase was slightly higher in the favelas than in the municipality overall, as the location quotients for 1991, 2000 and 2010 indicate: 0.23, 0.27 and 0.32, respectively.

The literate population rose considerably between 1991 and 2000, and then practically remained the same over the following decade with the behavior of this indicator in favelas and the municipality almost equal. The difference that still remains may be related to the higher presence of young families in the favelas.

In sum, over the last twenty years we can observe a younger age structure being maintained in the favelas with a slow and gradual increase—quicker in the favelas than in the rest of the municipality—of the older population. The literacy indices in the favelas and the municipality converged most in the 1990s when the illiterate population fell more sharply across Brazil as a whole.[10]

In terms of income, we can observe that the presence of household heads with no income or earning up to 3 minimum wages was practically double in the favelas during the 1990s. In the last decade, however, this stratification altered drastically with around 70% of household heads in the municipality and more than 95% of household heads in favelas being located in the band from 0 to 3 minimum wages. This has been caused by a substantial rise in the value of the minimum wage from the start of the 2000s, as analyzed in Chapter 1.

However, the average income of household heads in favelas remained practically the same over the last decade, in contrast to the small decline in income among the household heads seen in the rest of the municipality. In 2000, the average income of household heads in favelas was R$334.55: this rose to R$664.44 in 2010, but the latter in fact corresponded to R$333.57 when deflated by the INPC for 2000. In the municipality over the same time frame, the average income of household heads in 2000 was R$325.13, rising to R$2,106.97 in 2010, or R$1,057.77 after deflation. Observation of the location quotients thus indicates a slight fall in income inequality between the poorest population residing in favelas and the population living outside them.

The indicators relating to infrastructure and services, on the other hand, reveal a considerable improvement in favela conditions, principally in relation to sanitary waste collection via the mains sewage system. In the last twenty years the percentage of favela households covered by the service rose from 25% to 68%, though still far from the average coverage for São Paulo as a whole: 91.9%. Observation of the location quotients indicates that the rise in coverage has been much more intense in favelas.

Water supply became more universal, practically reaching parity between favelas and municipality. It is important to emphasize that these figures, replicated in the case of sewage services, are derived from the responses given by residents themselves and do not reveal the actual quality of service, nor the existence of clandestine connections.

Meanwhile, waste collection services, which at the start of the 1990s covered around 95.2% of the municipality compared to just 63.3% of favela households, showed a good improvement in favelas over the decade, rising to 82%, and a certain stability in the 2000s. At the end of the 2000s, however, the service still showed 15% lower coverage in favelas.

We can therefore observe that the socioeconomic and urban conditions of the favelas have become closer to the conditions of the formal city. While

Table 8.2 Socioeconomic indicators in São Paulo, favelas, their neighboring areas and urbanized favelas 1991, 2000 and 2010.

	Favelas	Urbanized nucleuses	Surrounding 300m (excludes favelas)	SPM
Children up to the age of 14	29.6	28.5	23.1	20.8
People aged 65 or over	2.6	3.4	6.0	8.1
Literate population aged five years old and over	89.6	90.6	94.2	95.2
Household head without income and up to 3 min. wages	95.6	94.5	81.6	68.6
Households connected to water supply network	97.3	99.4	99.4	99.1
Households connected to sewage system	68.2	87.7	91.4	91.9
Households covered by waste collection service	79.4	80.7	95.3	95.1

Source: Author's elaboration based on favela maps by PMSP and IBGE Demographic Censuses.

the gap separating these two realities indicates the need for coverage by specific public policies, the hypotheses of urban dualization are not verified, corroborating the analyses presented in the first chapters of this book.

To complement this observation of changes in São Paulo's favelas, I shall compare them now to the urbanized nucleuses and to their immediate surroundings.[11] As remarked earlier, the urbanized nucleuses are favelas that, according to the São Paulo Municipality, have already received basic infrastructural improvements.

Overall we can note a gradient toward better conditions as we move from the favelas to the urbanized nucleuses, the areas surrounding the favelas and the municipality as a whole. However, it is important to emphasize that the indicators for the urbanized nucleuses are very similar to those found in the favelas. This may indicate that urbanization does not lead to rapid social change in the settlements.

The main improvement relates to the percentage of households connected to the sewage network, although the urbanized nucleuses still show a level of coverage lower than the formal city. The same applies to the waste collection service, indicating that although the urbanization of precarious settlements has improved access to infrastructure and services, these areas still have lower levels compared to the formal city.

The quality of the urban services provided in urbanized favelas is not always equivalent to the quality of services in the "formal city." Indeed, problems related to a lack of maintenance in urbanized favelas are detected in almost all those cities that have implemented urbanization programs (Denaldi 2003, Uemura 2000). Additionally, the inadequate provision of social housing means that favelas are subject to a new wave of densification even after urbanization, very often accompanied by territorial expansion.

Inversely, the percentage of household heads with no income or earning up to three minimum wages is considerably higher in favelas (around 95.6 percent) compared to the wider municipality (68.6 percent) or even the area surrounding favelas (81.6 percent). Comparing the favelas to urbanized nucleuses, we can observe that the income of household heads in the latter areas—94.5 percent—is only slightly better than the percentage found in the favelas: 95.6 percent.

This slight increase in the income of household heads in urbanized nucleuses compared to favelas may perhaps suggest a tendency toward the "expulsion" of poorer families from these areas due to the valorization of properties after the interventions. Indeed, this is a recurrent argument in the literature. However, it has proved impossible to advance beyond the hypothesis stage in this study. Discussing this phenomenon, Silva (2000) argues, based on research conducted in eight Brazilian favelas, that the valorization of properties does not necessarily lead to the substitution of poorer residents but establishes a price pattern for new purchases or leases of properties that tends to increase the income band of those living in the urbanized favela.

As already pointed out in Saraiva and Marques (2005), the areas surrounding the favelas generally show the characteristics of a transition zone between the favelas and the city as a whole. When we disaggregate the indicators by district, we observe that the same situations highlighted in this previous study are repeated here. In other words, São Paulo municipality contains favelas in very poor districts where the average income of the household head differs little from the average found in the rest of the district; favelas in high-income districts where the average income of the household head is more than three times less than the surrounding average;[12] and favelas in districts with a potentially higher social mixture where the surrounding area shows average conditions compared to the favela and the district as a whole. This time, I look to incorporate into the analysis the behavior of the infrastructure and services indicators.

Hence, the first group comprises districts located on the outskirts of the municipality, part of the precarious urban frontier experiencing significant demographic growth (Torres 2005): Capão Redondo, Jardim Ângela, Grajaú, Pedreira and Parelheiros to the south; Brasilândia and Perus to the north; and Sapopemba, Lajeado, Itaim Paulista, Iguatemi, Vila Curuçá, Jardim Helena, Cidade Tiradentes, Guaianases, Anhanguera, José Bonifácio and São Rafael in the extreme east. In this group, the average monthly incomes of household heads in the favelas, in the surrounding areas and in the districts differ little, amounting to less than R$3,000 in all three kinds of locality. In relation to infrastructure, we can highlight the districts of Jardim Helena, Itaim Paulista, José Bonifácio and Cidade Tiradentes, where the sewage drainage conditions are much worse in the favelas compared to those found in surrounding areas or in the district as a whole, where more than 80 and 90 percent of households are covered, respectively. It is worth emphasizing that the latter two districts include a large number of public housing developments.

The second group, favelas in high-income regions, include districts concentrated to the west and south of São Paulo's historic center[13] as well as Tatuapé and Santana. However, only the districts of Campo Belo and Vila Andrade encompass a more representative number of favelas. In Campo Belo, the average monthly income of household heads is around R$5,700, while in the favelas the average is R$950 and in areas surrounding the latter around R$3,300. In Vila Andrade, the average monthly income of household heads is around R$4,000, while in the favelas the average is around R$700 and in the area around the latter around R$2,200. This variation suggests that favelas in high-income districts produce a degree of "devalorization" in their surrounding areas—higher than in the socially mixed districts, as we shall see.

In relation to infrastructural coverage, we can observe that in Vila Andrade, the percentage of households connected to the sewage system and waste collection services is very similar among the favelas, surrounding areas and overall district at over 90 percent. The proximity between the indicators is probably due to the "effect" of the Paraisópolis favela, which contains a large proportion of the district's households and has already received urbanization projects at different times. However, it is not alone: As well as Paraisópolis, other favelas from the district like Pullman and the Peinha favela are fairly well consolidated. The same does not apply to Campo Belo, where the favelas are more like "islands of vulnerability" on the shores of the Avenida Água Espraiada, with the percentage of households integrated with the sewage system below 40 percent. In the district's largest favela, for example, Sônia Ribeiro, many of the households within the nucleus are still not made of brick.

Finally, in the third group, which contains most of the districts with a higher social mixture, these trends are less evident. However, observation of this group confirms that the higher the average income of the district, the more the favelas tend to be differentiated from their surroundings in terms of income, with the same not being verified in relation to urban conditions.

Towards a Typology of Favelas in the São Paulo Metropolitan Region

In this section, I look to compare the dynamic of the favelas in São Paulo municipality with the rest of the SPMR, exploring the existence of a typology of favelas within this overall region.

The first hypothesis to test is related to the discovery of a degree of relative stability in the population dynamic of São Paulo's favelas—that is, the extent to which this stability may be related to an explosive growth of the metropolitan region's favela population. In absolute terms, the total population in substandard tracts in the SPMR was around 756,400 people in 2000, rising to 885,900 people in 2010. Hence, the average annual geometric growth rate of the population in substandard tracts during the period was 1.59 per year.

Meanwhile, the growth rate of the SPMR's population as a whole was 1.26 per year. These results might suggest a higher growth in the favela population compared to the overall population. However, comparison of the data from the census for the São Paulo municipality with the information on favelas supplied by the municipal council does not support this conclusion. If we take just the information from the census, we can verify an average growth rate of 3.52 per year in the substandard tracts. However, the analyses presented here based on the cartographic databases produced by the municipal administration indicate a growth of 0.41 per year.

Testing the hypothesis of explosive population growth in favelas encounters problems because of the changes on the limits of substandard tracts, as mentioned in the first section of this chapter. Unlike São Paulo municipality, we lack favela maps for the other municipalities of the SPMR that would enable the analyses to advance. Just considering the census data, though, it does not seem that the low growth of the favela population in São Paulo is related to any large growth of the favelas beyond its frontiers.[14]

In terms of socioeconomic indicators, we can also note a considerable similarity between the indicators (age group, income and literacy) encountered in the favelas of São Paulo municipality and the other municipalities.[15]

The main difference is found in the indicators for household integration with the sewage system, which were slightly better in the municipalities of Diadema, Santo André and São Bernardo compared to the capital and worse in the other municipalities. These results are less related to the per-capita GDP of the municipality than the existence of favela urbanization policies for uninterrupted periods.[16] To explore the characterization undertaken so far in an disaggregated form, and with the objective of analyzing any potential changes to the heterogeneity observed in Saraiva and Marques (2005), I also made use of cluster analysis based on the 2010 census data. This analysis considered indicators for access to infrastructure and urban services (the proportion of households connected to the main water supply, the sewage system and the urban waste collection service), schooling (the proportion of literate people five years old or over and average years of study of the household head) and income (average monthly income of the household head). The aggregation method used was two step,[17] which indicated the existence of four groups, distinct from each other and internally homogenous, whose relative share is very similar to São Paulo municipality and to the other municipalities of the metropolis.

In socioeconomic terms, the favelas presented much lower conditions than the average for the metropolis as a whole. The average time of study of the household head, for example, was around 8.2 years in the metropolis as a whole and 5.6 in the favelas, while the monthly average income of the household head, around R$1,842.00 in the metropolis, was just R$664.00 in the favelas. The persistence of this inequality highlights the importance of the modules for the social and economic integration of favelas contained in urbanization programs, such as the More Equal Santo André Program,[18] developed by the municipal administration of this municipality for around 10 years. The infrastructure indicators proved to be more relevant to differentiate groups of favelas.[19]

In the *consolidated favelas*, a group containing the majority, that is, 1,620 favelas, the social and especially physical conditions were revealed to be higher than average for the favelas as a whole. The proportion of households connected to the sewage system is 93.81 percent and households with waste collection 96.24 percent. The percentage of elderly people is also higher, around 3.2 percent, and there is a lower presence of children up to the age of 14: 27.4 percent. The average monthly income of the household head is R$697.00. In this group are the four largest favelas in the metropolis—Paraisópolis, Pantanal 2, Heliópolis and São Francisco Global—as well as a substantial portion of the favelas in the protection areas for the river sources of the Billings and Guarapiranga reservoirs, as illustrated in Figure 8.1.[20] It might be expected that all the urbanized nucleuses were contained in this group; however, just 255 of the 354 nucleuses belong to this type.

A set of favelas with intermediary conditions was subdivided into two groups with low urban consolidation and differentiated primarily by sewage system coverage. The *low-consolidated favelas*, 616 cases, possess infrastructure indicators, as well as social conditions, below the average of the favelas. The percentage of households connected to the sewage system is 58.36 percent, if we consider the average, and 73.69 percent, if we consider the median, but still below the average found in the metropolis as a whole, around 89.7 percent. Coverage of households by waste collection service is just 26 percent on average. However, it is highly probable that these are favelas where waste is collected from dumpsters, due to the narrow and/or steep roads. Finally, the indicators for age structure, schooling and income are very close to those to the next group to be described.

Low-consolidated favelas with precarious sewage system coverage total 788 cases, where social conditions are slightly better than the previous group. The population up to the age of 14 represents around 30 percent and the elderly around 2.8 percent of the total. Average time of study of the household head is 5.5 years, and the literate population age five years old or over is 89.5 percent. Meanwhile in relation to infrastructure, although the proportion of properties connected to the main water supply is over 98 percent, as among the previous groups, and 95 percent of households are covered by waste collection, just 20 percent of the households are linked to the sewage system.

Finally, the *precarious favelas*, totaling 196 cases, have the worse infrastructural and socioeconomic conditions. Coverage percentages are very

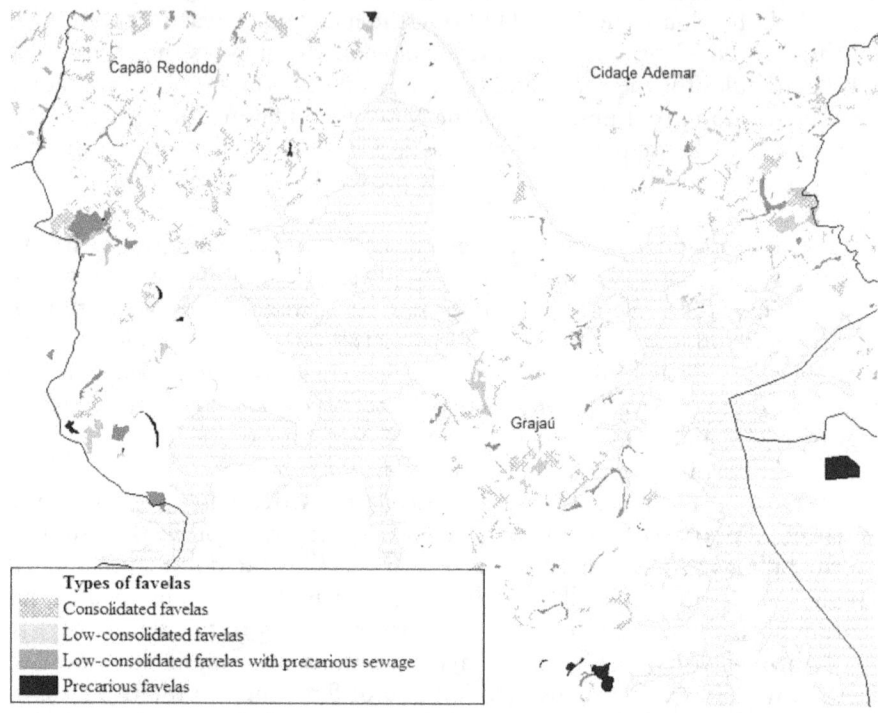

Figure 8.1 Types of favelas in the area around the Guarapiranga and Billings reservoirs, southern SPMR, 2010.

Source: Author's elaboration based on the PMSP maps and IBGE demographic censuses.

low, even in terms of the number of households linked to the main water supply, around 55 percent. The waste collection service covers 52 percent of households, and the sewage system connects 32 percent; in the case of the latter, however, there is a significant difference between the average and the median, with the latter covering just 13 percent of households. In terms of age structure, this is the group with the most young people and the least old people. In relation to the monthly average of the household heads, there is a significant standard deviation between the values, making the median more reliable. The median income was R$575.00.

The correlation between precarious conditions, adopting the proportion of households with sewage network connection as a proxy, and the implantation date of the favelas in São Paulo municipality, where the latter information is obtainable, proved to be insignificant (Pearson = 0.023). Just 13 of the 103 favelas in these conditions were initiated after 2000, and 40 predate the 1980s, again suggesting the hypothesis that some settlements cannot be consolidated.

The different types of favelas described here are not exactly comparable to those analyzed in Saraiva and Marques (2005) due to a set of factors: The polygons are no longer the same, not all the variables used coincide, and another aggregation method was used to create the clusters. However, it is worth emphasizing that, as pointed out a decade ago, the heterogeneity existing in the favelas of the São Paulo metropolis remains significant.

The main change worth emphasizing seems to be the improvement in conditions in the favelas, confirming the analyses of the previous sections. In 2000, the type with the best social conditions and infrastructure was associated with just 18 percent of favelas, while in 2010 the type with consolidated urban conditions represented one half of the favelas. The favelas with the worst or most precarious social conditions and infrastructure, however, rose from 6 to 8 percent of the total.

Final Considerations

In São Paulo municipality, the presented information indicates the consolidation of the favelas in the territory of the city. This is suggested by the low population growth and the relative reduction of the favela population as well as by an increase in housing density and an improvement in infrastructural and socioeconomic indicators. Finally, the analysis showed a certain exhaustion of areas in the capital that in previous decades were occupied by favelas, especially public plots and environmental protection areas.

This exhaustion, however, does not appear to be related to the explosive growth of favelas in the metropolitan region. Although growth of the favela population has been higher in the other municipalities of the metropolitan region than in the capital, even in these areas rates were lower than those found in the overall population.

Despite this increasing trend toward consolidation, in São Paulo municipality it was possible to observe the existence of a gradient toward better conditions among favelas, urbanized nucleuses, the areas surrounding favelas and the municipality as a whole, with the conditions found in the urbanized nucleuses being the closest to the favelas. The observation of a stronger gradient among favelas, their surroundings and the overall district in those districts with an average income in the capital allows us to hypothesize a devalorization in the surrounding areas due to the favela effect. Following this logic, favelas in the high-income districts would be much more segregated, without any influence on their immediate surroundings.

Finally we can note that the same diversity in favela types in the capital is also encountered in the metropolitan region's other municipalities, as in 2000. Over the last decade, however, favelas have become a little more homogenous due to urban consolidation, observed in around half of São Paulo's favelas.

Notes

1. The Brazilian national census is carried out every 10 years by IBGE.
2. See Chapter 1 for a broader historical context.
3. This is because very small favelas are ignored by IBGE since a minimum of 51 households is required to constitute a substandard cluster. Moreover, the realization of the demographic census at national level depends on a prior logistics, involving a physical-financial timetable and the hiring of field researchers. To this end, IBGE makes use of information provided by the municipal councils, which do not always possess updated records of favelas. For more details on the differences in definitions and their consequences, see Marques et al. 2003.
4. IBGE introduced various methodological and operational innovations to the 2010 census, improving the identification of substandard tracts. These innovations included the use of high-resolution satellite images, specific research on the morphological characteristics of particular areas, and meetings on the topic at the Municipal Commissions of Geography and Statistics (http://www.ibge.gov.br/home/presidencia/noticias/noticia_visualiza.php?id_noticia=2051).
5. This exercise involved the selection of substandard sectors from 2010 that touch on or are contained within the 2000 census sectors (utilizing the "select by location" tool of the Maptitude software). The result indicated that 2,460 of the 3,305 polygons, or around 74 percent, albeit possibly with geometric corrections, had already been mapped in 2000. Next we selected the substandard tracts for 2010 that touched the already-selected sectors, that is, those already mapped in 2000. We repeated this procedure one more time until the number of sectors was stabilized, and the final result was a selection of the substandard sectors for 2010 that already existed in 2000 as well as those contiguous with the latter. The unselected sectors, therefore, can be considered "new"; that is, nonexistent or unmapped in 2000 and not the result of the expansion of the substandard sectors existing in 2000 (i.e., continuous sectors). A total of 635 substandard sectors were encountered in this situation in the SPMR, 423 of them in São Paulo municipality. The figures illustrating this exercise can be found in a preliminary version of the present chapter published in Portuguese: Saraiva, C. "Revisitando a dinâmica social das favelas." In: Marques, E. (ed.) (2015). *São Paulo, 2010: Espaços, Heterogeneidades e Desigualdades na Metrópole*. São Paulo: UNESP.
6. The map based on the 2000 census used for the analysis, resulting from the collaboration between the CEM and the São Paulo Municipality, contained 2,018 favelas. In 2008, the municipality launched a digital platform providing access to the public, Habisp, which enables permanent updating of the social, economic, legal and urban records for precarious settlements. The favela map database was also updated, resulting in 1,573 favelas and 222 urbanized nucleuses (totaling 1,795 settlements) at the time of the platform's launch. This update process involved the merging or elimination of favelas, as well as the elimination of overlaps between favelas and irregular housing developments, based on field surveys carried out by technical officers. Additionally, a new category was created, "urbanized nucleuses," that is, favelas that already possess connection to the main water supply and sewage systems, street lighting, water drainage and waste collection (cf. http://www.habisp.inf.br/theke/documentos/estudosepesquisas/relatorioanalitico/index.html).
7. In the analysis made in 2000, I combined the overlay and tag techniques, reflecting the fact that at the time I lacked any recent parameters for analyzing the household and population results since the last census conducted by the municipality dated from 1987. In this exercise, however, I used the data to help choose between the techniques or a combination of both. Although the Habisp platform

had initially been fed with data from geostatistical estimates, these have since been continually updated in the field by SEHAB officers. We concluded that the overlay tool showed a tendency to underestimate the numbers when the census sectors are much larger than the polygons defined for the favelas and/or possess relatively large, empty areas. This means that is an option only when favelas and census sectors present a very proximate geometry. I discovered, however, that even in this situation the tool can lead to distortions since some information is withheld for sectors with few households due to questions of census confidentiality.

8. Correction of the favela areas continued to be adopted to match them to the geometry of the census areas designed on the basis of the centerlines of the road network, as highlighted in Marques et al. 2003.
9. In a study commissioned by the Ministry of Cities, the CEM developed a methodology for resolving the problem of underestimating substandard tracts in demographic censuses. Using discriminant analysis techniques, the method compares the average social composition of substandard sectors with the composition of non-special areas and discriminates those sectors similar to the substandard sectors, though they have not been classified as such. This methodology was recently applied to the data from the 2010 census concerning the metropolitan regions of São Paulo State in a study commissioned by FUNDAP (Foundation for Management Development). The growth rate of the population in precarious settlements in the SPMR was 0.76 per year. Hence, the relative stability observed in São Paulo municipality has been reproduced in the rest of the SPMR.
10. Analysis of the literacy rate disaggregated by age ranges shows that the fall in illiteracy was not related to the "aging" of the population since this rate is actually higher among older sections of the population. See http://www.iets.org.br/biblioteca/Analfabetismo_no_Brasil.pdf.
11. The term "immediate surroundings" refers to a 300-meter band around the favelas obtained through the use of the bands tool of the Maptitude software. To improve capture of the conditions around the favelas, I extended the band by 100 meters, set out in Saraiva and Marques (2005), which aims to minimize those cases where the band includes just empty areas or urban barriers.
12. To analyze the behavior of the indicators, I reduced the universe of 96 districts in the municipality to those 55 districts with more than 10 favelas since the data in the districts with few favelas is inconsistent.
13. The exceptions are Alto De Pinheiros, Jardim Paulista, Perdizes, Moema, Bela Vista, Consolação, República, Sé, Cambuci, Brás and Bom Retiro districts, which do not contain favelas.
14. Other studies conducted by CEM using a different methodology from the one used here confirm the low population growth in precarious settlements over the last decade.
15. As in an earlier study (Saraiva & Marques 2005), to avoid introducing any bias to the analysis, we discounted information for municipalities with less than 10 substandard tracts. The analysis included the municipalities of Carapicuíba, Diadema, Embu, Ferraz de Vasconcelos, Francisco Morato, Franco da Rocha, Guarulhos, Itaquequecetuba, Mauá, Osasco, Santo André, São Bernardo do Campo, Suzano and Taboão da Serra.
16. According to IBGE data (2012), the per-capita GDP for Osasco and São Bernardo is higher than São Paulo's, while the per-capita GDPs for Diadema and Santo André are lower.
17. The distance average used was log-likelihood and the selection of the final number of clusters was fixed at four. The percentage attributed in manipulating the noise caused by outliers was 5 percent. The result of the analysis indicated a

good quality of cluster cohesion and separation. The variance analysis, ANOVA, indicated the desired level of significance, lower than 0.05 for all variables.
18. The More Equal Santo André Program consists of the joint and simultaneous application within the same territory of the city of 19 social programs designed to improve social inclusion.
19. The favelas and urbanized nucleuses in the São Paulo municipality and the substandard tracts of the other municipalities (containing at least 10 substandard tracts) from the metropolitan region comprised a total of 3,224 polygons.
20. On this point, it would be interesting to verify the impact of the Guarapiranga Program, launched in 1996, aimed at the socio-environmental recuperation of the favelas and precarious housing developments located in the region of the Guarapiranga Reservoir in São Paulo city. Frozen in 2001, the program was relaunched four years later when it was also expanded to include the areas around the Billings Reservoir and was renamed the Mananciais Program (or River Source Program).

Bibliography

Denaldi, R. (2003). *Políticas de Urbanização de Favelas: evolução e impasses*. FAUUSP: PhD thesis.
Leeds, A. (1969). The significant variables determining the character of squatter settlements. *America Latina*, 12(3), pp. 44–86.
Mangin, W. (1967). Latin American squatter settlements: A problem and a solution. *Latin American Research Review*, 2(3), pp. 65–98.
Maricato, E. (1996). *Metrópole na periferia do capitalismo*. São Paulo: Hucitec.
Marques, E., Torres, H. and Saraiva, C. (2003). Favelas no Município de São Paulo: estimativas de população para os anos 1991, 1996 e 2000. *Revista Brasileira de Estudos Urbanos*, 5(1), pp. 15–30.
Pasternak, S. (2006). São Paulo e suas favelas. *Revista do Programa de Pós-Graduação em Arquitetura e Urbanismo da FAUUSP*, 19, pp. 176–197.
Pasternak, S. (2000). Degradação ambiental em favelas. In: Torres, H. and Costa, H. (eds.) *População e Meio Ambiente: debates e desafios*. São Paulo: Editora do Senac, pp. 271–297.
Pasternak, S. and Bógus, L. M. M. (2001). São Paulo: o caleidoscópio urbano. *São Paulo em Perspectiva*, 15(1), pp. 31–44.
Pearlman, J. E. (1976). *The myth of marginality: Urban poverty and politics in Rio de Janeiro*. Berkley: University of California Press.
Saraiva, C. and Marques, E. (2005). A dinâmica social das favelas da Região Metropolitana de São Paulo. In: Marques, E. and Torres, H. (eds.) *São Paulo: segregação. pobreza e desigualdades sociais*. São Paulo: Ed. SENAC, pp. 143–167.
Silva, H. M. B. (2000). *Programas de urbanização e desenvolvimento do mercado em favelas brasileiras*. Paper prepared to Lincoln Institute of Land Policy.
Torres, H. (2005). A fronteira paulistana. In: Marques, E. and Torres, H. (eds.) *São Paulo: segregação. pobreza e desigualdades sociais*. São Paulo: Ed. SENAC, pp. 101–120.
Torres, H. and Marques, E. (2002). *Tamanho populacional das favelas paulistanas. Ou os grandes números e a falência do debate sobre a metrópole*. Paper presented at XIII Meeting of ABEP.

Turner, J. (1968). *Uncontrolled urban settlement: Problems and policies, Urbanization: development policies and planning, International social development review No 1*, New York: United Nations.
Uemura, M. M. (2000). Programa de saneamento ambiental da bacia do Guarapiranga: alternativa para proteção dos mananciais? FAU-PUC Campinas: MA dissertation.
UN-Habitat. (2003). *The challenge of slums: Global report on human settlements.* Nairobi: United Nations Human Settlements Programme.
Valladares, L. do P. and Figueiredo, A. (1981). Habitação no Brasil: uma introdução à literatura recente. *BIB*, 11, pp. 25–49.
Vekemans, S. J. R. and Giusti, J. (1969). Marginality and ideology in Latin American development. *Studies in Comparative International Development*, 5(11), pp. 221–234.

9 Public Housing Production

Eduardo Cesar Leão Marques and
Leandro de Pádua Rodrigues

In this chapter we analyze the production of social housing (*habitação de interesse social* [HIS]) by public authorities over the recent period in the SPMR. Given the competitive nature of the division of institutional responsibilities in the provision of housing policies in Brazil, this production includes policies at three government levels: municipal, undertaken by the São Paulo Popular Housing Company (*Companhia de Habitação Popular São Paulo* [COHAB]); state, implemented by the Urban Housing Development Company (*Companhia de Desenvolvimento Habitacional Urbano* [CDHU]); and federal, principally those implemented by the My House My Life Program (*Programa Minha Casa Minha Vida* [MCMV] Program). Since the creation of the federal program in 2008 and 2009, however, the first two agencies have practically ceased developing policies for producing their own housing units, concentrating instead on favela urbanization and the reform of housing projects built over the last decades. In fact, over the last five years, MCMV Program has produced close to 130,000 housing units,[1] while CDHU produced less than 12,000 housing units, some of them in association with the federal program itself. On the other hand, the new agency created by the São Paulo state government—Casa Paulista—is too recent to have produced significant effects on new social housing projects in the region up to the date studied.[2] For this reason, the present chapter focuses its attention on the production of the MCMV Program, including construction projects contracted up to June 2014.

It is worth pointing out that the very distinction between public and private housing production is increasingly artificial given the recent transformations of the sector. Traditionally, the difference between these two fields was clearer since the private market was uninterested in supplying housing for low-income families. More recently, though, these two fields have tended to converge, first as a result of the gradual reform of the housing sector at national level (Dias 2012) and later following the introduction of a new mechanism for implementing the MCMV Program that was unconventional by Brazilian standards, involving direct contracting of private construction firms by the Caixa Econômica Federal (CEF). Despite this convergence, however, the two forms of production still encounter significant differences in terms of demand, especially for the low-income bands of the MCMV Program. Hence, while we study the production of this program in this chapter, Telma Hoyler analyzes the market production in the next chapter.

The program delivered 619 construction projects up to June 2014, totaling 131,363 contracted units. Among these, 35 percent were contracted for Band 1 (zero to three minimum wages), 38 percent for Band 2 (three to six minimum wages) and 27 percent for Band 3 (six to 10 minimum wages). Despite the high production volume, which undoubtedly represents an advance in relation to the previous housing sector situation, the program has been criticized mainly from two directions. First, for allocating to the lowest-income bands (families in Band 1), who represent around 70 percent of the housing shortage at national level and at 76 percent in the SPMR (Ministry of Cities 2009), a share of financial resources lower than their actual share of the housing deficit (initially 40 percent and later 60 percent nationally). Second, the program was blamed for generating a new wave of peripheralization and the reinforcement of segregation in Brazilian cities, considering the small role allocated to local governments in the implementation and the considerable discretion allowed to private constructors when proposing housing projects. The present chapter empirically tests these hypotheses for the SPMR, analyzing not only the localizations of the building projects but also their relation to the urban structure already in place. When these dimensions are considered, we obtain results that qualify the conclusions reached by existing studies of the topic.

The chapter is organized in three parts in addition to the present introduction and the conclusion. In the following section, we briefly survey housing policies in Brazil and explain the general outlines of the program as well as the criticisms directed toward it. In the second section, we describe public housing production in the SPMR, both in quantitative terms and in terms of its overall geographic distribution. In the third part, we investigate the spatial dimension of the program in detail, analyzing the segregation patterns of the housing projects, comparing them to the localizations of the projects constructed by COHAB and CDHU and to the social composition of the residents living in the areas surrounding the new projects in 2010. At the end, we summarize the chapter's main findings.

Housing Policies and the My House My Life Program

As already discussed in the first chapter, the main moment in the expansion of the public housing supply occurred during the military dictatorship as part of the system organized by National Housing Bank (*Banco Nacional da Habitação* [BNH]) and the Housing Financing System (*Sistema Financeiro da Habitação*) created in 1964. These federal institutions funded state or metropolitan companies,[3] which in turn produced new housing units in projects in urban peripheries, built by private construction firms, for financed sale. This policy led to a considerable expansion in the mass production of federal housing, although these projects were marked by low-quality construction, widespread corruption and a highly peripheral pattern of localization, adding to the high levels of segregation already present in Brazilian cities (Maricato 1987). Additionally, lower-income social groups were never covered by the policy since they were unable to meet the funding criteria.

Between the shutting down of BNH in 1986 and the creation of the Ministry of Cities in 2002, the federal government maintained a low presence in public housing policies (Cardoso & Aragão 2013), although important institutional initiatives were gradually introduced over the 1990s, especially in terms of regulating private-sector production (Dias 2012). The creation of the ministry began the process of intense institutional construction already discussed in Chapter 1, although perhaps with less insulation from party political maneuvering than desirable (Rolnik 2012).

Returning to the central topic of this chapter, the federal government launched the MCMV Program in 2008, injecting public housing policies with an unparalleled volume of resources in the last few decades. Organized along very different lines to previous initiatives, the program was developed in two phases, the first launched in 2009 and the second in 2011. It has been also gradually transformed over time with the issue of numerous inter-ministerial ordinances and presidential decrees, adding a myriad of rules not always easy to comprehend as a whole. The program's initial goal was to build 1 million new homes for families on an income below 10 minimum wages per month. However, the program in fact tried to achieve more general objectives, becoming included in a series of measures for boosting economic activity in a context of international economic crisis (Lima et al. 2013). Some of the most important decisions in terms of program design stemmed from the imperative to produce immediate results, in line with the economic objective, which critics argued, explained why the program mostly failed to follow the guidelines set by the 2004 National Housing Plan (Bonduki 2009, Lima et al. 2013). The first phase was concluded in 2011 with the construction of 4,493 housing projects totaling 743,430 units (Cardoso et al. 2013). The program's second phase was launched in 2011 and set the even more ambitious target of building more than 1 million homes at the cost of R$126 billion by 2014, including R$73 billion as subsidies for families in Bands 1 and 2. The production target for Band 1 families was initially set at 400,000 units in the first phase but was later increased in the second phase to 860,000 units by 2014.

To implement the program, an atypical arrangement was made for its implementation, very different from any previous Brazilian experience in housing policies. Because of the scale of the program's targets and the political and economic objective of immediately enabling the projects to be built, construction firms were allowed to present projects to CEF directly to obtain funding. Local governments were mainly responsible for making land available after joining the program via CEF, the program's financial administrator.

The program proposed to reduce the national housing shortfall by 14 percent and established three bands targeting families with monthly incomes between zero and 10 minimum wages, with each band involving different financing conditions. The main innovation in terms of the program's design was precisely the conditions given to the poorest families: a high subsidy for families with an income up to three minimum wages (initially R$1,395 and later R$1,600, in Phase II) and moderate subsidy for families with an income between three and six minimum wages (initially R$2,790 and later R$3,100 in Phase II). The third band, ranging from six to 10 minimum wages (from R$2,791 to R$4,650 and later from R$3,101 to R$5,000 in Phase II) was not subsidized. The financial arrangement also includes the Housing Assurance Fund (*Fundo Garantidor da Habitação* [FGHab]), a compensation system in case of income instability among borrowers, as well as two subprograms[4] and economic subsidies, which simplifying, can be summarized as follows:

(1) Residential Lease Fund (*Fundo de Arrendamento Residencial* [FAR]): This fund provides financial resources (in the form of subsidies) to those families in Band 1 and to the construction firms (in the form of financing) wishing to build housing units for this band. In the case of this income band, the final borrowers cannot choose the housing project in which they will live: Instead units are allocated via a random draw made by the municipal council.
(2) Social Development Fund (*Fundo de Desenvolvimento Social* [FDS])-Entities: Also exclusive to Band 1, but with resources allocated to families organized in cooperatives, this fund is aimed exclusively at housing movement entities that operate housing construction firms.
(3) National Urban Housing Program (*Programa Nacional de Habitação Urbana* [PNHU]): This program is aimed at families earning up to 10 minimum wages. In practice, however, only families in Bands 2 and 3 manage to acquire a home since the sales limit price over the housing unit is higher than that provided by FAR: Currently, in the PNHU funding lines, homes can be sold to a maximum value of R$170,000, while the FAR limit is R$76,000. The two main lines of funding in the SPMR during the period studied here are: "off-plan property," for individuals collectively forming an organized entity, and "support for production," which enables financing for construction firms during the building phase.
(4) Urbanization: The financial resources are released by the Brazilian Development Bank (*Banco Nacional de Desenvolvimento Econômico e Socia*: [BNDES]) and channeled toward the urbanization of precarious settlements.

As of June 2014, 2.12 million units had been contracted, approximately 60 percent in Band 1, 28 percent in Band 2 and 12 percent in Band 3. However, not all the states of the federation maintained the program's general pattern of targeting mostly Band 1. The distribution of housing production by states roughly matches urban population, with São Paulo producing around 407,543 units, Minas Gerais 195,229 and Bahia 191,628, followed by Rio de Janeiro with 150,435 and Rio Grande do Sul, with approximately 132,000 (Marques & Rodrigues 2013). The distribution by bands also varies substantially between states, although most of them have concentrated production on Band 1. The states that proportionally targeted Band 1 more were located in the North, led by Roraima and Amapá. São Paulo, whose production will be analyzed in detail in the remainder of this chapter, is among the group that least provided for Band 1, with its production concentrated in Band 2 and Band 3.

The program was enthusiastically welcomed and at the same time criticized by the urban policies community. On the other hand, people welcomed the volume of investments made and praised the creation for the first time of a financial solution that enabled the production of homes for relatively low-income bands by the private sector, injecting a considerable volume of subsidies. On the other hand, criticisms were made mainly concerning two points. First, there is some wariness in relation to the targeting of Band 1: Phase 1 of the MCMV Program allocated 47 percent of its financial resources to subsidize the families in Band 1 (Brazil 2009), while Phase 2 of the program increased the resources for Band 1 by 60 percent. However, the housing shortage in the band up to three minimum wages is 89.6 percent, according to the calculations of the João Pinheiro Foundation (Brazil 2011). The consequence of this mismatch is that the housing deficit in the band up to three minimum wages "might be reduced 7.13% by the MCMV Program, while in the band from 3 to 10 MW would be reduced by 99.63%" (Nascimento & Tostes 2011). Furthermore, the MCMV Program would tend to "[benefit] sections of the middle class . . . generating a market for the private sector at a lower risk" (Bonduki 2009, p. 13). Along the same lines, Arantes and Fix (2009) argue that the tendency to not target the classes that really need the subsidy will continue. Bonduki (2009) point out the clear risk of the program producing poor-quality housing that largely fails to respond to the profile of the housing shortage, concentrated in the band up to three minimum wages. In fact, the author argues that even if the program goal of building 400,000 housing units for this band was achieved, "just 6% of the shortfall would be met" (Bonduki 2009, p. 14). Hence, once again in Brazilian history, a program would target officially (on paper) the lower-income social groups but in practice would reach mainly the middle classes—the same as occurred during the BNH cycle.

As we have argued, however, the distribution of production by bands across Brazil suggests that in most states a higher proportion of housing projects were built for Band 1 than Bands 2 and 3. Nonetheless, more precise analyses comparing the results of the MCMV Program with the proportions set out in the National Housing Plan suggest an excessive concentration of the housing program production in smaller cities in the interior of states, which possess smaller levels of housing problems but easier conditions for construction (Lima et al. 2013). The mechanism behind this concentration seems to be the wider availability of cheap land, although this helps take the program beyond the more general objectives of housing policy. The production of a higher number of studies on specific cities may or may not confirm this tendency.

Another set of criticisms concerns the construction projects themselves. The program merely established a set of basic characteristics for the types of units and projects to be produced, with 39 square meters for apartments and 36 square meters for houses.[5] This schema included two rooms, a living room, kitchen, bathroom and service area. The first studies investigating satisfaction levels among project beneficiaries revealed a variety of criticisms concerning building types and standards (Cardoso et al. 2013). The projects were limited to 500 units in the case of building blocks and 300 in the case of condominiums, but no restriction was imposed on building adjacent projects. As we shall show in the analysis of the São Paulo data, this happened in various cases, substantially increasing the scale of the built spaces, though it cannot be taken as the overall pattern of the program.

According to most critics, this mismatch is derived from a radical dissociation of the program from the principles and targets of the National Housing Plan (*Plano Nacional de Habitação*: see Balbim et al. 2013) as well as local urban policies (Cardoso et al. 2013, Pequeno 2013).[6] Some studies, however, report more continuities than ruptures in relation to the policies already implanted previously by local housing agencies, as in the case of Belém (Lima et al. 2013).

The literature has criticized in particular the absence of greater controls on the localization of the construction projects, held responsible for generating yet another cycle of poor-quality housing being produced in highly peripheral locations, reinforcing social segregation in space and to a certain extent repeating the experiences of the BNH period (Arantes & Fix 2009, Bonduki 2009, Cardoso et al. 2013, Pequeno 2013, Rolnik 2012). This, critics argue, has been reinforced by the lack of any regulatory framework concerning the localization of housing projects financed by the CEF. In cities with more than 50,000 inhabitants and in metropolitan regions, the cost of urban land is very high, meaning that construction firms look for lands distant from urbanized areas to reduce their costs and maximize their profits (Cardoso 2013, Cardoso et al. 2013). In fact, a pamphlet on the program produced by the Ministry of Cities recognized this risk when it stated that "[i]t is important to take care to avoid reproducing the past practices of housing programs that constructed poor quality and badly located projects" (Brazil 2010, p. 22). Responding to this problem, the program prioritizes states and municipalities that have assigned "land plots located in a consolidated urban area for implanting construction projects linked to the program" (Brazil 2010, p. 35). However, this is the only incentive available for trying to curb the potential distant localization of housing projects, and no stronger controls are established to ensure that the "care" expressed in the official texts is transformed into a feature of the implemented policy.

This problem is, critics argue, reinforced by the program having been pushed into the background of state and municipal government actions: "[H]ence the projects are not formulated through the interaction of public authorities or organized demand. . . . [T]hey are not defined as part of the municipal strategy of urban project and may even work against it" (Arantes & Fix 2009, pp. 3–4). As the projects are presented by the construction firms, they are "strictly conceived as commodities, generating profits for their proponents" (Arantes & Fix 2009, p. 4). This is seen to encourage a strong market logic in the program, as happened too during the BHN period, which impedes catering for the low-income band up to three minimum wages.

The existing empirical analyses confirm these hypotheses concerning segregation. Araújo et al. (2013) analyzed the distribution pattern of projects in the Rio de Janeiro Metropolitan Region (RJMR), emphasizing their peripheral localization. Pequeno (2013) undertook the same exercise for the Fortaleza Metropolitan Region (FMR), reaching similar conclusions in terms of the tendency toward peripheralization. The data reported by Mercês (2013) and Moysés et al. (2013) also highlight the peripheral pattern in the case of the new projects in Belém and Goiânia, respectively.

However, we think that the analyses of segregation conducted up to now by the existing studies can be refined. First, some studies analyze just the program's production for Band 1, overlooking a substantial portion of the housing production (and deficit) for Band 2, which in some cities may be highly relevant and follow the differentiated spatial pattern.

Additionally, and more importantly, any analysis of segregation cannot limit itself to an analysis of the general distribution of the projects using maps or a more detailed discussion at most at the level of municipalities. Although these dimensions are important, they represent merely an initial approach to the problem since it would be unreasonable to presume that the MCMV Program would promote housing projects in very central locations or in districts occupied by higher income classes when no other public housing program does. To analyze segregation patterns, therefore, we need to methodologically establish comparative parameters for distances and localizations. This is the only way that we can take into account the scale differences of different cities and the existence of polycentric urban structures as well as evaluate the program in comparison with existing public housing projects. In relation to the latter, the debate has also largely overlooked the fact that the stock of housing units produced by the state through housing companies is more clearly comparable to Band 2 of the MCMV Program in terms of income than to Band 1 since the BNH production model prioritized income groups similar to the former.

The next sections analyze the spatial pattern of the MCMV Program's housing projects in the SPMR taking into account these dimensions. Next, we analyze the general characteristics of the program's housing production by band within the space of the metropolis. In the third section, we test the critical arguments relating to social segregation in space, employing geoprocessing tools to provide a more precise analysis of the segregation patterns associated with the projects constructed in the three program bands.

The My House My Life Program in the São Paulo Metropolitan Region

As of June 2014, 619 new projects[7] were contracted in the SPMR by the MCMV Program, totaling 131,363 units, with 39,923 units already delivered by that time and another 52,611 units under construction. Among the contracted units, 35 percent were targeted for Band 1 (zero to three minimum wages), 38 percent for Band 2 (three to six minimum wages) and 27 percent for Band 3 (six to 10 minimum wages). By way of comparison, Cardoso et al. (2013) indicate that 42,492 units were built in the RJMR, 53 percent of them for Band 1. Fortaleza, on the other hand, received 15,285 units, 80 percent for Band 1 (Pequeno 2013), while Belém had 7,243 units, 49 percent for Band 1 (Mercês 2013).

In terms of housing projects, the distribution is a little different, considering the varied average sizes of the projects. Band 1 presents, in the SPMR, slightly larger housing projects with 258 units, on average, resulting in 178 projects, while Band 2 had an average of 177 units and 263 projects, and Band 3 has 170 units per housing project and 178 new projects.

Lima et al. (2013) estimate the Band 1 share to be just 9 percent of the national housing shortage in 2007. This deficit calculation uses the methodology of the João Pinheiro Foundation (Brazil 2011) and includes units to be replaced due to precarious conditions and to alleviate excessive densification, excessive rent and cohabitation. In São Paulo's case, 76 percent of the deficit in the metropolitan region is located in Band 1, 13 percent in Band 2 and just 2 percent in Band 3. Overall, the program's housing production reduced the shortage by 18.9 percent, but by just 8.8 percent in Band 1 and 55.2 percent in Band 2, as well as exceeding the deficit in Band 3. Although the program helped reduce the deficit in the SPMR, therefore, it did at much lower proportions than the investments made by the implemented program.

In terms of the program's subcomponents, this new housing production in the SPRM followed a fairly clear pattern of distribution. In Band 1 FAR production was widely predominant (120 projects), with FDS-entities a distant second (with 43 projects) and urbanization in third (16 projects). Bands 2 and 3 present different profiles with most involving "support for production" (233 projects for Band 2 and 172 for Band 3), followed by "off-plan property" (48 projects in Band 2 and 36 in Band 3). In general terms, therefore, when we talk about Band 1, we are discussing FAR projects, while we are analyzing "support for production" when referring to Bands 2 and 3.

The biggest concentration of units was in the largest municipalities of the metropolitan region: São Paulo, Guarulhos, Mogi das Cruzes, Suzano, São Bernardo do Campo, Cajamar, São André, Osasco and Mauá.

Subsequent tests will allow the segregation involved in these housing projects to be verified with more precision, but an initial approach to the question can be made through observation of maps. Since the spatial distribution of projects varies substantially according to the band, we have opted to present the localization of each band separately. Figure 9.1 displays the information by band. As can be seen, the pattern for Band 1 is peripheral but also affects more consolidated areas of the periphery. We can also highlight the Itaquera region and the outskirts of the East Zone of São Paulo as well as regions in Jardim Ângela, Guarulhos, Mogi das Cruzes, Poá and Suzano and in the São Paulo ABC, especially in Diadema, Santo André and Mauá. As we shall see later, an important portion of these localizations on the periphery are close to existing housing projects. We can also observe the location of some projects (three) in the center of São Paulo, contracted very recently and yet to be built.

The localization pattern for Band 2 is much more dispersed and much less peripheral, with innumerable projects in the more inner region of São Paulo municipality as well as the Center and the North Zone. It is important to note the contrast between this presence and what Cardoso et al. (2013) report concerning the absence of projects in central areas of Rio de Janeiro. In São Paulo, more than a few Band 2 and 3 projects are located in areas of the traditional center. However, more peripheral localizations are

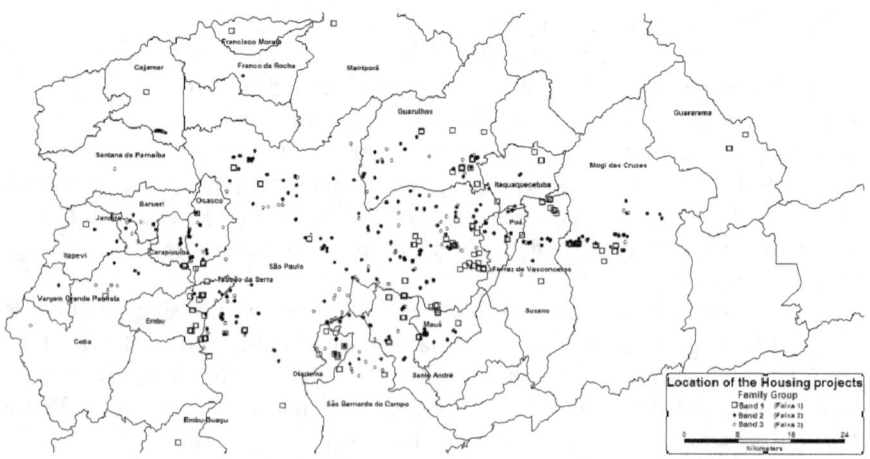

Figure 9.1 Localization of housing projects by MCMV Program band, SPMR.

Source: Data from the Caixa Econômica Federal elaborated using CEM cartographies.

also found, including the large agglomeration in Cajamar and projects in the West in Barueri, Jandira, Itapevi and Osasco, with numerous projects in Mogi das Cruzes and the São Paulo ABC region, in particular Diadema, São Bernardo, Santo André and Mauá, where another large agglomeration is found. The East Zone of São Paulo municipality also received a lot of projects but in more consolidated regions.

Finally, Band 3 has a very similar pattern to Band 2. It can be said, in fact, that in terms of macro-localization, the Band 3 projects as a whole are more peripheral than Band 2, at least in terms of the presence of housing projects in the more inner region of the metropolis. Attention is also drawn to the lower number of projects in Mogi das Cruzes. The map shows an ample distribution of projects in the East Zone of São Paulo, to the southeast and southwest, as well as projects in municipalities to the west of the metropolis, Guarulhos and the ABC region.

It is also worth emphasizing the clusters of projects found in Cajamar, Mauá and the southwest of São Paulo municipality. These are housing project clusters for Bands 2 and 3, built by a variety of different construction firms, including 19 projects in the south of Cajamar and 30 projects in Mauá. Additionally, there are some projects intended for Bands 2 and 3 simultaneously. Finally, we should mention that the housing units for some projects are sold by the MCMV Program and the rest sold outside the program to families that earn more than 10 minimum wages.

Residential Segregation and the MCMV Program

Our analysis of segregation patterns in the MCMV Program housing projects will be provided in various stages of increasing detail, allowing us to investigate segregation not only in geometric terms, but also sociospatially, taking care to differentiate the program's various bands. First, we assess the scale of the projects. Second, we investigate the distances of the projects from centralities in the metropolitan region. Next, we examine the distances of the projects from important elements of urban infrastructure, such as the subway network and the CPTM rail system, as well as projects already built by COHAB and CDHU. Third, we compare the social composition of the areas surrounding the projects to assess whether the construction of these housing projects situates their residents in wealthier or poorer and more precarious areas in urban terms.

In relation to the scale of the projects, 33 clusters present more than 500 units, the biggest being located in Guarulhos, with 2,380 units in one project, and in Cajamar, with various closely located projects that together number 3,098 housing units. Although most of the housing projects are not on a large scale, therefore, some large projects do exist.

To analyze the distances from the centralities, we considered not only the distances to the main centralities of the metropolis but also the regional subcenters since, although job distribution is strongly radial and concentric from the expanded center outward, diverse other services are disseminated through various centralities. We, therefore, considered not only the distances to the most important centralities—Praça da Sé (historical center) and Berrini-Marginal Pinheiros (current business center)—but also the closest centrality based on a polycentric structure composed of: Praça da Sé, Berrini-Faria Lima and the centers of Santo Amaro, Penha, São Bernardo do Campo, Santo André, Osasco, Mogi das Cruzes and Guarulhos. It should be noted that the reported distances are the simple Euclidean distances between the location of the housing project and the closest centrality. The information is presented in Table 9.1. As it is difficult for us to analyze the distances without an external standard of comparison, we also calculated and included in the table the distances of COHAB and CDHU housing projects to the same centralities.

First, we can observe the distances involved in the MCMV Program projects. As can be seen, the distance varies between the three bands but tends to be relatively stable within them, as the low deviations in relation to the averages testify. The patterns of distances are clearly ordered, with Band 1 more distant and Band 3 the closest to the analyzed centralities. The table shows large average distances between the projects and the most important centralities of the metropolitan region (Sé and Berrini)—between approximately 19 and 28 kilometers. However, when we consider secondary centralities within the metropolis, the distances fall substantially to between 8 and 10 kilometers. Another interesting point is that the difference between the distances of the program's bands shrinks when we consider secondary centralities, though the first band continues to show higher distances. Despite these observations, the distances of the MCMV Program projects to centralities are significant, even in relation to secondary centralities, enabling the maintenance of a reasonable degree of segregation of these projects at the level of the metropolis.

Table 9.1 Distances for housing projects to centralities—MCMV, COHAB and CDHU (km).

	Band 1	Band 2	Band 3	CDHU	COHAB
Distance from Sé	25.8	20.8	19.5	21.1	18.4
Distance from Berrini	27.4	22.8	20.2	23.7	20.9
Distance to nearest centrality	10.1	7.8	8.1	10.4	10.3
Subway station	4.3	4.1	4.7	2.4	3.9
CPTM station	3.7	2.6	3.3	3.4	2.9
SUS (public) hospital	4.8	4.1	4	1.6	2.9
School	0.3	0.3	0.3	0.2	0.2

Source: Data from the Caixa Econômica Federal elaborated using CEM base maps.

The distances of COHAB and CDHU housing projects from centralities, however, provide an external standard of comparison that adds some interesting information. The average distances of the projects in the SPMR vary between 18 and 24 kilometers from the most important centralities and approximately 10 kilometers from any centrality, figures close to those found in the MCMV Program housing projects, especially the Band 1 projects. Band 3 V Program projects, on the other hand, have distance patterns similar to the COHAB projects in relation to Sé and Berrini but present smaller distances (of around 8 kilometers) than the latter (around 10 kilometers) in terms of the other centralities.

Hence, in terms of distance to centralities, the MCMV Band 1 projects are fairly similar to COHAB housing and particularly to CHDU housing. The Band 2 and 3 projects present smaller distances than the low-income housing projects already found in metropolitan São Paulo. It is worth emphasizing that the income band traditionally targeted by COHAB and CDHU does not coincide with Band 1 but with Band 2. Hence, this is the band that we can effectively compare to the BNH model policies. From this viewpoint, therefore, the localization of the MCMV housing production is less peripheral to the previous policies.

But what is the pattern of accessibility of these housing projects to urban infrastructure? Furthermore, how do we use the existing COHAB and CDHU projects as a parameter; are the latter located closer to the MCMV Program's housing? To test these dimensions, in the final rows of the table, we list the simple Euclidean distances of the MCMV projects to the subway and CPTM stations, the nearest school and the existing housing projects.[8]

The distances to the CPTM rail stations are lower than those to the subway stations for all bands, which is to be expected given the more peripheral pattern of the former network. The difference is higher for projects aimed at Bands 2 and 3. The distances of the existing COHAB and CDHU housing projects to subway stations, on the other hand, tend to be much lower, the result of the concentration of projects in Itaquera, but similar to the MCMV projects in relation to the CPTM rail stations.

The presence of school facilities is fairly similar for all bands, which is unsurprising given the widespread diffusion of schools across the metropolitan region today, even in the most outlying peripheries. On the other hand, the distance to public hospitals is substantially higher for the MCMV Program projects, especially in Bands 1 and 2, compared to the existing low-income housing projects. The short distance of the COHAB projects results from their high concentration in Cidade Tiradentes.

Given the program's design, it might be expected that Band 1 projects were the closest to the existing housing projects, while those of Band 3 would be the furthest away, and that the higher distances to the transport system were observed in relation to Band 1 projects (and the lowest among Band 3). This is not exactly the picture observed in the table. Although Band 1 projects tend to be closer to existing housing projects, Band 3 is not the most distant. On the other hand, the Band 3 projects are the most distant to the subway, which has a less peripheral network than the CPTM rail system. Additionally, the MCMV Program projects present higher proximity with the CDHU projects than the COHAB projects for all bands.

Residential segregation concerns the homogeneity of the social composition of the city's areas, separated by distances from other similarly homogeneous spaces. Consequently, another way for us to apprehend the dimensions relating to segregation is by comparing the characteristics of the areas surrounding the projects with those that we can imagine would be those of future residents of the housing projects. Geoprocessing tools help us in this task once again since we can generate estimates using the data from the 2010 census for the social characteristics of the residents from the areas surrounding the projects at a given distance. In this case, we analyzed a 500-meter surrounding area. Table 9.2 presents the information, including similar data relating to COHAB and CDHU housing projects and to the metropolitan region as a whole to establish parameters for comparison.

As can be seen, in terms of social characteristics, the area surrounding the Band 1 projects diverges considerably from the averages of the metropolitan region and approximates those of the CDHU projects and, in particular, the COHAB projects. The areas surrounding Bands 2 and 3, as would

Table 9.2 Average social characteristics of the area surrounding projects (1000 meters), 2010.

	MCMV Program			CDHU	COHAB	SPMR
	Band 1	Band 2	Band 3			
Social characteristics						
Average income (R$)	1,187	1,640	1,713	1,284	1,235	2,029
Household heads with nominal monthly income up to 1/2 minimum wage (%)	2.1	1.3	1.1	1.5	1.5	1.2
Average years of study—in years	6.9	8.0	8.1	7.1	7.1	8.7
Population age under 10 years (%)	17.8	15.7	15.3	17.0	17.4	14.2
Population in favelas (%)	12.0	8.6	9.0	10.8	11.3	3.3
Households and infrastructure						
Rented home (%)	17.2	20.4	20.9	17.5	17.3	7.6
Home with main water (%)	97.8	99.1	98.7	98.0	99.1	98.9
Home with own sewage disposal (%)	83.9	89.6	88.9	87.8	90.8	92.0

	MCMV Program			CDHU	COHAB	SPMR
	Band 1	Band 2	Band 3			
Households and infrastructure						
Home with waste collection by truck (%)	94.3	95.1	93.5	93.6	93.3	80.1
Home with waste collection by dumpster (%)	2.9	3.1	3.6	5.0	6.2	2.7
Home with metered electricity (%)	80.8	85.5	86.4	84.9	84.5	86.7
With paved road (%)	93.2	97.1	96.8	95.6	96.7	95.8
With sidewalk (%)	85.3	91.6	89.9	90.1	91.1	90.1
With curbs (%)	91.3	95.1	94.3	91.9	92.7	93.3
With culverts/manholes (%)	42.3	45.7	46.2	43.7	52.1	49.1
With tree planting (%)	71.4	74.3	74.8	71.8	64.0	75.1
With garbage accumulated on streets (%)	5.2	4.5	4.4	4.7	6.0	4.1

Source: Data from the Caixa Econômica Federal elaborated using CEM base maps.

be expected given the localization patterns already presented, show higher income, schooling and literacy rates and an older age structure, though still distant from the metropolitan averages.

In relation to the characteristics of the households and access to infrastructure, the projects again show conditions below the city averages. The conditions of Bands 2 and 3, on the other hand, are also better than those surrounding Band 1 and almost identical between themselves. Attention can be drawn to the similarity between the Band 1 projects and those of the CDHU and COHAB housing projects. It is also worth stressing that the areas surrounding the COHAB and CDHU condominiums tend to have large proportions of waste collected by dumpster, while band 1 of the MCMV Program has fewer electricity meters, both indicators of low-quality infrastructural services.

As the traditional production of housing companies was concentrated in bands similar to Band 2 and not Band 1, the earlier argument concerning the program's impact on sociospatial segregation is reinforced here, in contrast to what the majority of analysts have concluded.

Finally, to complete our analysis of the characterization of the locations of the program projects and provide a view of segregation from another angle, we cross-referenced their localization with the types of space formulated in Chapter 6. While in the preceding analysis we analyzed the characteristics of the residents in the space immediately surrounding the project, in this case the comparison is between these social characteristics and the social composition of the spaces in which they are located at a broader scale. As would be expected, the localization of the bands varies substantially by type of space, although it does follow a clear order. Band 1 is strongly concentrated in spaces of manual workers—69 percent—though with a fairly substantial portion too in lower, middle-class mixed spaces: 25 percent. Bands 2 and 3 show relatively similar profiles with a predominance in mixed middleclass and lower, middle-class mixed spaces, though with inverted emphases. There is practically no project in elite spaces and very few Bands 2 and 3 projects in the space of upper middle-class spaces. This information confirmed the previous data and reinforced the similarity in terms of localization of Band 1 with the traditional São Paulo (and Brazilian) public housing production as well as indicating that Bands 2 and 3 tended to produce a different and less peripheral pattern in sociospatial terms.

Conclusion

As we have seen, the MCMV Program saw a substantial investment in production in the SPMR from its outset, building around 130,000 units. Differently to other regions of Brazil, the program catered for a relatively small portion of Band 1 and higher proportions of higher income bands. In the SPMR, the proportion of Band 1 covered was relatively small—around 35 percent (this proportion attained 60 percent on average nationally), which represented a low proportion of the housing shortage in this income band—around 8.8 percent. On the other hand, around 55 percent of the estimated deficit for Band 2 was attained, while the deficit for Band 3 was fully attained and amply exceeded.

In terms of localization, the analysis has confirmed the peripheral pattern to the localization of the projects already highlighted by the literature. The program's projects are located relatively far from centralities and large transport systems, though not diverging significantly from what public authorities have traditionally produced in the region. Generally speaking, the distances of Band 1 projects from centralities tend to be relatively similar to those of existing COHAB and CDHU housing projects, while projects for income Bands 2 and 3 show better access to centralities. In terms of the social composition of the surrounding areas, those areas around Band 1 projects are once again very similar to those of existing low-income housing projects, while those for Bands 2 and 3 diverge more and are closer to the averages for the metropolis. This scenario is confirmed by the analysis of the type of space where the projects have been built. While Band 1 projects are predominantly constructed in manual worker spaces, maintaining the pattern of segregation, projects in Bands 2 and 3 have been launched primarily in lower middle-class mixed and mixed middle-class spaces, respectively. As existing housing projects primarily benefit an income band matching Band 2 of the MCMV Program, the pattern of localizations in the SPMR can be said to be less peripheral than the earlier housing production, though the distances are fairly high.

In terms of residential segregation, therefore, the program's projects in the SPMR have followed the general logic of segregation patterns in the metropolis, but without worsening them, as suggested by a significant portion of the existing literature. Given the volume of housing production involved, however, it is also clear that an important chance has been lost to contribute to a more intense alteration of the patterns of social segregation present in the São Paulo metropolis.

Notes

1. According to the Caixa Econômica Federal's Executive Report of 30 June 2014—all the data on the MCMV Program's housing production in the SPMR has been taken from this report.
2. This figure includes some very different modalities of housing production, including a large number of letters of credit, but also global ventures, *mutirões* (communal projects) and production for specific corporations, like the military police or SABESP (water and sewage company of the state of São Paulo), among others. See http://www.cdhu.sp.gov.br/producao-new/producao-habitacional.asp?destHab=0&Pag=producao-habitacional
3. Including COHAB-São Paulo, run by the São Paulo Municipality. CDHU, belonging to the state government, was created later in 1989.
4. The National Rural Housing Program (*Programa Nacional de Habitação Rural* [PNHR]) is not described here since no construction project was contracted under this modality in the SPMR.
5. These averages have altered since the creation of the MCMV Program (in 2009) with the specifications for Phase 1, the transition and Phase 2. For more information on Band 1, see http://www.caixa.gov.br/habitacao/mcmv/habitacao_urbana/pp_const_mov_soc/construcao_civil/recursos_far.asp.
6. Pequeno (2013), for example, reports that no project produced by the MCMV Program in the municipality of Fortaleza is located in the areas designated by the urban master plan for this use.
7. Among the 619 projects, one project from Band 1 could not be georeferenced. Hence, the analyses concerning localization relate to 618 projects.
8. The largest distances occur between six projects located in Guararema municipality and COHAB and CHDU housing projects (40 and 11 kilometers, respectively) as well as subway stations (45 kilometers). The biggest distance among all those analyzed is 13 kilometers between CPTM rail stations and these same housing projects. These results are to some extent expected since the subway network only covers São Paulo municipality and COHAB is a municipal public company.

Bibliography

Andrade, L. and Azevedo, S. (1982). *Habitação e poder: da fundação da casa popular ao banco nacional da habitação*. Rio de Janeiro: Zahar.

Arantes, P. and Fix, M. (2009). *Como o governo Lula pretende resolver o problema da habitação (Parte 1, 2 e 3)*. Available at: http://passapalavra.info/?p=9445, Consulted 9 May 2009.

Araújo, F. S., Cardoso, A. L. and Jaenisch, S. T. (2013). Morando no Limite: Sobre Padrões de Localização e Acessibilidade do Programa Minha Casa Minha Vida na

Região Metropolitana do Rio De Janeiro. *XV Encontro da Associação Nacional de Pós-Graduação e Pesquisa em Planejamento Urbano e Regional*, pp. 1–16. http://unuhospedagem.com.br/revista/rbeur/index.php/anais/article/view/4538/4407

Arretche, M. (2002). Federalismo e relações intergovernamentais no Brasil: A reforma de programas sociais. *Dados*, 45(3), pp. 431–458.

Arretche, M. (2001). Uma Contribuição para fazermos avaliações menos ingênuas. In: Carvalho, Maria do C. B. de and Moreira, Maria C. R. (eds.) *Tendências e Perspectivas na Avaliação de Políticas e Programas Sociais*. São Paulo: IEE/PUCSP, pp. 7–224.

Arretche, M. (1990). Intervenção do Estado e setor privado: o modelo brasileiro de política habitacional. *Espaço & Debate*, 31, pp. 21–36.

Balbim, R. N., Krause, L. H. and Neto, V. C. L. (2013[0]). Minha Casa, Minha Vida, Nosso crescimento: como fica a política habitacional? IPEA. Textos para discussão 1853. Brasília: IPEA.

Bonduki, N. (2009). Do Projeto Moradia ao Programa Minha Casa Minha Vida. *Teoria e Debate*, 82, May/June, pp. 8–14.

Bonduki, N. (2002). *Origens da habitação social no Brasil: arquitetura moderna, lei do inquilinato e difusão da casa própria*. 3rd edition. São Paulo: Estação Liberdade: FAPESP.

Brazil, Ministério das Cidades. (2011). Déficit Habitacional no Brasil 2008. Ministério das Cidades. Secretaria Nacional de Habitação, p. 140.

Brazil, Ministério das Cidades. (2010). *Secretaria Nacional de Habitação. Como produzir moradia bem localizada com recursos do programa minha casa minha vida?* Brasília: DF.

Brazil. Ministério das Cidades. (2009). *Secretaria Nacional de Habitação. Avanços e Desafios: Política Nacional de Habitação*. Brasília: DF.

Cardoso, A. (2013). *O Programa Minha Casa Minha Vida e seus efeitos territoriais*. Rio de Janeiro: Letra Capital.

Cardoso, A. and Aragão, T. (2013). Do fim do BNH ao Programa Minha Casa Minha Vida: 25 anos da política habitacional no Brasil. In: Cardoso, A. (ed.) *O programa Minha Casa Minha Vida e seus efeitos territoriais*. Rio de Janeiro: IPPUR/Letra Capital, pp. 17–66.

Cardoso, A., Nunes Junior, D., Araújo, F., Silva, A, Aragão, T. and Amorim, T. (2013). Minha Casa Minha Sina: implicações da recente produção habitacional pelo setor privado na Zona Oeste da cidade do Rio de Janeiro. In: Cardoso, A. (ed.) *O programa Minha Casa Minha Vida e seus efeitos territoriais*. Rio de Janeiro: IPPUR/Letra Capital, pp. 143–160.

Dias, E. (2012). *Do Plano Real ao Programa Minha Casa, Minha Vida: negócios, votos e as reformas da habitação*. University of São Paulo: Master dissertation.

Lima, J., Ponte, J., Rodrigues, R., Ventura Neto, R. and Melo, A. (2013). A promoção habitacional através do Programa Minha Casa Minha Vida na Região Metropolitana de Belém. In: Cardoso, A. (ed.) *O programa Minha Casa Minha Vida e seus efeitos territoriais*. Rio de Janeiro: IPPUR/Letra Capital, pp. 161–186.

Maricato, E. (1998). Política urbana e de habitação social: um assunto pouco importante para o governo FHC. *Revista Praga*, São Paulo: Hucitec, 1(6), pp. 67–78.

Maricato, E. (1987). *Política habitacional no regime militar: Do milagre brasileiro à crise econômica*. Petrópolis: Vozes.

Marques, E. (2010). Urbanização e integração de assentamentos precários. *Projeto Perspectivas dos investimentos sociais no Brasil (PIS)*, draft. 1–34. Available at: http://www.cedeplar.ufmg.br/pesquisas/pis/Estudo%2025.pdf

Marques, E. and Rodrigues, L. (2013). O Programa Minha Casa Minha Vida na metrópole paulistana: atendimento habitacional e padrões de segregação. *Revista Brasileira de Estudos Urbanos e Regionais*, 15, pp. 159–177.

Mercês, S. (2013). Programa Minha Casa, Minha Vida na Região Metropolitana de Belém: localização dos empreendimentos e seus determinantes. In: Cardoso, A. (ed.) *O programa Minha Casa Minha Vida e seus efeitos territoriais*. Rio de Janeiro: IPPUR/Letra Capital, pp. 187–204.

MINHA CASA, Minha Vida. (2009). Available at: http://www.sinduscon-rio.com.br/mcmv/CARTILHADACAIXA.pdf, Consulted 31 August 2009.

Ministry of Cities (2009). http://www.cidades.gov.br/index.php/minha-casa-minha-vida

Moysés, A., Cunha, D., Borges, E. and Maia, T. (2013). Impactos da produção habitacional contemporânea na Região Metropolitana de Goiânia: dinâmica, estratégias de mercado e a configuração de novas espacialidades e centralidades. In: Cardoso, A. (ed.) *O programa Minha Casa Minha Vida e seus efeitos territoriais*. Rio de Janeiro: IPPUR/Letra Capital, pp. 255–278.

Nascimento, D. and Tostes, S. (2011). Programa Minha Casa Minha Vida: A (mesma) política habitacional no Brasil. Arquitextos. Available at: http://www.vitruvius.com.br/revistas/read/arquitextos/12.133/3936

Pequeno, L. (2013). Minha Casa, Minha Vida em Fortaleza: novas periferias? *XV Encontro da Associação Nacional de Pós-Graduação e Pesquisa em Planejamento Urbano e Regional*, pp. 1–18.

Rolnik, R. (2012). Democracy on the edge: Limits and possibilities in the implementation of an urban reform agenda in Brazil. *International Journal of Urban and Regional Research*, 35(2), pp. 239–255.

Shimbo, L. (2012). *Habitação Social, Habitação de Mercado: A confluência entre Estado, empresas construtoras e capital financeiro*. Belo Horizonte: Ed. C/Arte.

10 Private-Sector Housing Developments
Who Produces What, How and Where?

Telma Hoyler

The topic of urban land has animated debate among economists since the 1960s, as Haila (1991) showed in her review and useful categorization of the literature. After the classic works of Topalov (1979), property development also became a central topic in urban studies. French urban sociology had advanced in understanding the specific logic of real estate development through its interpretation of the city as the outcome of production processes carried out by different fractions of capital, despite the conclusion of this school of thought concerning the state's action as a blind and agency-less subject. As Topalov pointed out, urban land has no production costs, and its value is determined through a relation of social dispute. Studies of how real estate capital was reproduced thus began to include an analysis of the processes behind the valorization of urban land.

Without challenging this interpretation, but taking into account global and local transformations, some authors have more recently made important progress by investigating the details of the sector's operation. Within this framework we can include, for example, the study of the instruments through which property developers transform urban land (David & Halbert 2013), the sector's cycles, its influence and the government decisions made in relation to the market (Fainstein 1994), the effects of the capitalization of the companies (De Magalhães 2002) and changes in land use and occupation, with a transformation in its values in the postindustrial period (Hamnett & Whitelegg 2007).

This chapter will seek to continue this work by attempting to understand the structure and dynamics of the São Paulo real estate sector over the recent period. With this aim in mind, I describe the dynamic of residential private-sector housing developments in the SPMR during the period from 1985 to 2013, paying special attention to the general attributes of price and size of housing units, the spatial distribution of the developments, the characteristics of the agents involved and the policy explanations concerning the different periods encompassing production.

In Brazil, a series of institutional reforms made by the federal government buoyed the development of the private housing sector in Brazilian cities during the 2000s. Predictably, São Paulo, the country's largest city and the base for nearly all the large property developers, expresses the impact of these reforms.

Exploring this scenario, the results of the present investigation show that the country moved to a new cycle of real estate development, the main feature of which was the diversification of the economic profiles targeted by the property market. Traditionally aimed at the high-income sector, the market significantly increased its production for middle- and low-income sectors beyond the developments commercialized by the MCMV Program, though a confluence exists between them.

The context in which these reforms took place can be seen, from one angle, as a government project that aimed to turn housing production into the motor for the country's development. From another angle, though, taking into account the effort made by authors like Guy and Henneberry (2000) and David (2012) to deconstruct the operative tools and logic of the economics and finances adopted by the real estate industry, it can be concluded that the government ceded to the rhetorical arguments made by agents in the property market, who insisted and continue to insist—notwithstanding the vast range of measures adopted—on the multiple financial risks to which real estate development is exposed. As a result, a series of instruments were created to provide more legal and financial security to the sector. Both these angles appear to be correct insofar as they reveal different parts of the story. However, a more comprehensive understanding reveals a confluence of interests between the government and actors from the real estate market. In the case of approval of housing developments in São Paulo, I study this confluence in Hoyler (2015).

In fact, the reforms undertaken by the federal government offered the companies favorable conditions for public listing from 2006 onward, making São Paulo an ideal case for comparison with other cities in terms of financialization of the property market. However, contrary to the general theory suggested by Theurillat et al. (2015), the entry of financial capital into the Brazilian real estate market did not involve passing through successive evolutions, as though the country had passed from the "self-provision and self-consumption real estate market" stage to the "metropolitan financialized real estate market stage" by way of a phase of specialized housing development. In Brazil, different forms of organizing property development—which, with the appropriate adjustments, could be taken as comparable to those described by the author—coinhabit and simultaneously dispute urban space.

This coexistence of companies of different sizes and strategies is indeed fairly useful for those linked to financial capital. As we shall see later, making use of a variety of partnerships, large companies can enter new geographic regions, access new sectors, expand to lower-income sectors, increase their opportunities in the traditional markets, test new markets with lower risk and learn about the strengths and weaknesses of commercial partners.

Here I shall describe residential property development in greater São Paulo in three main sections. The first is a description of real estate developments in the period in question, including general characteristics of the developments and the cycles behind this production. In the second section

I present the types of developers working in the region and what this means in terms of new housing developments. Finally, the third section provides an analysis of the spatial distribution of private-sector housing projects over the market production cycles.

Dynamics of the Real Estate Developments

Before proceeding, it is worth remembering that private-sector housing production does not cover all housing production in the SPMR. This also includes the market associated with the construction firms that build homes commissioned by the owner-occupier or long-term tenant, public housing production, generally associated with low-income groups, and the construction of dwellings by the residents themselves—a common practice among the low-income population in the peripheries and one difficult to measure. Here, therefore, we shall focus on the typical capitalist market of housing production where the main agents are development companies.

The collection, organization and sale of information on new housing developments in the city of São Paulo are undertaken by EMBRAESP. The database of residential property developments produced by EMBRAESP covers all developments advertised through the mass media and informed by the brokers contacted by the company. Even if the developments have yet to be delivered or completely sold, they appear in the records, which is why I refer to the category as *released* housing developments.

The data presented here include the São Paulo capital and the entire SPMR since housing production in the surrounding cities is closely linked to the dynamic of the metropolis. Land availability, current regulations, the construction costs involved and the type of effective demand influence the spread or concentration of this housing production. Furthermore, the home-workplace commuter dynamic provided additional security for the big developers to produce housing for lower-income sectors living in the adjacent municipalities where working-class residences are generally found.

In the period from January 1985 to December 2013, a total of 16,935 developments were released in the SPMR, covering an area of more than 154 million square meters, with a little more than half of this total comprising floor space (i.e., the area effectively located in the internal environments of the housing unit—in Brazil this is differentiated for tax purposes). This floor space was distributed throughout the SPMR in 1,088,110 housing units made up of 2,326 houses and 14,609 apartment blocks.

The measures of central tendency for the prices[1] of housing developments indicate an average of R\$5,637.87/m^2 of floor space (equivalent to US\$1,879.29/m^2),[2] but given the glaring variability in the data, this information proves of little use: The most expensive square meter was sold in 1989 and is located in Higienópolis, a traditional district in the city center featuring buildings designed by famous architects, costing the equivalent of

R$43,430.88/m² (US$14.286,47/m²) for floor space, although this was not the most expensive unit sold over the period. Meanwhile, in Taboão da Serra, a city in the metropolitan region of São Paulo, the cheapest square meter of floor space was sold for R$944.15/m² (US$310.57/m²) in 2003.

The dispersion of housing unit floor space is also considerable: Around 68.2 percent of the developments have units up to 100 m², 30 percent of developments have units between 100 m² and 300 m² and just 1.8 percent of developments have units equal to or over 300 m² (the largest unit sold in the period being 2,000 m²).

Comparatively speaking, the prices found in São Paulo for high-income apartments are in some cases comparable to those of New York. In the Jardins, Moema and Morumbi districts, new apartments can be sold for up to R$32 million for 1,000 m², equivalent to similar-sized Upper East Side apartments costing US$11 million at the current exchange rate, though higher levels and prices are found in Manhattan. Prices in London are much higher than both cities. For a similar standard in London, an apartment will be sold in Chelsea, for example, for £10 million. However, this comparison is exploratory given the large number of variables involved in determining a property's price,[3] and the aim is merely to situate non-Brazilian readers vis-à-vis the standards of São Paulo developments. For a more comprehensive view of the residential property market, we can also consider factors such as average income, living costs and the alternatives available for buying one's own home in other cities.

The average sale price of 1 m² in Manhattan is equivalent to approximately 25 percent of the amount that a New York resident earns each year. In London, the average sale price of 1 m² in the most central region of the city is equivalent to approximately 43 percent of the amount that a London resident earns each year on average. In São Paulo, this proportion is equivalent to much less, around 13 percent on average.[4]

The dynamic of the residential property market in the period under study passed through three production cycles, detectable in terms of the total volume of units, the total number of developments and the financial amount released. Figure 10.1 illustrates this dynamic:

Cycle 1 covers the period from 1985 to 1993, with a large peak in terms of amount released in 1986, followed by a fall and a new spike in 1989, despite the maximum amount having been some way below the 1986 figure. The production of R$17.5 billion (US$5.75 billion) in 1989 fell rapidly, along with the total number of residential units released.

In 1994 Cycle 2 began, marked by a rapid increase in the number of units and amount released until 1997, followed by a brusque fall to figures close to those of 1994, though the housing production level was actually slightly lower than that year. A period of stability then ensues until 2004, marked by production oscillating at relatively low levels. The production peaks for each cycle coincide with the years during which Brazil experienced economic crises, suggesting that the country's real estate sector is a niche to

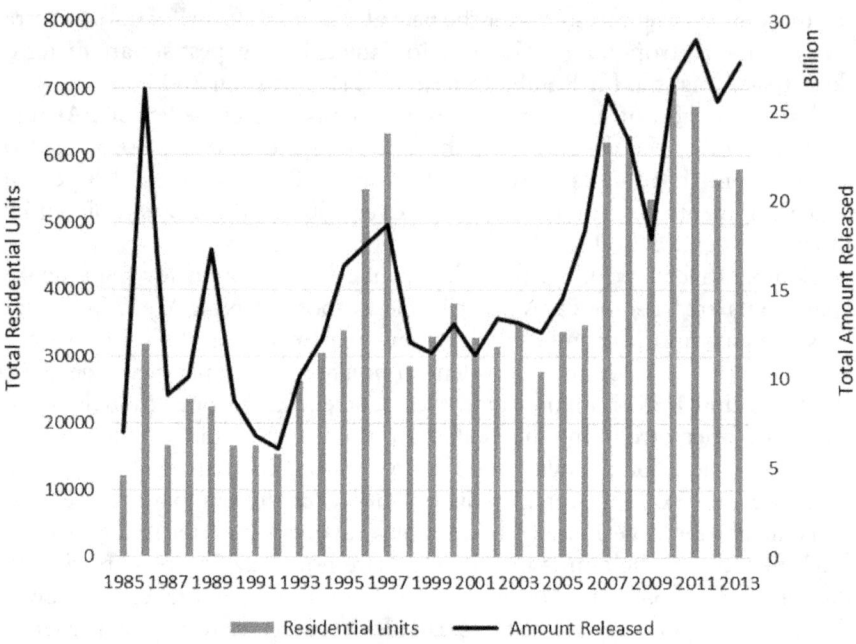

Figure 10.1 Number of residential units and amount released (1985–2013).
Source: Author's elaboration based on EMBRAESP data.

which investments converge at moments of risk and low investment profits, though this topic requires a specific analysis.

Cycle 3 began in 2005 when the number of units rose rapidly along with the overall amount released on the market. In 2007, the number of releases and the total amount released were already comparable to 1986, until then the highest peak in this time series. In 2011, the amount released on the market exceeded R$29 billion (US$9.5 billion), the largest over this historical period. In 2012, the overall amount and the number of developments released fell slightly before rising again until 2013. Based on this brief description, we can observe that the dynamic of released units in each period reveals a new cycle emerging in the real estate sector from the second half of the 2000s.

In relation to this third cycle, it is important to point out that the intense growth in production from 2005 is associated with the series of incremental reforms to housing policy made from the Fernando Henrique Cardoso government onward, culminating in the Lula government and its introduction of a wide-ranging legal framework for guaranteeing property transactions.

From 1986, when the BNH, responsible for financing production during the military dictatorship, was closed, the country's housing policy underwent intense institutional fragmentation and an increase in legal and economic insecurity.

During the Fernando Henrique Cardoso administration (PSDB, right-wing, 1995–2001), although government actions had been fragmented and sector oriented, responding in isolated form to demands from different areas linked to housing production and home loans, the research carried out by Dias (2012) indicates that a context broadly favorable to the private housing sector had already begun to emerge, subsequently expanded by the Luiz Inácio Lula da Silva government (PT, left-wing, 2003–2010). This primarily occurred through the creation of the Property Financing System (*Sistema Financeiro Imobiliário* [SFI]) in 1997, which established a regulatory framework for property financing and the operations of financial institutions on the capital market. The SFI works by raising funds in the secondary securities market and channeling them to the real estate sector through instruments enabling the securitization of receivables, quickening the turnover time of capital fixed in housing developments. The main criticism directed at the system is that it was not created to solve the housing shortage but as a financing model intended to ensure security in the sector's transactions and allow large inputs from the financial market to the benefit of groups with higher purchasing power (Royer 2009).

The same law that instituted the SFI also designed instruments for debt securitization of buyers in the residential market, such as Certificates of Real Estate Receivables (*Certificados de Recebíveis Imobiliários* [CRI]). Securitization in Brazil operates as follows: When a property developer sells the units of a building already constructed or that is planned to be constructed, he or she can opt to securitize the debts of the buyers and sell them on the market. He or she then receives back the capital used to finance the purchasers and can reinvest the funds in another development or repay any outstanding debts on the latter. Whoever buys the securitized shares receives earnings from the debt amortization and servicing directly from the purchasers. However, the policy design proved unattractive to investors. This situation only changed with the advent of Lula's political project, which included institutional reform to redress the disconnected way in which the housing sector had been treated. In the process, more funds were raised for the housing sector, and changes were made at bureaucratic levels.

The redesign of housing policy also depended on improvements to make it more attractive to the private sector, both in terms of housing production and in the granting of loans. With this aim in mind, a federal law issued in 2004 reinforced the legal framework of the SFI, needed to expand the real estate sector by encouraging banks to invest their saving funds in housing. This stimulus came through some guarantees making it easier to repossession a property in the case of nonpayment or delays in loan repayments, the creation of segregated assets[5] and increasing the legal security of the investor and buyer of the property in the case of the developer experiencing financial problems.

These measures made the environment more secure for the capitalization of property developers. From mid-2006, therefore, the relation between housing policy and private home production acquired even newer dimensions with the entry of financial capital into the development companies that made a primary offering of shares on the São Paulo Stock Exchange, as studied by Fix (2011) and Shimbo (2012).

At the same time, the Brazilian economy grew and stabilized, while purchasing power increased—essential for the mixture of public and private funds surrounding the real estate market to be connected to effective demand, which began to benefit from ample access to home loans.

Stimulated by the new federal government regulations, large companies began to consider this new consumer sector as effective demand. Moreover, these large developers were able to cater for this new market niche since, as well as being financially strengthened by capitalization, they internally developed corporate strategies (mergers and acquisitions, creation of subsidiaries, joint ventures, etc.) and measures relating to production and control (standardization of developers and control systems for costs and schedules in the construction work) that enabled them to diversify production.

The number of developers that formed partnerships to release a housing development was nonexistent during the first and second cycles, but amounted to 200 such developments in the third cycle. Corroborating this finding, a study by Souza (2011) identified 86 cases of horizontal partnerships, 12 joint ventures, 16 acquisitions and three mergers into stock market-traded companies during the period from 2005 to 2010 alone.

In relation to the developers that went public, the literature has argued that the intense capitalization also enabled the centralization in the same company of the functions of property development, construction and sale, even though this strategy has been accompanied by the difficulty of cost control, managing partners and executing developments, given the distance of the construction sites and the organizational inefficiency that these large companies gradually develop (Shimbo 2012).

The time series of residential housing releases showed a change in profile in the types of product favored during each cycle of production. To perform this analysis, the developments were separated into four distinct types of product, the latter taken as a set of matching characteristics, developed for a particular target public sharing the same aspirations and capacity for payments.

The first type of product is targeted at the low-income population. These are developments possessing up to 50 m^2 of surface area, one bathroom, up to one garage space and a total sale price as high as R$250,000 (US$82,236.84). The second type of product, aimed at middle-income groups, possesses up to 80 m^2 of surface area, up to two bathrooms, up to one garage space and a cost as high as R$450,000 (US$148,026.31). The third type of product, targeted at the upper middle-income bracket, possesses up to 200 m^2 of surface area and costs up to R$650,000 (US$213,815.78). Finally, housing units intended for high-income groups have a sale price and attributes based on Type 3 and higher.

The data show that housing production for low-income groups expanded constantly over the three cycles, increasing from 5.13 percent of production in the first cycle to 18.30 percent of total production of the third cycle. It is also notable that the other income categories displayed similar behavior in the second and third cycles, indicating a degree of stability in the volume of production for higher-income groups.

Comparing the housing development databases systemized by EMBRAESP with the information on units sold by the MCMV Program (see previous chapter) reveals a 20 percent overlap—that is, a total of 20 percent of low-income developments commercialized from 2009 onward were sold by the MCMV Program, costing less than R$196,000 (US$64,400).

This data suggest a confluence of the market and the government in the production of housing for low-income groups. Benefitting from economic policy and from learning about business operations for this economic sector pursued by the MCMV Program, companies were able to produce for low-income groups without direct government subsidies by raising the final price marginally and using other mechanisms to finance production and purchases developed and improved over the last decade.

The private-sector housing production for low-income groups in São Paulo is fundamentally different from similar sectors in cities like New York City, Paris and London since, in the latter, developments of an equivalent standard are not sold through the market but produced through public housing policies. Alternatively, the low-income population can also be assisted through government rent subsidization. In New York, 47 percent of the stock built for leasing has a price limit regulated by the government at half the market value. In London, some rent is also subsidized by the government with the benefiting population paying the equivalent of 15 percent of the average monthly salary of a London resident.

In Brazil, by contrast, home ownership has been historically encouraged, a variable to be considered when looking to understand the conditions of its urban housing market. While rent in New York, already very expensive, on average consumes 52 percent of the population's monthly income, average rent in the city of São Paulo exceeds the population's average family income. In the São Paulo case, this needs to be interpreted in light of the fact that the rental prices of the central region push the average figures upward, while the poorer population builds precarious dwellings on the peripheries to live in themselves or to rent out informally, meaning that these homes are not computed in the official statistics.[6]

Private Agents Involved in Housing Production

The real estate developer is responsible for interconnecting all the other agents involved in the construction project. It is the developer who commissions a construction firm to produce an apartment block or house and assumes responsibility for selling it on completion. It is the developer too who chooses and buys the terrain, raises the capital needed for its purchase and construction, hires the architectural and engineering projects, adapts the project to the zoning regulations applicable to the terrain, and obtains the licenses for sale and construction.

The EMBRAESP database includes information concerning three types of agent: cooperatives, public agents, and private companies—all legally termed developers, though they have distinct socioeconomic profiles. The public agent operating in São Paulo is the Metropolitan Housing Company (*Companhia Metropolitana de Habitação*), an entity set up by the federal government in the 1960s and tasked with implementing the housing policy established at that time by the BNH. Since 1985, it has released just 205 housing units in 17 developments, 16 of them concentrated in the first cycle. It produced units with an average of 48 m^2 floor space and a total sale value of R$218,000 (US$71,710). Over the period as a whole, 220 developments were produced for low-middle and low-income groups, released by 77 cooperatives: Here I can highlight the number of housing releases in the second cycle when 190 developments were built, compared to 11 in the first cycle and 19 in the third. Given the prominence exerted by private companies in property development, I shall turn to them next.

A total of 3,178 different developers involved in the residential housing developments were identified across the period, either as the sole company or in partnership with one or more other companies. The portion of developers that released developments increased by more than 50 percent between the first and second cycles, rising from 1,076 to 1,642 different companies, but decreased from the second to the third cycle, suggesting that the large developers strengthened by the federal policy began to concentrate the market.

The development firms are also strongly differentiated in terms of the spatial coverage of their projects within the SPMR. The 10 developers with 150 releases or over distributed their production over 50 districts or municipalities on average (varying between 25 and 73). Among the 27 developers that released between 50 and 150 developments, the average was 16 districts (varying between 16 and 30). This measure of central tendency fell to 10 districts among the 84 developers that produced between 20 and 25 developments and 5.5 districts among the 194 developers that produced between 10 and 20 apartment blocks.

Another way of exploring the activities of the developers and better comprehending the political economy of this sector is through the intensity of production,[7] categorizing them as contingent, active or structural (Logan & Molotch 1987). The first comprises isolated cases where the developer decided that it would be more profitable to invest in the sector without planning to do so systematically. Despite being similar in terms of the prediction of movements made by other developers when it comes to decision making, the latter two categories can be distinguished by the intervention made—or not—to alter the structural conditions of the market, an activity performed by structural-type developers.

Inspired by this categorization, analysis of the database allowed the developers to be separated into three types according to the volume of production and number of property releases. These are: small developers, who individually released an amount below R$465,500 (US$153,125) in the period and just one or two developments (representing 66.3 percent of total developers); the mid-range producers (33 percent of total developers) with a production between R$1.5 million and R$2 billion (US$493,421 and US$657,894.736); and the large developers (0.7 percent of total developers), which individually released between R$2 billion and R$25 billion (US$657 million and US$8 billion).

Apropos the latter type, it is worth highlighting that just 18 developers that went public released a total of 297,799 housing units during the period. If we compare this figure with the lower-producing developers, 2,924 companies would be needed to produce the equivalent number of property developments.

On average the large developers offer a cheaper sale price for the products aimed at the low-income market compared to the price offered for the same type of product by medium and small developers (R$165,000 compared to R$198,000 for medium companies and R$200,000 for small companies, equivalent, respectively, to US$54,276, US$65,131.57 and US$65,789.47) and a much lower average floor space (49 m^2 compared to 55 m^2 for medium companies and 60 m^2 for small companies).

Securitization, which in turn, forms the base of the SFI fund-raising system, involves a set of essential requirements for the property investment to be attractive to the investor and for the developer to be able to transform the creditor's debt into receivables through the SFI: generation of cash flow, quality of receivables, diversification of the portfolio, regularity of payments, homogenous schedules, form of amortization and ease of marketing securities, type of property, maximum value of each credit, the debt/property value ratio and the buyer's payment capacity. In this new context, the real estate development sector, with the aim of ensuring a real guarantee to a complex financial operation—like those measured by the CRIs—became structured from the outset to meet these framework criteria. These, in turn, were more achievable for the larger developers, which helps explain their prominence in real estate production over the recent period.

The Distribution of Housing Developments in the Metropolitan Space

The analysis of the spatial distribution of real estate releases is another important dimension in comprehending housing production patterns over the decade, a task made possible by geographic information system tools. Figures 10.2 and 10.3 show how the spatialization of the releases reflects the recent change in the market, considering the form in which the different social groups in the metropolis are divided.

224 Telma Hoyler

The first cycle is characterized by production concentrated fairly heavily on high-income products within the borders of São Paulo. The city peripheries, however, received practically no developments during the period. This is explained by the fact that, until the recent reforms, the low-income population residing in the peripheries did not represent effective demand. In the second cycle, the data show an increase in the production for the popular sector but still concentrated mostly in São Paulo city, especially in the East and North Zone. The third cycle, shown in Figure 10.2, was characterized, in turn, by the concomitant spread of production toward municipalities adjacent to São Paulo city, where the low- and middle-income population lives and where land prices are cheaper, as well as by the intensification of

Figure 10.2 Location of private sector developments, Cycle 1 (1985–1993).
Source: Author's elaboration based on raw data from EMBRAESP.

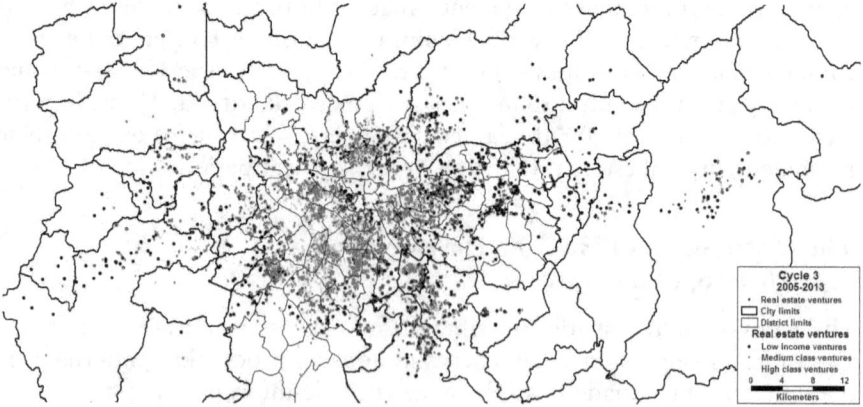

Figure 10.3 Location of private-sector developments, Cycle 3 (2005–2013).
Source: Author's elaboration based on raw data from EMBRAESP.

verticalization in older, consolidated, industrial areas in the capital, which have not experienced any significant change in their land use profile since becoming urbanized. These areas became targeted for middle-high income production. At the same time as observing a spread in production in the third cycle, we can also identify substantial levels of production in the center of São Paulo, highlighting the Santa Cecília and República districts with small apartments sold at prices that can be categorized as middle income.

Summing Up

The dynamic of real estate production in the SPMR proved to be cyclical and closely related to the macroeconomic conjuncture and the political options available for governments.

The data suggest that the real estate dynamic of the formal market during the period under study went through three production cycles in terms of volume and amount released. The last period was recently influenced by a series of incremental reforms to federal housing policy that culminated in the Lula government's establishment of a legal framework guaranteeing transactions and increasing home loans.

These measures were followed by a period of growth and stabilization in the Brazilian economy, a rise in purchasing power and the introduction of the biggest program of subsidies for purchasing homes in Brazil, leading to a resumption of housing production on a large scale. The largest volume of this production, in turn, was executed by developers that capitalized and were able to rely on their own financial and organizational framework for responding to the new demand.

Contrary to what was expected, the introduction of tools for the financialization and capitalization of the main property development companies did not lead to a shift to elite production due to the home loans available for low-income groups. This new consumer sector was discovered by the large developer companies, which were already coming to the fore, benefitting from the new financial regulations introduced by the federal government. Indeed, housing production for low-income groups increased over the course of the cycles, beyond the housing production by the MCMV Program.

In spatial terms, the last decade has been characterized by the spread of production toward the municipalities bordering São Paulo city and by the intensification of verticalization in older consolidated industrial areas in the capital, which have not experienced any significant change in their land use profile since becoming urbanized.

Notes

1. The prices from the EMBRAESP database have been adjusted and updated to the prices of December 2013 using the IGP-DI, one of the indices adopted for readjusting home mortgages. This is a composite index, which as well as the IPA

includes the Consumer Price Index and the National Civil Construction Index, enabling a more comprehensive adjustment.
2. Dollar conversion made May 13, 2015, based on the exchange rate of US$1 to R$3.04.
3. These include localization, nearby amenities, construction materials, number of bedrooms, bathrooms, garage spaces and so on. Overall, comparability between cities is also made more difficult by the diversity in types of residential property: detached houses, semi-detached houses, terraced houses, mobile and park houses to cite just some of the types marketed in other cities of the world but not in São Paulo as a market category that affects pricing.
4. Information based on consulting http://www.kpmg.com/uk/en/issuesandinsights/articlespublications/newsreleases/pages/london-real-estate-prices-will-increase-in-2015-but-growth-will-slow-in-2016-says-kpmg.aspx; http://www.corcoran.com/.
5. In Portuguese, "patrimônio de afetação"—this separates the assets of a development from the others held by the developer so as to ensure that the home purchaser does not suffer any loss if the developer goes bankrupt, as occurred in the case of Encol.
6. Information based on data obtained from the following sites: https://www.london.gov.uk/priorities/housing-land and http://www.secovi.com.br/pesquisas-e-indices/estudo-de-precos-de-imoveis-de-terceiros.
7. Developers have also been categorized as either conservative or speculative, according to the expectation of rate of return and the level of certainty of the rental sector; however, this separation is not feasible using the available database. On this question, see Fainstein, S. (1994). *City Builders: Property, politics and planning in London and New York*. London: Basil Blackwell.

Bibliography

David, L. (2012). The social construction of real estate market risk. The case of financial investments cluster in Mexico City. *Journal of Urban Research*, 9. DOI: 10.4000/articulo.2163. http://articulo.revues.org/2163

David, L. and Halbert, L. (2013). *Finance capital, actor network theory and the struggle over calculative agencies in business property market in Mexico City metropolitan region*. Available at: https://louisedavid.files.wordpress.com/2012/10/david-halbert_regional-studies-2013.pdf

De Magalhães, C. (2002). Global players and the re-shaping of local property markets: Global pressures and local reactions. In Guy, S. and Henneberry, J. (eds.) *Development and developers: Perspective on property*. Oxford: Blackwell, pp. 224–246.

Dias, E. (2012). *Do Plano Real ao Programa Minha Casa Minha Vida: negócios, votos e a reforma da habitação*. University of São Paulo: Master dissertation.

Fainstein, S. (1994). *City Builders: Property, politics and planning in London and New York*. London: Basil Blackwell.

Fix, M. (2011). *Financeirização e transformações recentes no circuito imobiliário no Brasil*. University of Campinas: PhD thesis.

Guy, S. and Henneberry, J. (2000). Integrating the economic and the social in property research. *Urban Studies*, 37(13), pp. 2399–2416.

Haila, A. (1991). Four types of investment in land and property. *International Journal of Urban and Regional Research*, 15(3), pp. 343–365.

Hamnett, C. and Whitelegg, D. (2007). Loft conversion and gentrification in London: From industrial to postindustrial land use. *Environment and Planning A*, 39(1), pp. 106–124.

Hoyler, T. (2015). *A two-way road: How real estate and the approval bureaucracy interact in São Paulo*. Paper prepared for the Research Committee 21—Sociology of Urban and Regional Development of the International Sociological Association, Urbino, Italy.

Logan, J. and Molotch, H. (1987). *Urban fortunes*. California: University of California Press.

Royer, L. (2009). *Financeirização da política habitacional: limites e perspectivas*. University of São Paulo: PhD thesis.

Shimbo, L. (2012). *Habitação Social, Habitação de Mercado: A confluência entre Estado empresas construtoras e capital financeiro*. Belo Horizonte: C/Arte.

Souza, F. (2011). *Análise das influências das estratégias de diversificação e dos modelos de negócio no desempenho das empresas de Real Estate no período de 2005 a 2010*. University of São Paulo: Master dissertation.

Theurillat, T., Rétrat, P. and Crevoisier, O. (2015). The real estate markets: players, institutions and territories. *Urban Studies*, 52(8), 1414–1432.

Topalov, C. (1979). *La urbanización capitalista*. México: Editorial Edicol.

11 Mobility Inequalities in a Road Transport System

Carolina Requena

Urban mobility is a topic explored by an ample academic literature, most of which, though, is dedicated to its supposedly technical aspects, with a minority of studies examining its sociopolitical dimensions. The present analysis fits into the latter category. Nonetheless, over the last two decades, this approach has grown in volume in countries belonging to the Global North and South alike, including studies of the relations between urban mobility and social exclusion (see Lucas 2004 and 2011), social stratification (see Vasconcellos 1999) and poverty (see Salon & Gulyani 2010). In general, these studies are associated with public policy frameworks, political-institutional phenomena and social protests and the interpretation that the question has been insufficiently explored in the North (the case of Salon & Gulyani 2010).[1]

In Brazil, the studies problematizing urban mobility as a sociopolitical issue can be divided into a first wave at the time of Brazil's return to democracy in the mid-1980s, and another much more recent wave, produced in the 2010s. This temporal dispersal seems to be influenced by the heating up of political questions: During re-democratization, the literature responded to the social burden persistently placed on users of public transport (the cases of Fagnani 1985, Itacarambi 1985, Vasconcellos 1999 [1988]). Recent texts, meanwhile, seem to be prompted mostly by the congestion experienced by Brazilian urban transport systems and the search for factors that might explain the problem (i.e., Gomide & Galindo 2013, Requena 2015, Silveira & Cocco 2013).

The European field of Anglophone sociopolitical studies on urban transportation also seems closely tied to the empirical conditions of the policy area: Its initial framework was the creation of the UK Social Exclusion Unit by the British Labour Party in the 1990s. Not only investigations in the UK but also in other Anglophone countries (outside the US) and in continental Europe emerged from this framework (Lucas 2011). The research agenda led by Karen Lucas since then has aimed, using case studies and the comparison between policies in the UK and in the US, to establish theoretical propositions concerning the relation between access to transport and social exclusion (Lucas 2004).

This chapter presents the case of São Paulo with the objective of making evident the range of different experiences of journeys within the metropolis. The intention is to problematize to some extent the idea of a "mobility segregation," observable when we spatialize the uses of transport modes in a disaggregated form in the city's metropolitan region. In this sense, its aim is to provide a sociopolitical analysis of mobility by observing the distribution of particular journeys within the finite and disputed space of the metropolis and the implications of this distribution.

Although the study by Vasconcellos (1999) performed a pioneering role in demonstrating a correlation between the uses of particular modes of transport and social stratification in Brazil, I argue that this approach is insufficient by itself to connect the question of mobility to the urban environment. In fact, the spatial expression of the uses of individual and collective modes of transport, as well as walking, reveals that it involves a system of wide-ranging inequalities—which span from the socioeconomic characteristics of citizens to their opportunities to use space and time in the city, limited in turn by the opportunities available to all other users in a finite system. This is the main contribution offered by this chapter.[2]

The analysis thus takes into account at least two factors that determine mobility in São Paulo: (1) the transport conditions (supply of structures designed for circulation and the adoption of modes of transport that circulate via these structures) and (2) the varied socioeconomic conditions in the spaces of the metropolis. We shall see that the picture emerging at the end of the 2000s reveals a clear predominance of road-based and motorized forms of mobility, with journeys by car exceeding journeys by bus. In this scenario, users of collective transport take on average more than double the travel time of users of individual transport. We shall also see that the circulation by car takes place at higher levels in the social spaces of the elite and upper-middle classes, as in the classification elaborated in Chapter 6, while journeys on foot are more common in the spaces of lower-middle classes and manual workers.

To contextualize the case study, the text includes an initial section describing the historical legacies of the São Paulo transport system. In the second section I describe in detail the pattern of metropolitan mobility expressed in the 2007 Metro Origin/Destination (O/D) data in comparison to two earlier surveys (1997 and 1987). In the third section, I focus on the diverse mobilities across the metropolitan region at the end of the 2000s. This movement from the general to the specific allows us to situate the frequency of travel by particular modes of transport in relation to the supply of infrastructure and the socioeconomic characteristics of the areas where these journeys are made.

The Radial-Concentric Road Model as a Legacy

Reading the history of the supply of transport services in São Paulo and how the space of the city evolved from the start of the 20th century tells us that two important aspects of the relation between these factors remain as legacies for the metropolis at the start of this century: (1) the feedback relation between the establishment of what tended to be radial-concentric routes and the spaces of interest to the real estate market, especially the housing developments for both rich and poor sectors and (2) the heated disputes over spaces of circulation in a socially segregated city whose population growth was intense and difficult to keep up with over the course of the century.

At the turn of the 20th century, the electric trams—run as a monopoly by the Canadian company Light & Power[3] and radiating out from the city center—established a commercial relation with the city in real estate terms with concrete consequences from the viewpoint of the metropolitan region's occupation (Sávio 2010). Light mostly acted as an urbanization company, concentrating its efforts on real estate valorization rather than on designing and structuring a transport system capable of meeting the population's needs (Brasileiro & Henry 1998).

The 1920s marked the beginning of the transition from a city built around rail tracks to the road-based São Paulo we know today. Another transport plan that radiated out from the city center was introduced, this time designed by the public authorities: the Avenidas Plan. Leme (2009) shows how European urban planning ideas inspired Prestes Maia and Ulhôa Cintra, authors of the São Paulo Avenidas Plan in the 1930s. They mixed the teachings of the German Joseph Stuben, concerned with opening up radial routes, and the Frenchman Eugene Hènard, interested in the relation between the automobile and the city. Inventor of the *ville pilotis*, in 1905, Hènard published "La circulation dans les villes modernes. L'autumobilisme et les voies rayonnantes de Paris," where he classified urban circulation through the use of indicators like the purpose of the journey, the time taken, the journey's start and end points, and the type of vehicle used. He proposed a hierarchy for the road system that valorized district and center commuter journeys. The urban circulation policies introduced over this period stemmed from the modernization process undergone by the city in the period after World War I, strongly marked by the introduction of the automobile. The car was "domesticated" by the São Paulo elite ever since the early foundation of the São Paulo Automobile Club in 1908 (Sávio 2010).

The new roads and avenues, sidewalks, the beginning of the process of institutionalizing the circulation of buses,[4] the presence of the automobile and the chaotic traffic in the city center where the entire transport network converged put pressure on the electric tram system to the point where Light & Power's monopoly eventually collapsed at the end of the 1920s. The buses or *auto-ônibus*, which first began operating as peripheral complements to the tram network, were already providing strong competition to electric trams in the 1930s, when the number of bus lines equaled the number of rail lines (Sávio 2010).

In the following decade, influenced by the discussion in favor of state regulation of public utility services, the city council created a municipal transport company (*Companhia Municipal de Transportes Coletivos* [CMTC]), which received Light & Power's assets and 17 bus companies and lines—without, though, putting the private bus companies out of business (Brasileiro & Henry 1998). In the 1950s, the situation favored the buses as Light & Power lost interest in supplying urban transportation following the national restructuring of the energy sector (the trams were finally taken out of service in 1968). The creation of the metro company—*Companhia do Metropolitano de São Paulo* (Metrô)—in the mid-1970s allowed the public authorities to regain some control over urban transport (Fagnani 1985). Urban transportation served as an instrument of federal economy policy during the military dictatorship, especially in the National Development Plan (*Plano Nacional de Desenvolvimento* [II PND]) introduced in response to the oil crisis. At the time, reformulations of metropolitan transport—the case of the metro in São Paulo—were conceived as a potential means of improving the use of the energy grid (Fagnani 1985).

However, the introduction of the metro system was unable to alter the predominance of the road industry, stimulated by the military government itself. São Paulo was seen by the dictatorship as an important hub of the national highway system, and the government invested in the metropolitan region—which it also instituted in 1973—through various programs intended to expand its road network. Between the 1960s and 1980s, the capital's express lanes increased from 69 to 687 kilometers (a 896 percent increase), while the slower lanes rose from 817 to 1,682 kilometers (a 106 percent increase), the equivalent to constructing 1.5 million linear meters of traffic lanes in the main system (Vasconcellos 1999). Furthermore, the automobile industry had been given fresh impetus by the federal government, first through the creation of the Automobile Industry Executive Group (*Grupo Executivo da Indústria Automobilística* [GEIA]) by the Juscelino Kubitschek government in the mid-1950s as part of its Targets Plan (Arbix & Zilbovicius 1997). The 1960s and 1970s, punctuated by the "economic miracle" induced by the military regime, saw important increases in the vehicle ownership rates in São Paulo. During these decades, the "transport question" grew in importance in the city, and its transit and transport agencies were transferred to municipal control, an unprecedented step in Brazil (Vasconcellos 1999). During the return to democracy, municipal governments sought in different ways to take control of the collective road transport system. However, the CMTC was deactivated in the 1990s and a mixed company introduced (São Paulo Transporte [SPTrans]) merely to manage the system operated entirely by the private sector under the umbrella of the Municipal Transport Office. Governed by the changes introduced by the 1988 constitution, the 1990s involved institutional building at the state level. The institutional fragmentation of metropolitan transport has been identified as one of the causes of the region's low mobility (Zioni 1999).

Mobility in São Paulo in the Recent Period

By using data from the Metro Origin/Destination surveys, I can measure the main mode of daily journeys[5] through the classification individual, collective and on foot[6] and through the differentiation between the modes on foot, by bus, car, metro, train, motorcycle, bicycle and others.[7] Although the O/D data presents certain limitations, the information is sufficient for us to analyze the diverse kinds of mobility experienced in São Paulo.[8]

The O/D data show that mobility in São Paulo has consolidated three main modalities: on foot, by car and by bus. Journeys where the main modes of transport are the metro and train account for only small proportions of the total number of trips made in the metropolis.

Breaking down the data on motorized road transport, car trips systematically prevail over bus trips. The 1987 survey indicated 26.2 percent by car compared to 23.6 percent by bus; the 1997 survey indicated 30.6 percent by car compared to 23.1 percent by bus; and the 2007 O/D survey indicated 27.3 percent compared to 23.7 percent. Journeys by motorbike, despite continuing to be a tiny part of the total at the end of the 2000s, increased sharply between 1997 and 2007, corroborating the predominance of road travel in São Paulo during this period. Journeys mainly using the metro and/or rail routes, for their part, never exceeded 8 percent of daily metropolitan journeys, which indisputably confirmed the minor role of rail transport in São Paulo mobility.

This predominance not only derives from the higher average number of daily trips in which the car is the main mode of transport, but it is also due to the disproportionate occupation of the road system made by this mode. Adopting the averages of 1.4 passengers per car (ANTP 2012) and 29 passengers per bus, we can calculate that a car user in traffic uses 42.8 m² of road, while a bus user in traffic uses 3.35 m². In other words, car use requires 12 times the space consumed by a bus passenger on average, a figure which may become even greater in rush hours.[9] According to the PMSP (2013), cars occupy 79 percent of the capital's road surface during rush hours, while buses cover 3 percent.

In this scenario, users of collective transport travel, on average, for more than double the time of users of individual transport. In the data obtained by the 1987, 1997 and 2007 surveys, users of individual transport traveled on average for half an hour (24, 28 and 33 minutes, respectively), while users of collective transport took around an hour on average to complete their journeys (59, 61 and 66 minutes, respectively). The gap between these averages has remained practically the same over the last few decades, even though the average journey time has increased for everyone.

Given that the average time spent on collective journeys corresponds to more than double the time used by individual transport, a kind of "mobility segregation" seems to be in operation in São Paulo, centered on travel time. In this sense, as well as being a value in itself, time has consequences for other aspects of everyday life. It might be argued that this situation is entirely a product of housing segregation, insofar as inhabitants of peripheral regions could be expected to take systematically more time to travel to metropolitan centralities due to the greater distances covered. However, the correlation between the average times spent on journeys made principally in individual mode and collective mode in the SPMR is positive and significant (0.411).[10] In other words, in regions where one time increases, the other also tends to increase, indicating that the issue is actually a problem of traffic congestion rather than one of the distances traveled.

The structure and vehicles supplied to the system, as well as the socioeconomic characteristics of the travelers, can help us comprehend the scenarios described so far. In this context of a strong rise in metropolitan mobility in the 2000s, the buses absorbed an enormous contingent of the capital's passengers. The number of passengers had gradually declined at the start of the 1990s, in the final years of the CMTC under the Luiza Erundina municipal government (PT, 1989–1992). From 1995, the year when SPTrans was introduced by the new mayor, Paulo Maluf (PDS/PP, 1993–1996), it began to fall steeply until the end of the government of Maluf's successor, Celso Pitta (PDS/PP, 1997–2000). It was only in 2002 that the number of bus passengers in the capital started to increase again, the sharp rise coinciding with the implantation of the Interlinked System (*Sistema Interligado*) by the 2001–2004 administration (Marta Suplicy, PT). This policy involved a 50 percent increase in the bus fleet (from 9,958 buses in 2002 to 15,293 the following year), absorbing bus lines run by illegal firms in the 1990s; fare integration that allowed users to make multiple bus journeys within a particular time span paying a single fare (the Single Ticket, or *Bilhete Único*); the separation of bus lanes for exclusive use by buses in long radial corridors (*Passa Rápido*); and the construction of peripheral bus terminals.

In relation to individual transport, when we examine car ownership among families living in the SPMR, the most important shift to occur during the decades analyzed here was between the 1987 and 1997 surveys. While most families (56.3 percent) did not own a car in the 1980s, this situation changed in the 1990s, when the number of families without a car fell to 47.2 percent.

The rate of vehicle ownership in São Paulo also rose sharply between 1987 and 1997 and continued to grow until 2007. While in 1987 there were around 14 cars for each 100 inhabitants, this rose to 18 in 1997 and to more than 20 in 2007. The São Paulo rate is the highest among the five large Brazilian cities analyzed by Balassiano (2010),[11] all of which showed a growth in the number of vehicles above the population growth rate between 2001 and 2008. The author compares the São Paulo rate with the indices observed in some European Union countries.

However, high levels of vehicle ownership do not necessarily imply a systematic use of the car—this is the case of metropolitan cities like London and New York, for example, with levels of vehicle ownership of 31.7 cars to 100 inhabitants and 23 cars to 100 inhabitants, respectively. These cities adopted policies regulating the use of the road system to reduce the use of private and individual transport on four wheels. London is known for its adoption of congestion charges.[12] New York, for its part, redistributed the road space toward increased use by pedestrians and cyclists.[13]

Using the O/D data, I tested the relation between the rate of vehicle ownership and the actual use of vehicles as the main mode of daily journeys in the SPMR. These results are shown in Figure 11.1,[14] which displays the dispersal and medians of these variables, accompanied by mapping of the average family income bands[15] in the O/D zones. Even using data aggregated by area and thus subject to the problem of ecological fallacy, the presence of a pattern is undeniable.

This combination of indicators makes it clear that the O/D zones with higher average family income (fourth quartile) have the highest rates of vehicle ownership in the metropolis (very different from the median) as well as adopting the car as the main daily mode at rates much higher than the median for the distribution of this kind of trip. The opposite end of the income spectrum, on the other hand, is confined to the lower left quadrant,

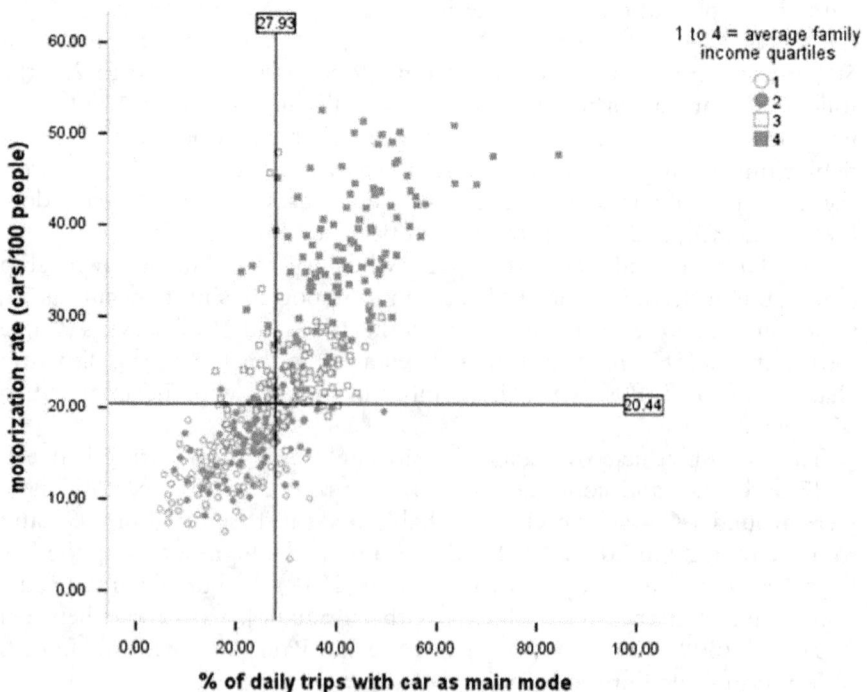

Figure 11.1 Vehicle ownership rate, income and car use: SPMR 2007.

Source: Author's elaboration based on 2007 O/D survey data.

below both medians. The second and third quartiles overlap in the middle of the graph, though not without showing a clear predominance of the third above the medians and the second below them. There are strong indications, therefore, that income, rate of car ownership and the number of car trips are positively correlated within the SPMR, even though we are dealing here with relations constructed at the level of area aggregated data.

These findings, along with the diverse inequalities in the SPMR demonstrated in this volume, make it essential to connect the daily trips to the metropolitan spaces in which they are made to test precisely what types of relations are established.

Expressions of Inequalities in the 2000s

To assess whether a concentration exists within the SPMR in terms of the adoption of certain modes of transport in daily journeys, I used the LQ tool.[16] The LQ consists of the ratio between the proportion of trips made using a certain mode of transport in a given space (O/D zone) and the proportion of trips made using this same mode across the metropolitan region as a whole. If we obtain values lower than 1, then the adoption of a certain mode is underrepresented in the location concerned, while values greater than 1 indicate overrepresentation. Hence, the higher the value of the LQ for a certain mode of journey, the more expressive its local frequency is.

Figure 11.2 shows the LQs of trips undertaken in individual and collective modes.

Map A reveals the concentration (dark gray areas) of trips made mainly in an individual mode in the expanded center of São Paulo municipality and also in the North Zone and the first ring of the capital's East Zone. The same pattern is observable in large portions of the ABC municipalities and Mogi das Cruzes, to the east of the metropolis, as well as toward the west and north of the metropolis, where closed residential condominiums are located, as we saw in Chapter 6.

Map B, on the other hand, shows the areas with under- and overrepresentation of daily journeys where the main mode of transport is collective. It reveals an underrepresentation of collective trips in the eastern portion of the SPMR. Across the remainder of the region, there seems to be a concentration of trips using collective transport in areas where a transport structure is provided, such as metro and train routes (dotted lines) and the bus corridors (solid black lines). Similarly, the northwestern portion of the SPMR, as well as metropolitan outskirts to the south, concentrate collective journeys more intensely compared to the overall average.

Within the O/D zone, I can also compare the frequency of trips in both modes. In making this comparison, it is notable that the regions where individual modes are overrepresented vis-à-vis collective modes are concentrated in the expanded center and in the entries to the North and East Zones of

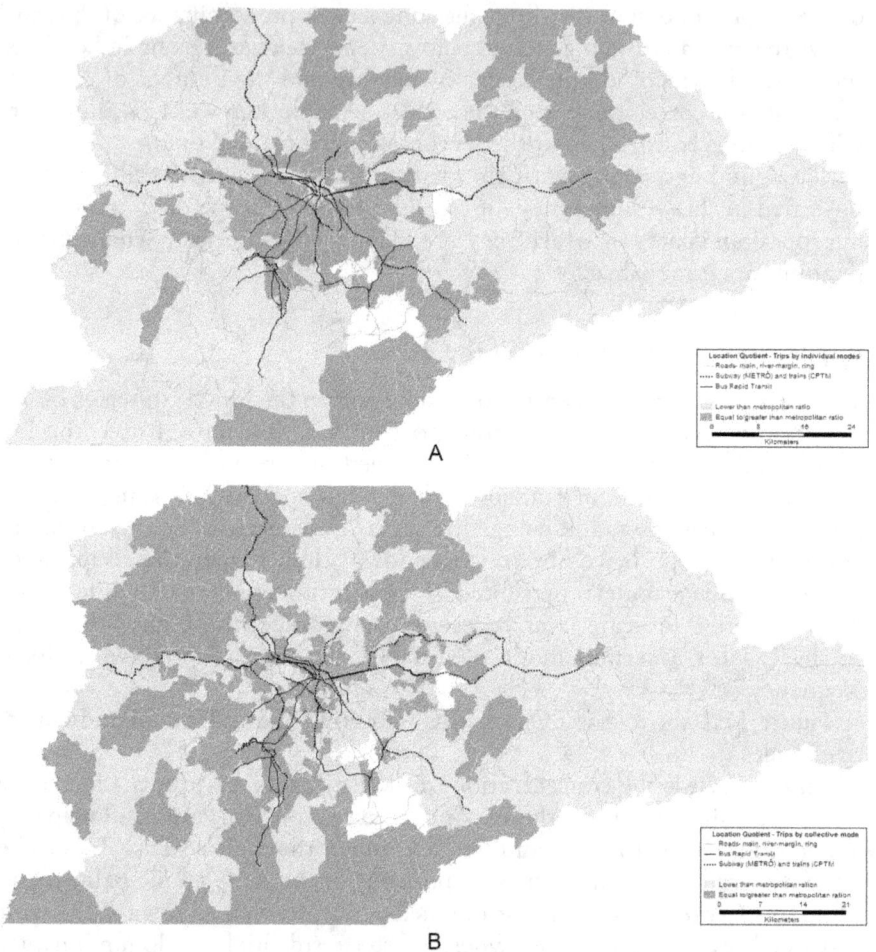

Figure 11.2 Location quotient of trips by individual modes (map A) and location quotient of trips by collective modes (map B), SPMR 2007.

Source: Author's elaboration based on 2007 O/D survey data.

the capital, as well as the ABC region, the centralities of some municipalities and the extreme East of the SPMR. Within the expanded center, I can also note that in the North, East and West in connection with the historic center, this overrepresentation is not found in the areas served by collective road transport (bus corridors) and rail transport (the metro and CPTM lines). On the other hand, in portions of the southwest vector and the first ring to the south of the municipality, served by this same collective transport structure, the use of individual transport is nonetheless still overrepresented.

Finally, exploring the relations between the adoption of modes of transport and the characteristics of the social spaces classified in Chapter 6 of this volume,[17] I can note the reinforcement of the same previously identified trends. Use of the car as the main means of locomotion in the most prevalent in elite spaces (41.3 percent of journeys made) and upper middle-class spaces (34.2 percent). Additionally, I can confirm that walking as the main mode of locomotion is widespread in lower-middle mixed spaces and manual worker spaces,[18] comprising 43.9 percent of journeys made in the latter. The frequency of trips by bus is distributed in a non-polarized form in the social spaces of the SPMR and does not predominate in any of them, maintaining an average of 23 percent of trips made. The fact that the bus is the most flexible means of collective transport in the metropolitan region and is available in geographic areas that span the full range of metropolitan socioeconomic profiles helps explain this non-polarization (given that the data are spatially aggregated).

Final Considerations

The analysis indicates that diverse inequalities affect urban mobility in São Paulo. The expressions of inequality between users of individual transport and users of collective transport are correlated to a certain degree with economic conditions (car journeys are made in areas with higher income), but not in unequivocal form, since the proportion of use of collective transport remains constant in the clusters of areas inhabited by the five social groups delimited for the metropolitan area. Unequivocal relations between individual and collective transport are found in terms of journey time (users of individual transport take half the time to complete their journey) and occupation of road space (users of individual transport consume 12 times more space).

Given this scenario, it is reasonable to argue that the São Paulo system of mobility, at least until 2007, historically reinforced, rather than mitigated, the inequalities present in the metropolis. All of the data used in this chapter refer to 2007, when the O/D survey was last undertaken. As the chapter is based on a historical narrative, it is important to point out that since 2013, 300 kilometers of exclusive bus lanes as well as bike lanes have been implemented in the municipality of São Paulo, but their effect on the pattern of journeys has not yet been analysed by specialists, except for City Hall servants. According to their data, bus speed on the exclusive lanes rose from 13,8 km/h to 20,4 km/h (Companhia de Engenharia de Tráfego 2013). For more on these recent policies and the political and institutional disputes behind them see Chapter 4 in Requena (2015).

Notes

1. There is also vast literature promoted by international bodies that problematizes urban mobility. However, since its goal is the dissemination of best practices and not necessarily the accumulation of knowledge on the topic, this literature will not be reviewed in the present article.
2. A description of this situation may assist future studies seeking to evaluate the impact of these relations on the lives of citizens, including health, access to education, work, leisure and so on.

3. A monopoly also existed prior to Light & Power: the Companhia Viação Paulista, which provided transport in animal-drawn trams and competed with the Canadian firm at the turn of the century.
4. "In 1930, the approximately 400 bus proprietors became subject to regulations imposing standards of service, speed limits, bus stops, etc." (Sávio 2010).
5. "Main mode of daily journeys made" refers to the trips undertaken in the O/D zones in the form of transport identified as the main mode by the interviewee. I shall refer to these journeys sometimes simply as "trips" since the analysis is undertaken only in relation to this type of movement.
6. Individual mode includes all the modes of individual journey except walking, that is, car driver and passengers, taxi users and motorcycle and bicycle riders. The collective mode includes the modalities of bus, metro, chartered bus and school transport.
7. The category "others" includes chartered bus, school transport, taxi and other modalities. São Paulo has no passenger water transport. On the other hand, private air transport by helicopter does exist, but this mode is not measured by the O/D survey, despite the SPMR having the second-largest fleet of private helicopters in the world (EMPLASA 2011).
8. Practically, the only source available on urban transport use in São Paulo, the O/D surveys are carried out with the aim of "serving as a base for transport planning studies . . . in order to evaluate projects for expanding or restructuring the transport network, whether by metro, train or bus" (Companhia do Metropolitano 2008). In other words, they are not designed with the primary objective of investigating mobility at an individual level. The metro publishes data aggregated in spatial units, or O/D zones, which entails the need for us to use this information cautiously to avoid making an ecological fallacy. The O/D zones have been redesigned between surveys, corresponding to 460 units in 2007, 389 units in 1997 and 254 units in 1987.
9. The calculations relating to car use are based on ANTP data: "Each car occupies a strip of road 3.0 to 3.5 m in width by around 10 m in length, that is, at least 30 m^2. However, in traffic this area increases by double at minimum, that is 60 m^2. . . . It is assumed that each car journey is made with 1.4 people travelling per journey" (ANTP 2012, pp. 75–76). The calculations relating to bus use were made by me, based on data on number, size and passengers carried by buses in the fleet managed by SPTrans in the São Paulo municipality in 2013, taking 3.5 m as the width of road used. Obtaining averages based on this data, I obtain an average road occupation of 96.8 m^2 by each bus in traffic. Adopting 40 percent as an average occupation by passengers in each bus, I obtain an average occupation of 28.9 passengers per bus.
10. To 0.01 significance.
11. São Paulo, Rio de Janeiro, Belo Horizonte, Porto Alegre and Recife.
12. Concerning the results of congestion charges on mobility in London, see, for example, Santos and Shaffer (2004).
13. See "Sustainable Streets Index," New York City Department of Transportation (2012).
14. The graph reproduced in this section refers to 2007, but similar graphs elaborated with data from 1987 and 1997 (not included here for space reasons) showed the same pattern of correlation between income, car ownership and car use.
15. The quartiles are (in rounded figures): R$1,080 to 1,727; R$1,728 to 2,271; R$2,272 to 3,355 and R$3,356 to 8,388.
16. Although LQ may seem somewhat fixed in space, it is adequate for the measurement undertaken here insofar as the data available to us depicts the areas from which journeys start.

17. An overlay was made using a geographic information system in which the O/D zone layer was superimposed over the layer with 633 weighting areas with data from the 2010 census used in Chapter 6. This overlay enabled the 2007 O/D data to be distributed in the polygons of the weighting areas. The average daily journeys made using each transport mode were then calculated for each of the five groupings of social spaces.
18. The motives given for traveling by foot remained constant in the responses to the 1997 and 2007 O/D surveys, with a predominance of the explanation that the trip made was short in distance. In both surveys, the motive "short distance" corresponded to 88 percent of responses, while "public-transport related problems" rose from 6.2 to 7.3 percent over the decade. It should be considered, however, that traveling short distances may in itself express a low level of mobility limited by the lack of income for transport costs.

Bibliography

ANTP. (2012). Premissas paea um plano de mobilidade urbana. Available at: http://files-server.antp.org.br/_5dotSystem/download/dcmDocument/2013/03/06/ABB0D95F-D337-4FF5-9627-F8D3878A9404.pdf

Arbix, G. and Zilbovicius, M. (1997). *De JK a FHC: A reinvenção dos carros*. São Paulo: Scritta.

Balassiano, R. (2010). Estudo 22: mobilidade urbana metropolitana. *Perspectivas de investimentos sociais no Brasil*. PIS, BNDES/Cedeplar. Available at: http:www.cedeplar.ufmg.br/pesquisas/pis/Estudo%2022.pdf

Brasileiro, A. and Henry, E. (1998). *Ônibus das cidades brasileiras*. São Paulo: Cultura Editores Associados.

Caldeira, T. (2000). *Cidade de muros: Crime, segregação e cidadania em São Paulo*. São Paulo: Ed. 34; Edusp.

Companhia De Engenharia De Tráfego. (2013). *Coletiva sobre faixas exclusivas à direita*. Available at: http://www.cetsp.com.br/media/255662/300kmexclusivas1.pdf

Companhia Do Metropolitano. (2008). *Pesquisa Origem e Destino 2007*. São Paulo: Metrô.

Companhia Do Metropolitano. (1998). *Pesquisa Origem e Destino 1997*. São Paulo: Metrô.

Companhia Do Metropolitano. (1988). *Pesquisa Origem e Destino 1987*. São Paulo: Metrô.

Empresa Paulista de Planejamento Metropolitano S. A. (2011). *Por Dentro da Região Metropolitana de São Paulo—RMSP*. Available at: http://www.emplasa.sp.gov.br/emplasa/RMSP/rmsp.pdf

Fagnani, E. (1985). *Pobres Viajantes: Transporte coletivo urbano Brasil Grande São Paulo 1964/84*. University of Campinas: Master dissertation.

Gomide, A. A. and Galindo, E. P. (2013). A mobilidade urbana: uma agenda inconclusa ou o retorno daquilo que não foi. *Estudos Avançados*, 27(79), pp. 27–39.

Itacarambi, P. A. O. (1985). *A administração da operação do transporte coletivo por ônibus em São Paulo: pública ou privada?*. Getúlio Vargas Foundation: Master dissertation.

Leme, M. C. (2009). A circulação de idéias e práticas na formação do urbanismo brasileiro. In: Pontual, V. and Loretto, R. (ed.). Cidade, Território e urbanismo, pp. 73–92.

Lucas, K. (2011). Transport and social exclusion: Where are we now? In: Grieco, M. and Urry, J. (eds.) *Mobilities: New perspectives on transport and society*. Farnham: Ashgate, pp. 207–222.

Lucas, K. (2004). *Running on Empty: Transport social exclusion and environmental justice*. Bristol: Policy Press.

New York City Department of Transportation. (2012). *Sustainable Streets Index*. New York: New York Department of Transportation. http://www.nyc.gov/html/dot/html/about/ssi.shtml

PMSP. (2013). A Prefeitura segue priorizando o transporte coletivo para oferecer viagens mais rápidas e confortáveis. *Jornal do Ônibus*, 930, pp. 17–25.

Requena, C. (2015). *O paradigma da fluidez do automóvel: burocracias estatais e mobilidade em São Paulo*. University of São Paulo: Master dissertation.

Requena, C. and Lopes Campos, M. (2014). *Trânsito e transportes em SP: uma política, duas burocracias*. Work presented at the IV Seminário Discente da Pós-Graduação em Ciência Política da USP, 7 to 11 April 2014. Available at: http://ocs.fflch.usp.br/sdpscp/IVsem/paper/view/185/136

Salon, D. and Gulyani, S. (2010). Mobility, poverty, and gender: Travel 'Choices' of slum residents in Nairobi Kenya. *Transport Reviews: A Transnational Transdisciplinary Journal*, 30(5), pp. 641–657.

Santos, G. and Shaffer, B. (2004). Preliminary results of the London congestion charging scheme. *Public Works Management & Policy*, 9(2), pp. 164–181.

Sávio, M. (2010). *A cidade e as máquinas: bondes e automóveis nos primórdios da metrópole paulista, 1900–1930*. São Paulo: Annablume.

Silveira, M. R. and Cocco, R. G. (2013). Transporte público, mobilidade e planejamento urbano: contradições essenciais. *Estudos Avançados*, 27(79), pp. 41–53.

Vasconcellos, E. (2001). *Transporte Urbano, espaço e equidade. Análise das políticas públicas*. São Paulo: Editoras Unidas.

Vasconcellos, E. (1999). *Circular é preciso, viver não é preciso: a história do trânsito na cidade de São Paulo*. São Paulo: Annablume/Fapesp.

Zandonade, P. and Moretti, R. (2012). O padrão de mobilidade de São Paulo e o pressuposto de desigualdade. *EURE*, 38(113), pp. 77–97.

Zioni, S. (1999). *O transporte público em São Paulo*. São Paulo: FAU/USP, unpublished MSc dissertation.

Contributors

Rogério Jerônimo Barbosa graduated in social sciences (Fafich/UFMG). He is a master and PhD student in sociology (DS/USP) and researcher at the Center for Metropolitan Studies (CEM).

José Marcos Pinto da Cunha is a statistician (IME/USP) and has a master's from the Latin American Center of Demography and a PhD in social sciences (IFCH/Unicamp). He is a full professor at the Department of Demography and researcher at the Nucleus of Studies of Population (NEPO/Unicamp) and at the Center for Metropolitan Studies (CEM).

Danilo França graduated in social sciences (FFLCH/USP). He is a master and PhD student in sociology (DS/USP) and a researcher at the Center for Metropolitan Studies (CEM).

Telma Hoyler graduated in public administration (FGV/SP) and has a master's in political science (DCP/USP). She works as a decision maker at the municipality of São Paulo.

Eduardo Cesar Leão Marques has a master's in urban planning (IPPUR/UFRJ) and a PhD in social sciences (IFCH/Unicamp). He is a livre-docente professor at the Department of Political Science (DCP/USP) and a researcher at the Center for Metropolitan Studies (CEM).

Ian Prates graduated in social sciences (FFLCH/USP) and is a master and PhD student in sociology (DS/USP). He is a researcher at the Center for Metropolitan Studies (CEM).

Carolina Requena is a journalist by training. She is a master and PhD student in political science (DCP/USP) and researcher at the Center for Metropolitan Studies (CEM).

Leandro de Pádua Rodrigues graduated in social sciences (FFLCH/USP) and has a master's in political science (DCP/USP).

Camila Pereira Saraiva is an architect and urbanist and a master and PhD student in urban planning (IPPUR/UFRJ). She works at the state of Rio de Janeiro with planning policies.

Index

ABC region 151, 153, 205, 236
access to transport 228
aglomerado subnormal 177
Arretche, Marta 42

Baeninger, Rosana 14, 37–8, 40, 58, 105, 109–10, 122, 139
Berrini region 47–8
Bonduki, Nabil 2, 11, 40, 47, 138–9, 198, 200–1
Brazilian cities 3–4, 31–3, 37, 39, 47, 58, 160, 162, 180, 197, 198, 214, 233
bus/buses 24, 37, 39, 45, 48, 49, 229–33, 235, 236, 237

Caldeira, Teresa 4, 43, 139, 160
car ownership 233, 235
case studies 228
census tracts 180
Center for Metropolitan Studies (CEM) 18, 57, 128, 139, 180
central areas 11, 21, 24, 34, 36, 38, 121–3, 126, 132, 134, 154, 204
classes/class 3, 14, 15, 19, 20–2, 15, 34, 38, 50, 57, 58, 62–5, 67–9, 73, 81, 86–7, 90–1, 104, 138, 142–5, 147–9, 151–3, 155–6, 160–2, 166–71, 200, 202, 210, 216, 229, 237
comparative urbanism 2, 4, 7–8
composition effect 80–1, 84, 87, 93, 94
consolidated periphery 168
counterfactual 81, 83, 93
cycle 14, 24, 62, 75, 90, 163, 200–201, 214–18, 220–2, 224–5

decomposition 79–80, 82, 92–4
demographic census data/demographic census/census data 24, 58, 64, 82, 107, 110, 161–2, 177, 179, 180, 188

demographic growth 2–3, 17, 20, 58, 101, 107, 109–11, 113, 120, 123, 126–8, 133, 186
dissimilarity index/indices of dissimilarity 142–3, 161, 166–8

East Zone 126, 152, 204–5, 235
Education/educational 17, 19–20, 24, 42–3, 45, 47, 49, 64–5, 67, 69, 74, 78–9, 81, 83–6, 91, 111–13, 138, 145, 162–5, 170; inequalities 163
EGP 19, 57, 63, 81, 86, 138, 142, 165, 166
elite 3, 7, 14–17, 21–5, 31, 33–6, 38, 43, 112, 121, 143, 145, 147, 149, 151–3, 155–6, 162, 167–70, 210, 225, 229, 230, 237
EMBRAESP database 128, 216, 221, 222
expressions of inequalities/expressions of inequality 235, 237

favelas/favela 1, 6, 8, 11, 23, 37–8, 40, 47, 120, 129–31, 134, 139, 151, 160, 177–91, 196
financial capital 215, 220
formalization 3, 19, 61, 62, 68, 75, 79, 86

Hamnett, Chris 59, 131, 140–1, 214
historical center 3, 22, 31, 34–6, 126, 152, 153, 206
housing production 3, 23–25, 40, 128, 130–2, 134–5, 196–7, 200, 202–3, 207, 210–11, 215–17, 219, 221, 223, 225; for low-income groups 221, 225
housing projects 8, 35, 40, 196–8, 200–10, 216

244 Index

income 1, 3, 18–25, 37, 40, 57, 59, 61–2, 64–5, 73–6, 79–82, 87–92, 111–14, 117, 120–1, 123–4, 127–35, 138, 141–2, 145, 147–8, 151, 155, 161–5, 170, 179, 184, 186–91, 196–200, 202, 207, 209–10, 215–17, 220, 221, 222, 223, 224, 225, 234, 235, 237; inequality 1, 3, 19, 59, 61, 73, 74, 75, 76, 78–9, 80, 81, 82, 86, 90, 163, 165, 184
inequality/inequalities 1–4, 9, 18–20, 22, 25, 33, 36, 42, 50, 59, 61, 63, 68, 69, 73–86, 90–3, 120, 141, 147, 154–6, 160, 162–5, 170–1, 180, 184, 189, 228–9, 235, 237
infrastructure 15, 17, 23, 33, 34, 36, 37–8, 45, 60, 123, 128, 131, 133, 134, 147, 148, 153, 160, 177–8, 180, 182, 184, 185–6, 188, 189, 191, 205, 207, 209, 229
institutions 6, 8, 10, 11, 17–18, 31, 40, 59, 62, 73, 76–9, 197, 219
internal migration 110–11
intrametropolitan migration 103, 111, 114
irregular settlements 11, 22, 37–8, 40, 44, 47, 137

job creation 79, 87

Kowarick, Lúcio 2, 4, 11, 35–6, 40, 57, 73, 75, 138

labor market 3, 6–7, 16, 19–20, 25, 35, 42, 58, 60–5, 67–9, 73, 74–9, 81–4, 87, 89–92, 102, 106, 140, 163, 165
Latin American cities 2, 4, 9, 11, 12, 31, 178
LISA maps 168

Machado da Silva, Luis Antônio 75
Maloutas, Thomas 59, 141, 165
Marginality theory/urban marginals 10
Maricato, Ermínia 11, 40, 139, 180, 198
mean effect 80–1
Metro 229, 231–2, 235–6
metropolitan mobility 229, 233
metropolitan regions 101–7, 109, 113, 120, 161, 201
Minha Casa Minha Vida 23, 44, 49, 196
mobility 8, 24–5, 39, 104, 106, 109, 111–12, 114, 120, 228–29, 231–33, 237; mobility segregation 229, 232

Modernization theories 10
Moran Index 141–3, 156, 168

occupational inequalities 91
occupational structure 59–60, 69, 74, 77–8, 87, 89–93, 140
Oliveira, Francisco de 2, 32, 73, 75

Paraisópolis 151, 187, 189
Pasternak, Susana 109, 179, 180
Paulista Avenue 34
peripheralization 11, 17, 21, 32, 36, 40, 122, 123, 126, 153, 154, 156, 197, 202
periphery 2, 4, 10, 11–12, 15, 17, 21–5, 32, 36–8, 40, 43–4, 48, 49–50, 57, 76, 103–4, 107, 111–14, 121–6, 130, 133–5, 139, 142, 145, 151–2, 154, 155–6, 160, 162, 168, 181, 197–8, 201–2, 204–5, 207–8, 210, 216, 221, 224, 230, 233
polarization 3, 18–9, 22, 50, 59, 64, 69, 73–4, 76–9, 81, 84, 86–7, 90–1, 140–1, 160, 237
politics 1, 11, 12, 14, 32, 41–2, 45, 49–50, 139
Praça da Sé 206
Preteceille, Edmond 11, 57, 62, 138–41, 161, 170
public policies 2–3, 37, 59, 114, 120, 141, 158, 163, 171, 185

race/race relations 3, 19, 22, 25, 58, 64, 69, 160–3, 165, 168, 170–1
racial inequalities 160, 162–5, 170–1
racial segregation 22, 160–2, 165–72
Radial-Concentric Road Model 229
real estate 7, 21, 126–7, 162, 214–23, 225, 230
real estate developer/developers 38, 214, 216, 219, 220–25
real estate production 225
residential mobility 111–12
residential segregation 21–2, 40, 138–41, 147, 160–2, 165–6, 170–1, 205, 208, 211
road transport 24, 37, 45, 228, 231–2, 236
Robinson, Jennifer 1, 2, 4–6
Rolnik, Raquel 2, 11, 40, 138, 139, 161, 174, 198, 201
Roy, Ananya 4–8, 15

Sabatini, Francisco 11
Santos, Milton 100–2, 104–7, 113
Santos, Wanderley 16, 36, 75, 113
São Paulo 1–6, 9, 12–14, 17–25, 31–9, 42–6, 49–50, 57–8, 60–3, 65, 68–9, 73–4, 79, 84, 102, 106–7, 109, 110–14, 120–3, 125–6, 134, 138–43, 145, 151–5, 161–2, 165, 167–8, 170, 177–82, 184–91, 196, 200–1, 203–5, 207, 210–11, 214–17, 220–2, 224–5, 229–33, 235, 237
São Paulo Metropolitan Region 23, 74, 109, 162, 165, 187, 203
Sassen, Saskia 58–9, 61, 102, 139, 141
securitization 219, 223
segregation 4, 11, 20–22, 24, 35, 38, 40, 43, 57, 127, 138–43, 145, 147, 151, 154, 155, 160–2, 165–8, 170–1, 197–8, 201–6, 208, 209–11, 229, 233
skill-biased 84, 90
slums/slum 7, 44, 47, 48, 50, 177–9
social housing 196
social inequalities 3, 25, 33, 160

Sorensen, Aage 62–3
spatial distribution 123–4, 141, 143, 151, 155, 204, 214, 216, 223
spread of production 224–25

technological change 77
Telles, Edward 58, 161, 171
tenements 33, 35, 37, 179
train/trains 37, 45, 232, 235

urban circulation policies 230
urban land 201, 214
urban mobility 25, 120, 228, 237
urban sprawl/territorial sprawl/sprawl of the metropolis 31, 37, 40
urban transportation 228, 231

variance effect 80–1, 93
Vasconcellos, Eduardo 228, 229, 231

walking 229, 237
weighing areas 123, 125, 126, 127, 128, 129, 130, 132, 133, 142, 166, 168
West Zone 126

For Product Safety Concerns and Information please contact our EU
representative GPSR@taylorandfrancis.com
Taylor & Francis Verlag GmbH, Kaufingerstraße 24, 80331 München, Germany

www.ingramcontent.com/pod-product-compliance
Lightning Source LLC
Chambersburg PA
CBHW071351300426
44114CB00033B/1754